ISLAM AND POLITICS IN THE MIDDLE EAST

INDIANA SERIES IN MIDDLE EAST STUDIES

Mark Tessler, *general editor*

ISLAM AND POLITICS IN THE MIDDLE EAST

Explaining the Views
of Ordinary Citizens

Mark Tessler

Indiana University Press

Bloomington and Indianapolis

This book is a publication of

Indiana University Press
Office of Scholarly Publishing
Herman B Wells Library 350
1320 E. 10th Street
Bloomington, IN 47405-3907

iupress.indiana.edu

Telephone orders   800-842-6796
Fax orders   812-855-7931

Manufactured in the United States of America

Cataloging information is available from the Library of Congress.

ISBN 978-0-253-01643-0 (cloth)
ISBN 978-0-253-01657-7 (ebook)

1 2 3 4 5 20 19 18 17 16 15

To Pat

Contents

Preface

I WAS INTRODUCED to questions about Islam and its place in Muslim society and political affairs when studying, many years ago, at the University of Tunis. The curriculum in the year-long program leading to a *certificat* in "Sociologie Maghrébine et Islamique" included courses with prominent Tunisian professors and a chance to interact in a classroom setting, and on campus, with Tunisian university students. One of my courses, the title of which was something like "Islam in Theory and Society," was taught by Professor Abdelwahab Bouhdiba and focused on many of the topics that Bouhdiba would later explore in his writings. Among these were Islam and social change, sexuality in Islam, and Islam and criminality.

My experience in Tunisia beyond the university also deepened my early interest in Islam. Under the leadership of its charismatic and determinedly modernist president, Habib Bourguiba, Tunisia was carrying out a bold program of reform that had implications for the place Islam would occupy in public life. Reforms included the promulgation of a personal status code that challenged traditional interpretations of Islamic law in family affairs and gave men and women equal rights in a number of areas. This was, and remains today, the most progressive body of family law of any Arab country.

Bourguiba's government also challenged the way that Islamic endowments and trusts were administered; and in one of his most notable and controversial actions, he called for Tunisians to refrain from fasting during Ramadan if this would reduce their effectiveness at work. Bourguiba argued that the country was in a war against underdevelopment and that Islam exempts warriors from fasting when in battle. Among Bourguiba's many speeches dealing with Islamic themes was one, made during the time I was in Tunisia, in which he told his countrymen, "Faith and spiritual values are only effective to the extent they are based on reason."

But Bourguiba's was not the only Tunisian voice speaking about Islam at the time; and although there were many other Tunisian advocates of reform during this period, there were also those who opposed the president's modernist project in the name of fidelity to a proper understanding of Islam and its place in a Muslim society. These individuals called the president's message misguided and harmful, however well intended it might be. Some also charged that Bourguiba's actions were politically calculated and that their true purpose was to reduce the influence of institutions that might challenge his authority and the dominant position of the political party he led.

This first year in Tunisia was spent while I was a doctoral student in political science at Northwestern University. I had completed my first year of study at Northwestern when the opportunity to spend a year at the University of Tunis unexpectedly presented itself. Like my experience in Tunisia, the graduate program at Northwestern introduced me to things with which I had previously been unfamiliar and that were soon to become part of my continuing scholarly interest. When I told my undergraduate advisor that I had accepted an NDEA fellowship from Northwestern and would be studying political science there, he replied that I had chosen a very "behavioral" department. This is a term with which I was completely unfamiliar at the time, but I soon learned that it referenced an approach to scholarly inquiry that included an emphasis on formulating and testing hypotheses that seek to account for variance and on the collection and analysis of quantitative (and other) data. Northwestern had one of a small number of departments that were in the forefront of the "behavioral revolution" in political science in the 1960s.

Survey research and the study of public opinion were an important part of the training I received at Northwestern, and with this began a lifelong professional interest in the attitudes and behavior of ordinary men and women. My first-year paper at Northwestern was based on a survey; and during my second year, spent in Tunisia, it was perhaps natural that I would seek to supplement my coursework and travel around the country by conducting a survey of Tunisian students. Items on my questionnaire asked respondents to indicate the extent to which, using a 10-point scale, they agreed or disagreed with statements like "It is necessary for contemporary Islam to take steps to modernize further."

Some of the questions I asked in the student survey seem naïve in retrospect. But these were formative experiences that reflected a coming together of my interest in questions about the proper role of Islam in present-day Muslim society and in the way that ordinary citizens were processing and evaluating different and often conflicting messages about these questions. Thus, after returning to Northwestern for another year of study, I returned to Tunisia for dissertation research. Over the course of the next year, I conducted face-to-face interviews with a large stratified sample of men and women in Tunis and three small towns in different parts of the countries. Questions about Islam's place in public life occupied an important place on my interview schedule, along with questions about women's status and other political and social issues. My findings were later published in my book *Tradition and Identity in Changing Africa.*, coauthored with William O'Barr and David Spain (1973).

Fast forward to the present and it is clear that these questions about Islam and its place of political and social affairs have never gone away. They are on the agenda today; and with many ups and downs, many of which are described in the present volume's introductory chapter, this has been the case in the Middle East and North Africa for half a century or more. Thus, as reported in a May 2012 *New York Times* article entitled "Egyptian Campaign Focuses on Islam's Role in Public Life," published on the eve of presidential elections in Egypt, debates among contenders "returned repeatedly to questions about the meaning of Islamic law, its place in Egypt, and the role of Islamist groups like the Muslim Brotherhood."[1] Or, in the case of Tunisia, as the *Washington Post* observed in a June 2013 article entitled "Tunisia Faces Political Struggle over Islam," the role of religion and political organization "touches on the main challenges facing reformers across North Africa and the Middle East."[2] The days of Bourguiba and other advocates of radical reform, or sometimes even secularism, seem very far away. And a lot has also happened in Tunisia and Egypt and other countries touched by the events of the Arab Spring since the heady and hopeful days of 2011. But between my first years in Tunisia and the present, public discourse, and disagreement, about Islam's role in public life has for the most part been a constant, with considerable variation in the views of ordinary citizens not only across the Muslim-majority countries of the Middle East and North Africa but also, and even more, within these same countries. Although the data on which the research in this book is based only go back about a decade and half, they show, as do those from my earlier surveys in Tunisia and a few other countries, that questions about the proper relationship between Islam and politics are contested, with division more common than consensus on many of the relevant issues.

It is against the background of both the region's recent history and my own long-standing scholarly interests that I have undertaken to construct and analyze a new dataset with which to explore what ordinary men and women think about Islam's political role—and not only to discern and report *what* they think but also to identify some of the drivers and dynamics that shape their differing judgments. Composed of data from forty-four surveys conducted one or more times in fifteen different countries, the dataset will make it possible to present a more comprehensive picture of individual-level attitudes and values relating to Islam than has previously been possible. Further, I have incorporated country-level variables into the dataset, and this will enable me to consider national-attribute conditionalities, as well as individual-level determinants, when seeking to account for variance and to explain as well as describe citizen orientations.

This is a big and ambitious task for which I have constructed a unique and unusual two-level dataset. Nevertheless, readers will find that the data sometimes only suggest, rather than explicitly tell us, how and why people come to hold certain views. In other words, the causal stories to which the data direct our attention are not always self-evident. In these instances, the pursuit of explanatory insight requires going beyond the data and offering informed but ultimately speculative ideas about the experiences and circumstances that predispose people toward one position or another regarding the relationship between Islam and politics.

When offering these ideas, I try to be explicit about what the data do and do not tell us and to make clear when I am presenting my own assessments for the purpose of encouraging additional reflection and identifying avenue deserving of further research. We would always want our analyses to leave less room for interpretation, of course, but a measure of ambiguity and uncertainty is inevitable, and so offering ideas about underlying causal mechanisms is a researcher's responsibility. Such "grounded theorizing" is essential to the incremental and cumulative way that social research moves forward.

Thus, confident that there are no one-size-fits-all answers to questions about what people believe should be Islam's place in political life or why they hold particular preferences or predispositions, this book addresses issues have that interested me for many years and that I believe to be more important than ever in the Middle East and North Africa. My interrelated goals are to undermine simplistic and unidimensional characterizations while simultaneously reducing uncertainty about attitude-shaping dynamics; to present findings and interpretations in a way that stimulates reflection and encourages additional inquiry; and in these ways to contribute building blocks for the ongoing pursuit of a fuller analytical understanding of the way Muslim publics think about Islam's place in the life and political affairs of their communities.

Acknowledgments

I AM DEEPLY grateful to the Carnegie Corporation of New York for the Carnegie Scholar award that supported the research reported in this volume and construction of the new two-level dataset on which this research is based. I have placed the dataset in the public domain through the Inter-University Consortium for Political and Social Research at the University of Michigan, and I have attached Carnegie's name to the dataset as an expression of my gratitude.

I also acknowledge with sincere appreciation the support of former University of Michigan president, Mary Sue Coleman, and the University's former provost, Phillip Hanlon, with whom I worked in my capacity as U-M's vice provost for international affairs during this period. President Coleman nominated me for the competitive Carnegie award, and Provost Hanlon provided support for a research leave in order that I might devote as much time as possible to the project.

I have had a scholarly interest in Islam and its place in society and politics for many years, going back to my days as an international student at the University of Tunis. The many colleagues and other scholars who have offered encouragement and shared their insights since that time are too numerous to name, but it is a measure of the value I place on their support that my 2011 book, *Public Opinion in the Middle East,* is dedicated to them, along with my wife, Pat. The dedication reads, in part, "to my coauthors and all the students and colleagues whose collaboration has helped to make this research possible." Ten of these individuals are coauthors of the articles reprinted in this 2011 volume.

Two of my former students, and subsequently my coauthors on data-based publications, deserve special mention. Michael D. H. Robbins and Carolina de Miguel were my graduate research assistants during the period of my Carnegie award. Both completed their degrees several years ago and are now emerging scholars, as well as very good friends. As research assistants, they were invaluable in helping me construct and analyze the dataset on which this book is based. I am deeply grateful for their numerous contributions.

Finally, this book is for my wife, Pat. Her consistent encouragement and support, and her loving companionship over the years on numerous trips, sometimes extended trips, to international destinations, have meant everything to me.

A Note on the Carnegie Middle East Governance and Islam Dataset

A GENEROUS CARNEGIE Scholar award from the Carnegie Corporation of New York provided support for the research reported in this volume and for construction of the dataset on which this research is based. This newly created "Carnegie Middle East Governance and Islam Dataset, 1988–2011" brings together forty-four nationally representative public opinion surveys carried out in fifteen countries in the Middle East and North Africa between 1988 and 2011. The dataset contains not only responses to questions asked in these surveys but also variables based on the political, economic, and demographic characteristics of the countries at the time they were surveyed.

The Carnegie Dataset has been placed in the public domain for use by others. It may be downloaded, along with accompanying documentation, from the Inter-University Consortium for Political and Social Research based at the University of Michigan. Those who obtain the dataset may also wish to expand it either through the incorporation of data from additional and possibly more recent surveys or by adding more country-level variables. The Carnegie Dataset has been constructed and is being made available with these possibilities for expansion in mind.

ISLAM AND POLITICS IN THE MIDDLE EAST

Introduction

The Decline and Resurgence of Islam in the Twentieth Century

ISLAM TODAY OCCUPIES a central place in discussions and debates about governance in the Muslim-majority countries of the Middle East and North Africa. Indeed, whether, to what extent, and in what ways Islamic institutions, officials, and laws should play a central role, or at least an important role, in government and political affairs are among the most important and also the most contested questions pertaining to governance in the region at the present time. As Ali Gomaa, the grand mufti of Egypt, wrote in April 2011 in connection with the political transition struggling at the time to take shape in his country, Islamist groups can no longer be excluded from political life, but neither does one group speak for Islam nor should the nation's religious heritage interfere with the civil nature of its political processes. Thus, he concluded, Egypt's revolution has swept away decades of authoritarian rule but it has also "highlighted an issue that Egyptians will grapple with as they consolidate their democracy: the role of religion in political life."[1]

Concerns about the place of Islam in political affairs are equally important elsewhere in the region, as they have been for some time. The secretary general of Tunisia's Islamist al-Nahda Party, Hamadi Jebali, described the political challenges facing his country in a May 2011 public lecture and asked, "What Kind of Democracy for the New Tunisia: Islamic or Secular?"[2] And again, about the same time, an Iraqi constitutional lawyer and media personality, Tariq Harb, wrote that a central element in the struggle to define his country's political future is the question of how "to balance religion and secularism."[3]

These and many similar statements addressed to the question of Islam's role in government and political affairs were made against the background of political transitions set in motion by the spontaneous and frequently massive popular uprisings that shook the Arab world at the end of 2010 and the first months of 2011—events popularly known as the "Arab Spring." Initially in Egypt and Tunisia, but soon elsewhere as well, most notably in Bahrain, Yemen, Syria, and Libya, protesters came into the streets and public squares to express their anger at decades of misrule by governing regimes that were authoritarian, corrupt, and, in the minds of ordinary citizens, concerned only with their own privilege and that of their friends. Regimes responded in different ways, sometimes introducing modest reforms, sometimes allocating additional resources to quiet the unrest, and sometimes using force to suppress the protests. In four countries—Tunisia, Egypt, Yemen, and Libya—regimes that had been in power for decades collapsed. In Tunisia, after first attempting to contain the protests, the president, Zine al-Abidine Ben Ali, fled the country in January 2011. The Egyptian president, Hosni Mubarak, surrendered power and was arrested less than a month later.

The Tunisian and Egyptian cases are particularly instructive because they brought transitions in which Islamist political movements played a leading role. Both countries held free and fair elections later in 2011, and in both cases well-established Islamist political parties were victorious. In Tunisia, al-Nahda outdistanced all others with about 40 percent of the votes. In Egypt, the Freedom and Justice Party, affiliated with the Muslim Brotherhood, won with a plurality of 38 percent. Not all who voted for these parties endorsed their Islamist platform, however. According to public-opinion polls, approximately half of those who cast their ballots for the Islamist party were actually voting for an alternative to the status quo, rather than *for* political Islam. This kind of "strategic" voting has been seen in elections in other Arab countries, as well as in electoral contests elsewhere. Thus, for many, a vote for an Islamist party has been a vote against corruption or authoritarianism—and in favor of fairness and accountable government, rather than a vote for Islam to play a significant role in government.

At the same time, the support that enabled these parties to win at the polls, as has been the case elsewhere in the region, also came from men and women whose vote was not strategic but, rather, reflected an endorsement of the parties' Islamist platforms. Survey research in Tunisia and Egypt indicates that approximately half of the votes that al-Nahda and the Egyptian Freedom and Justice Party received were cast by individuals who want their country to be governed by a political formula that is meaningfully Islamic and who thus constitute a core constituency for political Islam.[4]

The story in Tunisia and Egypt does not end there. In 2013, each country experienced new protests that expressed strong and apparently widespread discontent with the performance of its democratically elected Islamist government. At least to many whose vote for al-Nahda or the Muslim Brotherhood party had been strategic rather than ideological, political Islam was clearly not as appealing, or even acceptable, in practice as it had been when the party represented an alternative to the regime in power. The Islamist governments in both countries collapsed in the wake of the new protests, voluntarily in the Tunisian case and through intervention by the military in Egypt. Political Islam's core constituency remained significant in each country, however, leaving unresolved, and contested, questions about what would be, and what should be, the role to be played by Islam in Tunisian and Egyptian political life.

Although Tunisia and Egypt have followed very different paths since these events, as have other countries on which the events of the Arab Spring left their mark, the experience of the two countries illustrates the complex and often divisive ways that Islamist platforms and parties intersect both with the political process and with the way that ordinary citizens think about Islam's political role. Thus, regardless of whether or not political transitions go forward in Tunisia and Egypt and elsewhere in the Middle East and North Africa, these experiences make clear why Ali Gomaa, Hamadi Jebali, and others would talk in early 2011 about the need to balance competing ideological perspectives and grapple with the challenge of determining Islam's place in government and political affairs.

How ordinary citizens think about these issues is the focus of the present study, which presents findings from extensive public-opinion research in Muslim-majority countries in the Middle East and North Africa. To lay a foundation for the investigation of divisions and debates in the thinking of Muslim publics about Islam's place in the political arena, it is important not only to take note of present-day events in Tunisia, Egypt, and elsewhere in the Middle East and North Africa but also, and even more, to review at least briefly both Islam's claim to a central place in the governing of Muslim-majority countries and, also, the ways in which support for and opposition to this claim have influenced political life during the last half century.

Islam's Primacy and Early Challenges

The view that Islam should have a place of prominence in the political life of Muslim-majority countries derives, at least in part, and in the first instance, from the character of the religion. Islam is actually more than a religion in the Western, or Christian, sense. It is also a culture and a political community. The foundation of Islam is the Quran, and the Quran is above all a set of principles and norms for organizing and governing a political community—a community of believers who accept that the Quran is the revealed world of God and understand for this reason that it should guide their individual and collective behavior in temporal as well as spiritual matters. Working from the Quran, and also from the Sunna, which is the record of the sayings and practices of the Prophet Muhammad during his lifetime, Muslim scholars gradually codified the body of Islamic law, the Shari'a, literally the "straight path," during the centuries following the Prophet's death.

The Shari'a is comprehensive, fusing religion and politics and, in effect, being the constitution of the Muslim community. As one scholar notes, the Quran emphasizes the societal dimension of service to God: "Guided by the word of God and the Prophet, the Muslim community has a moral mission to create a moral social order."[5] The Shari'a thus addresses matters of governance, commerce, property rights, inheritance, taxation, crime, dispute resolution, the rights of non-Muslims, and much more, as well as such personal-status concerns as marriage, divorce, and the rights of women. As a result, the Muslim community created not only a science of jurisprudence to derive from the Quran and the Sunna a body of codified substantive law but also the institutions needed for the application and adjudication of this law. As Judith Tucker writes, "When we talk of Islamic law, we are referring as well to a series of Islamic courts that operated at varying levels of autonomy over the centuries."[6]

The understating of the relationship between Islam and governance embodied in this legal system reflects a view that Islam cannot be privatized and that there is no Islam other than *political* Islam. As in every legal system, there are differing views about the proper interpretation of the Shari'a on many questions, sometimes beginning with differing views about the applicability of particular Quranic verses. In addition, legal rulings are sometimes influenced by external considerations, with jurists and scholars offering interpretations that reflect their social position or political loyalties as much as an objective reading of the law. None of this is peculiar to Islam, of course, and it does not call into question the principle that the Muslim community should be governed in accordance with the Shari'a and, when questions arise, that it is for clerics, jurists, and Islamic scholars, known collectively as the *ulama,* to say what Islam requires of the community and its members. This understanding of the relationship between Islam and governance has not only been advanced and defended by the *ulama* themselves, it has also for centuries been considered self-evident and beyond dispute by most ordinary Muslims.

There are nonetheless alternative understandings and viewpoints, and these began to appear and exert influence in the nineteenth century. Currents of modernization and reform emerged in a number of Middle Eastern counties, most notably, but not only, in Turkey, Egypt, Syria, and Tunisia, bringing with them new political and administrative institutions and, sometimes, new conceptions of government. Among the new developments were educational reforms and the establishment of modern schools, which challenged and provided an alternative to traditional institutions of Islamic learning. In Egypt, for example, new educational institutions, which incorporated modern subjects and foreign languages into their curricula, were established alongside the country's traditional Quranic schools and mosque universities. By 1840 there were approximately fifty primary schools of this sort scattered throughout the country, as well as large preparatory schools in Cairo and Alexandria. There were also a number of specialized post-primary schools devoted to such practical fields as veterinary science, medicine, translation, and civil administration. The students in all of these schools soon numbered more than 10,000.[7]

Although less pronounced, there were similar developments in Tunisia. New primary schools were built, and a modern secondary school, the Bardo Polytechnic School, was established in 1840. Designed to train officers for the new Tunisian army, the Bardo School taught modern subjects, including mathematics and the French and Italian languages, as well as Arabic and the Muslim religion.[8] Later in the century, Tunisia established Sadiki College on the model of European lycées. Sadiki's declared purpose was to teach writing and useful knowledge, including "juridical sciences, foreign languages, and the rational sciences that might be of use to Muslims," as well as the Quran and "being not contrary to the faith."[9]

Equally important, if not more so, were reforms related to government and to the administration of Islamic courts and other religious institutions. An extensive program of reform, known collectively as *Tanzimat,* was undertaken in Ottoman Turkey toward the middle of the nineteenth century. It included sweeping internal political reorganization, the creation of a modern bureaucracy, reorganization of the military, and, as elsewhere, the establishment of new schools and overseas study missions. These reforms also laid a foundation for the diffusion of modernist currents to a number of the empire's Arab provinces.

With respect to Islamic legal institutions, modern-style civil and penal codes were introduced in Turkey toward the middle of the century. These involved a restructuring of the judiciary and the transformation of Islamic law from the fairly independent terrain of jurists into that of a "highly formalized and centralized agency of the state."[10] In Egypt, reforms included the establishment of "Mixed Courts" in 1876. These courts limited the jurisdiction of Shari'a courts and administered a new series of laws based mostly on French civil, penal, and commercial codes. In still another area with implications for the religious establishment, Islamic trusts and estates, known as *awqaf,* or *habous* in North Africa, were incorporated into a centralized administrative system in some countries. These trusts included lands set aside for religious purposes that were an important source of revenue for the *ulama.*

Challenges to the traditional Islamic institutions and conceptions, as well as to traditional society more generally, intensified in some countries with the introduction of European colonialism. Indeed, some of the reforms and innovations implemented during the latter years of the precolonial period, such as the Mixed Courts in Egypt, were in part a response to the growing involvement and influence of European powers.[11] The Europeans usually did not seek to dismantle Islamic courts or other traditional religious institutions. In Egypt, for example, the British were respectful of local sensitivities and avoided any interference in Islamic practice and administration.[12] The only clear counterexample is Algeria, where the French ruled the country directly and, as Wael Hallaq reports, the Islamic legal class was already in disarray by the latter part of the nineteenth century.[13]

Nevertheless, in Egypt, the Maghrib, and parts of the Levant, especially after World War I, the introduction of European rule was accompanied by the growth of new social classes and by politically conscious debates about whether and how

Islamic institutions should be reformed. On one side of the ideological and political divide were intellectuals, professionals, and others who embraced liberal or even leftist formulae. These individuals were often devout Muslims and strongly opposed to European rule. But they were modernists, as well as nationalists, and they advocated programs of change that would significantly reduce the role of the *ulama* and the institutions through which they exercised influence. On the other side were individuals and movements, such as the Muslim Brotherhood in Egypt and its affiliates elsewhere, who opposed European rule in the name of Islam and whose conception of reform involved strengthening the religion and ensuring its preeminent place in governing Muslim society. In this environment, early versions of the debates that would later become widespread in the Muslim Middle East could already be seen. As described by Nadav Safran with respect to Egypt, "the result was a kind of see-saw" characterized by "ambiguity and confusion attaching to the whole issue of religion and the state . . . an issue that had not been definitely settled when the revolution of 1952 broke out."[14]

Turning Away from Islam

The years following World War II brought an end to colonialism and saw the emergence of a new political dynamic in the Muslim Middle East. Moreover, much of the region witnessed a turning away from Islam during the early years of this period. This was evident during the 1950s and 1960s in both the ideological and the political formulae that had the greatest influence in the newly independent Muslim-majority countries of the Middle East and North Africa and also, at the individual level, in the attitudes and behavior of many ordinary citizens. With respect to the latter, particularly among the rapidly increasing number of younger and better-educated men and women, religious observance declined and new cultural norms and fashions were embraced. In major cities, where Islamic dress would become much more common a decade or two later, few young women wore the hijab and fewer still wore the abaya. Rather, as a Kuwaiti political scientist has written about the situation in the eastern part of the Muslim Middle East, "in Baghdad, Beirut, Cairo, Damascus, Kuwait and Tehran, short skirts—even miniskirts—were the fashion of the day. Male and female swimmers occupied some of the same public beaches in Kuwait and other parts of the region. Only Saudi Arabia, a center of conservative Islamic thinking, remained untouched by such trends and lifestyles."[15]

Similar patterns were present in Arab North Africa. As a prominent student of the Maghrib reported in 1966, most educated persons had abandoned the observance of Islamic ritual and, more generally, mosques were poorly attended, public prayer was rarely seen, and even the polite greetings with an Islamic context appeared to be less in use.[16] Thus, not surprisingly, a survey of Tunisian university students conducted in 1965 found that 64 percent of the respondents agreed, and in most cases agreed strongly, that it is necessary for contemporary Islam to take steps to modernize, whereas only 17 percent disagreed or disagreed strongly.[17]

With respect to political regimes and their ideologies, the turning away from Islam that marked the 1950s and 1960s is best illustrated by the experience of Egypt, where the regime of Gamal Abdul Nasser came to power in a 1952 coup that overthrew a corrupt, indulgent, and highly unpopular monarchy. Placing an ideological stamp not only on Egypt but also on much of the Arab world, Nasser advanced a quasi-leftist political philosophy based on socialism and Arab nationalism that struck a popular chord throughout the Arab Middle East; and this, along with his modernist and populist policies, his calls for improving the lives of ordinary citizens, and his embrace of Third World causes, soon made Nasser the most influential leader in the Arab arena.

Nasser did sometimes include Islamic references in his speeches, particularly when on the defensive, but the religion did not have a meaningful place either in the ideological vision or in the policies and programs that guided the revolution the Egyptian leader and his government sought to implement. Rather, Islam was either ignored or exploited. To the extent he responded to questions about Islam's place in his political formula, Nasser declared, as one scholar reports, not only that "ours is a scientific socialism" but also that "our religion is a socialist one" and that in the Middle Ages Islam "applied the first socialist experiment in the world."[18] Moving quickly to consolidate his power, Nasser banned the Islamist Muslim Brotherhood and imprisoned a large number of its members. This not only removed the most important source of opposition to his regime, it also silenced, at least for a time, the most powerful advocate of an alternative political formula, one that called for governance based on Islamic principles, institutions, and laws.

Nasserism, as the charismatic Egyptian leader's ideology was often called, inspired student and other movements in many Arab countries. It also contributed to, and was reflected in, the discourse of numerous Arab intellectuals. Ba'thism, meaning "renaissance," was another leftist ideology that was influential in the Arab world during this period. Ba'thists were in power in Syria, and the Ba'th Party had branches and was active in many other Arab countries, including Iraq, where it came to power in the late 1960s, Lebanon, Egypt, Jordan, Sudan, and Yemen. Ba'thism, like Nasserism, emphasized socialism and Arab nationalism. It was also explicitly secular in orientation, although it recognized Islam as a part of Arab heritage, and Ba'th intellectuals frequently lauded the socialist and revolutionary character of early Islam. According to one analyst writing during this period, the Ba'th Party, "while secular in orientation, embodies a renaissance of the Arab spirit similar to that embodied in Islam."[19]

Nasser's involvement in Arab affairs during this period was not limited to the appeal of his ideology and modernist policies. He also provided support for revolutionary movements in a number of Arab countries. Egypt assisted the anticolonial struggle in Algeria in the 1950s, for example, offering political support and broadcasting messages on behalf of Algeria's National Liberation Front through the Cairo-based Voice of the Arabs radio network. This led France to join Israel (and Britain) in attacking Egypt in 1956. A more consequential initiative, although it turned out to be short lived, was the political union that Nasser formed with the Ba'th regime in Damascus. Between 1958 and 1961, Egypt and Syria were joined in a political federation, the United Arab Republic.

In still another important contemporary development, revolutionary forces in Yemen, inspired by Nasser and the Ba'thists, overthrew the country's feudal monarchy in 1962 and established the Yemen Arab Republic. Nasser immediately recognized the new government; and, when forces loyal to the old order sought to reinstate the monarchy, with support from Saudi Arabia, he sent Egyptian troops and supplies to help the republican regime. In all of this, the behavior of key actors, including Nasser, was politically calculated and motivated by pragmatic as well as ideological considerations. The Egyptian leader's commitment to a revolutionary socialist and Arab nationalist agenda was nonetheless genuine, and his program inspired many and gave a distinctive character to politics and ideology in the Arab Middle East during most of the 1950s and 1960s.

Modernist or leftist governments with little interest in or tolerance for political Islam also appeared in the North Africa during this period. Socialism was the dominant ideology in Tunisia and Algeria; and in Morocco, although the country was ruled by a conservative monarch, there were strong leftist parties and factions. All three countries were authoritarian, or perhaps quasi-authoritarian in the case of Tunisia and Morocco, and while each emphasized or at least paid lip service to its Muslim identity, in no case were traditional religious officials permitted to exercise any independent political influence. Nor was any political space given to movements seeking to organize under the banner of Islam. Scholars of the region thus reported that men of traditional Islamic learning were on the defensive against a secular and Western-oriented leadership class,[20] and that even in the countryside the position and authority of religious figures were being eroded, principally because they did not represent the values emphasized by national elites and, therefore, could not provide their followers with access to central government resources.[21] The result, according to another observer: Religion was more relevant as a matter of individual conscience than of collective organization.[22]

Although each was characterized by its own unique experience and political formula, the non-Arab countries of Turkey and Iran were also led during this period by governments that had little interest in seeing Islam play a significant political role. In Turkey, although most ordinary citizens were personally devout, the Turkish republic had been militantly secular since its founding by Kemal Ataturk after World War I. Among the actions of the new state were the abolition of the Sunni Caliphate, which had been based in Istanbul; the abolition of the traditional religious school order as part of broader educational reforms; and the replacement of Shari'a courts by secular courts. During the years after World War II, democratic multiparty politics emerged in Turkey, and the government for a time took a somewhat more tolerant attitude toward Islamic activities in the public arena. In response, even though the political role of religious institutions and officials actually remained quite limited, the military intervened in 1960 in the name of preventing what it claimed was an emerging drift away from secularism. Democratic politics and competing ideological currents marked the years following the military's return to the barracks in 1961, and in this environment a party with strong Islamist leanings, the National Order Party, was established in 1970. The following year the military intervened for a second time and the Constitutional Court ordered the dissolution of the party on the grounds that it was seeking to advance a theocratic platform. The military intervened for yet a third time in 1980, declaring that it was acting to ensure civil order, national unity, and secularism. Military rule continued until 1983.

In Iran, following the ascent to power of Mohammad Reza Shah during World War II, Iranian politics initially witnessed a political confrontation between traditional Islamic authorities and the new shah. The increasingly autocratic shah prevailed in this conflict, and in 1963 he implemented a modernist and secularist "White Revolution" that the country's Shi'i clerics opposed for economic as well as religious reasons. Particularly important were the revolution's land reform program, which threatened the clerics' material interests, and its calls for women's emancipation, which challenged both the clerics' values and their role as guardians of Islam. Clerics who continued to oppose the program were suppressed by the shah, who called them "black reactionaries" and "lice-ridden mullahs."[23] Nor did the shah tolerate opposition from others; widespread demonstrations opposing the shah, fueled for some by his autocratic rule much more than his reformist program, erupted in 1963 and were brutally put down. The demonstrators, large numbers of whom were killed, included not only religious leaders but also students, teachers, *bazaaris*, workers, and others. In this environment, some Shi'i clerics went into exile, while others, largely to protect their positions, quietly went along with the shah's program, or at least bided their time.

As this admittedly incomplete snapshot of politics and Islam in the Middle East and North Africa in the 1950s and 1960s makes clear, the dominant ideological current of the period, and the one championed by those in power in many states across the region, ran directly counter to the view that politics in a country with an overwhelming Muslim majority should be organized in accordance with the principles, institutions, and laws of Islam. Leaders and governments with modernist, reformist, and largely secularist programs were not unchallenged by proponents of political Islam, and such programs were not even present in a few countries, most notably Saudi Arabia, or were a much less important part of the government's agenda in others, such as Jordan and Morocco. Overall, however, infused with a modernist and essentially revolutionary political sensibility, many national leaders, as well as numerous intellectuals and significant sectors of the population, embraced models of governance and societal organization that emphasized change and excluded traditional and Islamic political formulae. Thus, as summarized by a leading scholar of modern Islam,

> By the middle of the 1960s, Arab socialism in various forms appeared to be the most dominant ideology in the Arab East. Nasserism and the Ba'th were the two leading exponents of that view, but there were many other movements based on similar principles in other areas. Most discussion of Islam at the time saw Islam's future within the Arab socialist framework. Traditional, conservative and fundamentalist movements were often seen as final efforts of the old styles of the Islamic experience that would eventually have to accommodate themselves to this new dynamic force or face destruction.[24]

The Islamic Resurgence

A different picture, increasingly marked by what observers often described as the "revival" or "resurgence" of Islam,[25] gradually took shape in the years that followed. This resurgence was visible in the growing interest in religious practice and frequently in Islamic political formulae, not only among the general public but also among many of the better-educated men and women who had earlier embraced the modernist and socialist vision of Nasser and others. Many were increasingly coming to the view that modernization need not require a turning away from religion. The origins of this resurgence were diverse, rooted to a significant degree in the enduring religious attachments of ordinary Muslims but shaped to a significant extent as well by events that were transforming the regional landscape in the Middle East and North Africa.

One important event that contributed to a transformation of the region's ideological landscape was the Arab-Israeli war of June 1967. The war brought the Arabs a crushing defeat and thus cast doubt on the development ideologies of those states, particularly Egypt and Syria, that had led in the struggle against Israel. In the wake of the Arabs' defeat in the 1947–1948 war for Israeli independence, traditional and feudalistic regimes had been swept away in Egypt and Syria, as well as elsewhere, to be replaced by governments that promised that a political formula based on socialism and some mix of pan-Arabism and secular nationalism would enable their countries to prosper. After June 1967, however, the deeply demoralizing conclusion was that two decades of progressive reform and determined attempts at modernization and socialist development had accomplished little. Egypt under Nasser had been defeated more easily and decisively than had Egypt under the monarchy twenty years earlier. Nor had the Ba'th regime in Syria fared much better, despite its pursuit of development in accordance with the principles of socialism and secularism. Thus, there was suddenly a new logic and credibility to the argument that progress could be achieved only if the Arabs were guided by an indigenous political formula, namely that provided by Islam.

Some Muslim thinkers asserted that the defeat was punishment for the Arabs' flirtation with foreign ideologies, and specifically for a turning away from the faith. More common, and almost certainly more persuasive to many thoughtful Muslims, was the assertion, summarized in a major study of Arab political thought during this period, that Islam "could do what no imported doctrine could hope to do—mobilize the believers, instill discipline, and inspire people to make sacrifices and, if necessary, to die."[26] Interestingly, both radical and conservative Islamic thinkers also placed emphasis on the importance of Israel's identification with Judaism, arguing that Israel was strong precisely because it accepted and embraced its association with an ancient religion. The implication, made explicit by Islamic theoreticians, was that Muslims should exhibit the same religious zeal and, as had the Israelis, reject the secularist fallacy of a contradiction between religion and modernity.[27]

The Islamic resurgence was further fueled, and in some countries fueled more directly, by the oil boom of the 1970s. Oil prices increased significantly early in the decade, with price hikes initially brought on by the embargo that Arab petroleum-exporting countries imposed in response to the U.S. decision to resupply Israel during the Arab-Israeli war of October 1973. The price increases brought substantial new wealth to some countries, particularly Saudi Arabia, Kuwait, and Libya, where revenue from oil sales greatly exceeded what was needed for, and could be absorbed by, the domestic economy. Accordingly, these countries used a significant share of their new wealth to fund Islamic and other projects elsewhere in the Arab and Muslim world. Generous funding was provided for the construction of mosques and the operation of Islamic educational institutions, welfare societies, and cultural centers in many Muslim countries in the Middle East and other world regions. Islamic business activity was also stimulated by the inflow of capital from petroleum-exporting countries. In secular Turkey, for example, Islamic organizations and networks used this capital to engage in investment activity of substantial scale.[28]

Saudi Arabia played a particularly important role so far as the Islamic resurgence is concerned, although it was by no means alone in providing funds to Islamic institutions in other countries. Islam permeated politics in Saudi Arabia; without a constitution or a parliament, the government and legal system were, as they remain, based primarily on the Shari'a. Wahhabism is the dominant form of Islam in the Saudi Arabia, and the kingdom drew upon its new wealth to spread the conservative Wahhabi ideology throughout the Muslim world. Describing this drive, one scholar notes that "Saudi money was instrumental in the building and operation of thousands of mosques and madrasas (religious schools) from Lahore to London, and from Morocco to Malaysia. There, the Wahhabi message was presented to ever expanding audiences." This effort to deepen attachments to Islam in other Muslim countries, and to spread Wahhabi Islam in particular, was undertaken, he notes, "partly out of conviction and partly to counter the appeal of ideologies it perceived as a threat to its national security."[29] Further, the Saudi's external initiative was complemented and reinforced by developments within the kingdom, where, as another scholar reports, the Islamic educational system fostered a new generation of sheikhs, professors, and students during the 1980s and helped to fuel an Islamic resurgence inside the country.[30]

In this changing environment, and in part because of it, although only in part, an Islamic revival was increasingly visible among ordinary men and women in much of the Middle East and North Africa during the 1970s and 1980s. Islamic dress became increasingly popular among the young, including the better educated, with beards for men and head coverings for women. On university campuses, leftist student organizations declined in importance, often to be replaced by Islamic student movements. According to one account of developments in Egypt:

> In the early 1970s, small clubs and circles broadly committed to the study of Islam began to appear on most Egyptian university campuses. The mid-1970s saw a dramatic increase in the number, activities and appeal of these groups, which came to be known by the generic term of *jama'at islamiyya* (Islamic societies). By 1977–78, the *jama'at islamiyya* controlled most of the student unions and had grown into a major political force on university campuses.[31]

The religion was also increasingly present in secondary schools. As one scholar reported with respect to North Africa, high schools, like universities, by the 1980s were "serving as centers of Islamic activity and recruitment."[32]

Nor were such developments limited to the Arab world. A similar trend was taking shape in non-Arab Iran during this period. One author describes it as a "paradigmatic shift,"[33] with many educated Iranians beginning to refuse the premise that modernization of necessity involved Westernization and secularism. As explained by another, "Whereas earlier generations of Iranian intellectuals had been concerned primarily with ways to modernize the country," by the 1970s "the search for progress had given way to a quest for authenticity and roots; the preoccupation with overcoming backwardness had been replaced with a fear of moral decay and the loss of cultural identity."[34]

The Islamic resurgence was visible among less well-educated as well as better-educated men and women in the Middle East and North Africa. One indication of this was a growth in the sale of what are sometimes called "Islamic books"— inexpensive, attractively printed texts that are accessible to a readership with limited literacy skills and that take advantage of new printing technologies. These books and pamphlets were capturing an increasing share of the market and, according to a study of new media in the Arab world, their popularity reflected "the changing nature of religious—and political—discourse." The study reports that many of these books resembled practical manuals, dealing with the way that Muslims should conduct themselves in a modern society and thus "reconciling Islam with science." The study also discusses the growing importance of audiocassettes at the time, noting that in some regions they had begun to supplement or even replace pamphlets as vehicles for the discussion of Islamic themes. These cassettes made the sermons of prominent clerics from Egypt, Lebanon, and elsewhere available to ordinary men and women throughout the region. Finally, drawing upon research in Egypt and Oman, the study reports that the influence of this array of new media was becoming visible in the content of Friday sermons: In a change from the past, preachers increasingly incorporated references and allusions to a wide range of texts and events because they believed these were now familiar to a much wider audience.[35]

These and other dimensions of the Islamic revival are nicely described in a 1979 journalistic investigation of the situation in Tunisia, a country which, if anything, had gone further in the 1960s than had Nasser and the Ba'thists in carrying out a reformist program that reduced the influence of Islamic institutions and officials. The investigation reported increased individual piety and growing interest in Islam among the educated strata of society; the formation of Islamic study groups and increased membership in other religion-orientated associations; the emergence and growing visibility of a number of charismatic sheikhs and imams, many of the latter in working in neighborhood mosques; and a rise in the sale of books, records, and cassettes devoted to Islamic themes, with cassette sales, for example, estimated to be in the thousands every month. The investigation also reported in this connection that a "parallel society," with its own rules, was in the process of developing and organizing itself. French was not to be spoken, for example, and men and women were not to shake hands. Women were not to participate in theater groups, and music ensembles were either all male or all female, never mixed, and their repertoires were composed exclusively of liturgical chants and celebrations of Islamic ardor.[36]

An interesting study of similar developments in Syria that focuses on women reports that for many women, and frequently for men as well, religious activity during this period was not only increasing but was also moving out of the mosque and into an array of study groups, or even homes, as individuals sought to deepen their personal involvement in Islam. The study describes "women's enthusiastic response to the new opportunities which Islamic revivalism opens up for them outside the private sphere of their houses." Women from all strata of Syrian society—ranging from older traditional women from conservative Damascus neighborhoods to the Western-educated daughters of government ministers—were coming together in regular meetings devoted to prayer and Quranic lessons, which were "a means of transmitting Islamic knowledge." They were motivated both by a desire to strengthen religious attachments and understanding and by the appeal of greater social interaction beyond home and family. The study also notes, though writing of a period closer to the present, that the desire for lessons in Islam is so great among all levels of society that "informal study groups in private houses and courses in mosques and schools can hardly cope with the demand."[37]

Regimes under Pressure

There was a political as well as a purely religious and cultural dimension to the Islamic resurgence. Discontent with the domestic political and economic situation was growing in many Middle Eastern and North African countries during the 1970s and 1980s. One result of this discontent was increased popular support for opposition political movements organized under the banner of Islam—parties, groups, and factions whose opposition was sometimes directed at established clerics aligned with the government as well as the regime itself.

The case of Egypt is particularly instructive, although it is by no means unique. Nasser died in 1970, and his successor as president, Anwar Sadat, pursued an economic policy of *infitah*, or "open door," sometimes also cynically described as the policy of *"enrichissez-vous,"*[38] which emphasized capitalist development and foreign investment and greatly increased the gap between rich and poor. Public frustration, indeed anger, increased dramatically in this environment, and in January 1977 there were "bread riots" in many of Egypt's major cities. The uprising was a spontaneous response by hundreds of thousands of less affluent Egyptians to a rise in the price of basic foodstuffs due to the removal of government subsidies mandated by Egypt's international creditors, the World Bank, and the International Monetary Fund. Rioters attacked targets that symbolized the prosperity and privilege of the elite and the corruption of the regime. Establishments believed to represent Western influence and decadence, including dozens of nightclubs on the road leading from Cairo to the Giza pyramids, were also attacked. An estimated 800 people had been killed, and many more injured, by the time the disturbances ended two days after they had begun.

Discontent was pronounced among better-educated Egyptians as well, particularly the young, and was by fueled a combination of objective hardship and unrealized expectations. The most prominent complaint was the scarcity of appropriate employment opportunities for educated Egyptians, forcing most into low-paying and dead-end jobs in the government administration. Another important complaint, which was of concern to less-well-educated as well as better-educated urban youth, was the severe housing shortage in major cities. This forced many young people to delay marriage and increased the proportion of bachelors among younger men. As explained by one knowledgeable analyst, frustration about these and other problems, such as the breakdown of the urban infrastructure and the attendant increase in the difficulty of daily life, were the product not only of unfulfilled expectations but also, and to an extent even more, of a "comparison of the good life in the West, as shown on TV, in movies and in ads," and especially of a comparison with the privileged segments of Egyptian society. Among the latter were the many officials who worked with foreigners, sometimes called "five percenters" because of the commissions they received.[39]

Under these circumstances, the message of Islamic movements and personalities opposed to the Sadat regime, often advanced with the slogan that "Islam is the Solution," found a receptive audience among many young people. It offered "a cogent panacea: a comeback to a puritanical and egalitarian way of life, reducing the social gap by taking from the rich and giving to the poor."[40] And, more specifically, the solution called for by some involved more than greater respect for Islam in daily life or even the establishment of a strong Islamic party that would ensure the inclusion of an Islamic perspective in the discourse among competing political factions. For many Islamist movements and personalities, the solution lay in an alternative political formula, in the establishment of an Islamic state governed by the Shari'a.

Developments in a number of other countries paralleled those in Egypt during this period. In Morocco, Tunisia, Jordan, and Algeria, for example, there were large-scale riots through which ordinary citizens expressed their anger at the policies and performance of their governments. But the event that was most consequential during this period, reflecting the kinds of complaints that were breeding support for political Islam elsewhere but involving a much greater upheaval, was the Iranian revolution of 1979.

Discontent with the regime of the shah in Iran was not unlike that found elsewhere. It was more pronounced, however, intensified both by the opulence and excess of the shah's court and by the regime's brutal suppression of dissidents. Clerics and many other critics, including Ruhollah Khomeini, who would later become the leader of Iran, called it a "plundering" regime.[41] By 1976, the shah had accumulated one billion dollars or more from oil revenue; his family—including sixty-three princes and princesses—had accumulated between five and twenty billion dollars; and his family foundation controlled approximately three billion dollars.[42] Describing the "enormity and visibility" of the corruption, a leading student of Iranian politics reported that there were "huge bribes, fraudulent land schemes, and extravagant commissions on contracts"—all reflecting a "mad dash for instant wealth," with the shah's family and close associates "at the head of the pack."[43] In addition, the White Revolution was failing to deliver a better life for many ordinary citizens, and so discontent was also fueled by economic hardship among substantial segments of the population and by a huge and growing income gap, particularly between the urban and rural areas. The shah and his lieutenants responded to the growing chorus of complaints by undertaking to silence critics and suppress dissent. One observer described their actions, led by the dreaded SAVAK, the government's security apparatus, as a "reign of terror" in which "the ugliest forms of torture became the order of the day."[44]

This situation led large numbers of Iranians to turn toward Islam. In part, this was due to the organizational efforts of prominent clerics, including those, like Khomeini, who had been driven into exile. Although joined by equally determined secular critics of the regime, clerics and other religious intellectuals played a leading role in mobilizing opposition to the shah and his government. During the 1960s and 1970s, they laid the organizational and political foundation for a movement that subsequently initiated a mass uprising against the shah and what one critic called his "pseudo-modernist state structure."[45] Beyond organization, however, the clerics also drew support from the appeal of their political formula—an alternative to the uncaring and self-serving secular nationalism of the regime, one promising justice, equality, and the rule of law in a political system governed by the Shari'a. Thousands of Iranians, particularly the young, thus came to see Islam as "a force of liberation and a refuge from the oppressive secular politics of Pahlavi rule." In the mid- and late 1970s, "men and women flocked to religious study centers, where they discussed social and political matters in terms of the lives of the infallible religious leaders of Shi'i Islam."[46] By 1974, according to one study, there were over 12,300 religious associations in Tehran alone.[47] The Islamic revival was particularly strong in secondary schools and universities, where large numbers of women put on the veil and where some now called for segregation of the sexes.

Early in 1978, popular anger culminated in protest demonstrations against the shah, and by the latter part of the year the country was paralyzed by strikes and in a state of virtual war as troops loyal to the regime struggled to restore order. The shah left the country at this time, in January 1979, for what was officially described as medical rest, and two weeks later Ayatollah Khomeini returned from exile and was greeted by cheering crowds. Street fighting continued for another few weeks as the military worked to confront protesters and rebels, but the troops returned to their barracks in mid-February, and in April the country voted in a national referendum to become an Islamic republic governed by a theocratic constitution. Khomeini became the supreme leader of Iran in December 1979.

These events not only transformed Iran, they also contributed much more broadly to the emerging political dimension of the Islamic resurgence. As observed by a student of Tunisian politics, the Iranian revolution provided a populist vocabulary that helped Islamic movements in other countries to broaden their appeal.[48] Indeed, as expressed by another scholar of the region, it became "a shining example" by demonstrating that Islam "could inspire the masses because it spoke to them in their own language (unlike 'imported' Western ideas of the left and the nationalists)."[49] In addition, the Iranian revolution held out the possibility that those working for change under the banner of Islam might be able, even if the support of those who did not share their theocratic aspirations was required, to overturn an entrenched regime that had powerful economic and military resources at its disposal and was strongly supported by one of the world's superpowers. Thus, although the Iranian revolution "was not the original spark for revivalist movements throughout the region but the climax of an already deeply rooted movement," as another student of the Islamic resurgence points out, it added momentum far beyond Iran's borders by sending the message that "Islam could be a successful idiom of opposition" against powerful regimes that, on the surface, might appear to be invincible.[50]

Although in no other case was the political map transformed as thoroughly as in Iran, regimes in other countries were also badly shaken by outbreaks of popular anger over economic and political conditions. The best examples during the 1980s are the riots that took place in Morocco in 1981 and 1984; in Tunisia in 1984; in Algeria in 1985, 1986, and 1988; and in Jordan in 1989, each of which, in the short run at least, increased public receptivity to the alternative to the status quo offered by Islamists.

The litany of grievances in these countries and elsewhere was generally the same. First, masses of people lived in impoverished conditions, and, for much of the population, especially the young, the prospects for social mobility and a higher standard of living were declining rather than growing brighter. Second, there was a large and growing gap between rich and poor, meaning that the burdens of underdevelopment were not being shared equitably and that, despite economic difficulties, there were islands of affluence and elite privilege, often involving luxury and excess. As a study of Algeria reported, people were asking why more than half of the university graduates were jobless while the country earned billions per year from natural gas and many of its leaders were living like kings.[51] Third, there was a widespread belief that elite status was determined in most instances not by ability, dedication, or service to society but, rather, by personal and political connections, the result being a system where patronage and clientelism predominated in decisions about public policy and resource allocation and where "even college graduates without necessary family connections cannot get jobs."[52] Finally, there were few legitimate mechanisms by which the populace could register complaints in a way that had a meaningful impact on the political process, and none whatsoever by which it could remove senior political leaders whose performance was judged unsatisfactory. Accounts of conversations with ordinary citizens from many walks of life consistently produced the same list of complaints, with the frequent addition that there was not a single Arab state to which one could point as a model of proper government.[53]

The intensity and scale of the disturbances provoked by these grievances, and of the anger that produced them, is reflected in the following account of events in Morocco. Comparable accounts could be offered for Tunisia, Algeria, and Jordan.

In June 1981, tensions associated with economic and political grievances exploded in the form of violent riots in Casablanca. The immediate cause of the disturbances was a reduction in food subsidies that the government had enacted in response to pressure from foreign creditors, but the scope and intensity of the rioting revealed the depth of public anger. As thousands of young men from the city's sprawling slums poured into the streets, roaming mobs attacked banks, auto dealerships, and other businesses and public buildings identified with elite privilege or government authority. In subduing the rioters, police sometimes fired into the crowd, and at least 200 protesters were killed. Some estimates place the number much higher.

Additional rioting broke out in January 1984. A rise in the price of basic commodities subsidized by the government was announced, and again the burden fell most heavily on the working class and the poor. The first disturbances took place in Marrakesh, where students and unemployed youth from poorer neighborhoods took to the streets, and these protests were then followed by demonstrations in Agadir, Safi and Kasbah-Tadla in the south and in Rabat and Meknes in the central part of the country. Disturbances of greater intensity thereafter developed in the north, the most neglected and underdeveloped region of the country. In Nador, for example, there were attacks on banks and the agency of the national airline, Royal Air Maroc, indicating anger at the government and special bitterness at institutions symbolizing elite privilege. Some protesters carried pink parasols to express their disdain for royal pomp and their indignation at the excesses of the king and the elite. In Al Hoceima, protesting students were joined by fisherman, sailors, port workers and many others, including women. Moroccan security forces used considerable violence in quelling the riots in these and other northern cities. Press reports spoke of 150-200 deaths, or in some cases even more, as well as hundreds of injured and approximately 9,000 arrested.[54]

Maturing Movements

During the 1970s and 1980s, and often throughout the 1990s, movements organized under the banner of Islam continued to gain strength and became increasingly important political actors. As noted, regional developments contributed to this. Prominent among these was the Arabs' crushing defeat in their June 1967 war with Israel, which led many to lose faith in the argument of reformers and revolutionaries that socialism, secular nationalism, and pan-Arabism would make the Arab world strong and prosperous. Another factor was the oil boom of the 1970s, which provided new resources for Islamists and for Islamic projects throughout the region, including educational, cultural, and charitable activities with an Islamist orientation. Finally, the Iranian revolution of 1979 sent the message that groups and citizens mobilized under the banner of Islam could remove from power a highly unpopular regime that had appeared to be too powerful to be successfully challenged.

At least equally important, and in most cases more so, was the domestic situation in many Muslim-majority countries in the Middle East and North Africa. As discussed, economic hardships fostered popular discontent and anger, with citizens not only complaining about their government's inability to address pressing problems but also laying blame for this situation squarely on a self-serving and essentially closed political elite whose primary concern was the preservation of its own power and privilege.

But while this situation made some more receptive to the message that "Islam is the solution," other domestic considerations also contributed to the increasing salience of Islamist parties and movements and to the emergence of political Islam as a potent factor in debates about governance. One of these was the weakness, and often the absence, of meaningful opposition to the existing political order from leftist parties and political movements. Such movements lost much of their former appeal during this period, with a discouraged Egyptian socialist stating in the mid-1990s, "I do not believe Islam has a *real* solution, but we are without even the *name* of a solution."[55] Leftist opposition movements also suffered from interference and sometimes outright repression by the state, which during the early years of this period considered them a more important challenge than political Islam. Indeed, the authorities in some countries for a time quietly encouraged and gave political space to Islamic groups in order to counterbalance the Left. This occurred in Egypt, Jordan, Tunisia, and Palestine, as well as elsewhere. Thus, in countries where the Left was weak or absent, support for political Islam was usually the best, and sometimes the only, option for citizens seeking to oppose the status quo.

Islamist movements did not gain strength merely by default, however, or simply because there was often no credible alternative for expressing opposition to the prevailing political and economic order. These movements used an expanding network of religious, social, and cultural institutions to spread their message and mobilize support, which permitted them to operate though channels over which the state had only limited control and thus freed them, at least partly, from the interference that constrained the organizational opportunities available to other potential opponents of the regime. As two Algerian scholars wrote about the rise of Islamist movement in North Africa, "at first, through a network of independent mosques, the Islamists preached educational and mobilizational sermons," and by the mid-1980s this had given rise to a well-structured political organization.[56] Similarly, as an American scholar of Egyptian origin observed about this phenomenon in the eastern part of the Arab world, groups associated with political Islam used religious and cultural institutions and programs, particularly those that target the poor, to "participate in the political process within the official parameters of permissible action while working to extract concessions from the state to allow the [Islamist] movement greater access to the masses and through them access to power."[57]

A careful study of Egypt describes how these factors contributed to the strength of the Islamist movement in that country. While frequently without access to formal political institutions, Islamists found numerous opportunities for organization and outreach in ostensibly "nonpolitical" settings, and specifically those beyond the control of the state. Moreover, while the Muslim Brotherhood had been banned by Nasser and remained so under his successor, Anwar Sadat, Sadat initially gave some political space to Islamist groups on university campuses and elsewhere. As a result, there developed in Egypt in the 1970s and 1980s a vast, decentralized network of Islamic institutions that furnished the infrastructure, resources, and cadres for the mobilization of young people. Islamic activists used this network not only to denounce the Sadat and later the Mubarak regime but also to promote a militant and activist interpretation of Islam. Claiming the authority to interpret Islamic texts, Islamists promoted a new ethic of civic obligation and called upon recruits to participate in the Islamic reform of society and state.[58]

Similar trends were in evidence in many other Middle Eastern and North African countries, including but not limited to those that experienced explosions of popular discontent during the 1970s and 1980s. In Morocco, a number of new Islamist organizations appeared in the 1980s. In the 1990s, the most important of these, al-Islâh wal-Tajdîd, joined with and gained influence within a small political party, the Constitutional and Democratic Popular Movement; and in 1997, having changed its name to the Justice and Development Party (PJD), this new party participated in Morocco's multiparty parliamentary elections and won seats in nine of the districts in which it entered candidates. In 2002, campaigning on a platform that sought to balance "the pragmatic demands of participation and those dictated by its Islamist frame of reference,"[59] and presenting candidates in slightly more than half of the electoral districts, the PJD won forty-two seats, more than all but two of the twenty-three parties that sent at least one representative to the parliament.

In Tunisia, the Association for the Protection of the Quran was officially recognized as a "cultural organization" in 1970. The association's center was at the national university, where it attracted both students and faculty. Several years later, seeking to go beyond the association's cultural agenda, some members formed a new organization, al-Jama'at al-Islamiyya, and by the early 1980s this had evolved into the more explicitly political al-Ittijah al-Islami, the Islamic Tendency Movement (MTI).[60] The government arrested the MTI's leader, Rachid al-Ghannouchi, several times during this period. The movement nevertheless continued to gain influence. Its confrontation with the country's aging president, Habib Bour-guiba, led to a coup in 1987. With the new government promising greater political freedom, the MTI reconstituted itself as al-Nahda, the Renaissance Party; signed an all-parties national pact promising to uphold democratic principles; and pre-pared to participate in the 1989 parliamentary elections. The party was ulti-mately denied recognition, however, and its candidates were required to run on lists of independents, but this did not prevent them from winning 15 percent of all votes cast and up to one-third of the votes in major cities. Soon thereafter, Tunisia turned away from its democratic opening. Al-Nahda was declared a terror-ist organization, a large number of its members were arrested, and Ghannouchi went into exile.[61]

The Algerian experience, although it ended tragically, illustrates particularly clearly the extent to which public anger was leading to support for political Islam during this period. Shaken by the riots of the 1980s, the government embarked on a bold experiment in democratization at the end of the decade. Factions across the political spectrum were permitted to organize and participate in the mu-nicipal, provincial, and parliamentary elections scheduled for 1990 and 1991. The Islamic Salvation Front (FIS) was founded at this time by Abbassi Madani, an elderly sheikh whose orientation was relatively conservative, and Ali Belhadj, a younger and more militant high school teacher and imam. Representing a broad spectrum of Islamist opinion, FIS drew support from many quarters, including many for whom the appeal was its opposition to the political and economic sta-tus quo rather than the content of its proposed Islamic alternative.[62]

The party scored a decisive victory in the 1990 municipal and provincial elec-tions, capturing 54 percent of all votes cast and winning a majority of the seats in 55 percent of the municipal councils and two-thirds of the provincial assemblies. FIS also prevailed in the first round of parliamentary voting in 1991, winning 48 percent of the overall vote and 188 of the 231 seats contested in that round. The government responded to the FIS victory by canceling the second round of bal-loting for the parliament, and soon thereafter, amidst growing unrest, it banned the FIS, arrested a large number of its members, and placed the country under the control of the military. The next years were marked by violent conflict, with atrocities committed both by Islamic splinter groups and by the military and the vigilante groups it sponsored. By the time the so-called civil war subsided toward the end of the decade, an estimated 150,000 Algerians had been killed.

In Jordan, the Muslim Brotherhood was, and remains, the foundation of the Islamist movement. Established in 1945 and loosely connected to the Muslim Brotherhood in Egypt, it has over the years maintained complex but frequently positive relations with the Jordanian monarchy. In the absence of interference from the government, the Brotherhood built support during the 1970s and 1980s through an expanding network of social, charitable, and educational institutions.

According to a report in the early 1990s, this network included "some 20 Islamic clinics, one of Amman's largest hospitals, well over 40 Islamic schools, some 150 Quran studies centers, and other elements of what anti-fundamentalists call 'the infrastructure of an Islamic republic.' "[63] This was a very sizeable operation in a country that at the time had only four million inhabitants. The Brotherhood also benefitted from the economic and political discontent of many Jordanians, particularly those of Palestinian origin. As described by a close observer a few years after the 1989 riots, "many people were not willing to tighten their belts to pay for an economic crisis which they felt was the result of widespread corruption." The problem, she continued, was that "a system of cronyism is persuasive" among the country's elite, with opportunities for enrichment channeled by insiders to their friends and with top positions always going "to the same old faces, families and clans."[64]

Against this background, and with the king responding to the 1989 riots by permitting greater political freedom, candidates affiliated with the Muslim Brotherhood ran in the parliamentary elections that took place later that year and won twenty-two of the eighty seats in the assembly, as did nine others who described themselves as independent Islamists. The ban on political parties was lifted in advance of the next election, in 1993, and the political wing of the Muslim Brotherhood, the Islamic Action Front (IAF), was then established. There were also changes in the electoral law, with voters now permitted to cast their ballot for only one candidate in multimember districts, and this removed what had been an advantage for Brotherhood candidates in 1989. The IAF nonetheless won sixteen seats in the assembly, a strong showing, and remained an important force in Jordanian politics.[65]

Comparable developments took place in many other countries. Although none experienced the riots that shook Egypt, Morocco, Tunisia, Algeria, and Jordan, local and regional circumstances fostered a significant increase in the salience of Islamic political movements in Lebanon, Turkey, Yemen, Kuwait, and among Palestinians in the West Bank and Gaza, as well as elsewhere, during the 1980s and 1990s. In Lebanon, Hizbollah, the Party of God, emerged alongside the largely secular Amal Party in the 1980s. Both parties drew most of their support from the Shi'i population, the country's largest confessional community, and Hizbollah was initially known as the Islamic Amal. Among the objectives set forth in the manifesto issued by Hizbollah in 1985 was the transformation of Lebanon into an Islamic state. In one capacity, the movement was, and remains, a paramilitary organization; it has done battle with Israel and has resisted calls by the Lebanese government to surrender its weapons. Beyond this, however, Hizbollah resembles Islamic movements in other countries and has become a major force in Lebanese politics and society. Its network of schools, clinics, and other social institutions expanded steadily during the 1980s and 1990s. It also operates a radio and television station. Hizbollah functions as a political party as well. It began taking part in Lebanese elections in 1992 and in that year won eight seats, the largest single bloc in the 128-member parliament. Its allies won an additional four seats. From that point on, as one scholar reports, Hizbollah "developed a reputation—even among those who disagree vehemently with its ideology—for being a 'clean' and capable political party on both the national and local levels."[66]

Islamist party politics in Turkey began with the founding of the National Order Party in 1970 and its successor, the National Salvation Party, in 1973. But competition from secular and nationalist parties and, especially, repeated interventions by the military prevented any sustained growth until the Islamist Welfare Party, Refah, was established in 1983. Refah gained strength steadily during the 1980s and 1990s. Its Islamist platform attracted support among businessmen and young professionals, including students and former students with secular family backgrounds. The party's constituency also included the urban poor. In the face of widespread poverty and a growing gap between rich and poor, Refah and other Islamist movements preached to this constituency about the need for social justice and an end to government favoritism and corruption. They also organized social service and antipoverty activities. In 1994, the party won the races for mayor in Ankara and Istanbul, and it captured nearly one-third of the seats in the parliamentary elections of 1995, becoming the largest block in the assembly. As in earlier elections, the economic complaints of the working class and poor, particularly in the cities, played an important role in Refah's victory. Contrasting the relative importance of the party's emphasis on fighting poverty and corruption with its moral appeal based on Islam, a close observer of Turkish politics concludes that most voters were motivated by economic considerations, including the government's failure to provide needed public services. With respect to Islam, she adds, the religion's moral appeal, "powerful though it may seem . . . cannot be assumed a priori to be the principal agent of political mobilization."[67]

North and South Yemen were unified in 1990, at which time political parties were made legal and the Yemeni Congregation for Reform, Islah, was established as the Yemeni branch of the Muslim Brotherhood. The party advanced an Islamist agenda and called for legislation to deepen the Islamic character of state and society in Yemen. Islah also had close ties to the country's largest network of charitable organizations, through which it supported the operation of schools, clinics, and religious societies and distributed food and other forms of assistance to the needy. Reflecting the realities of Yemeni society, Islah had a tribal as well as a religious wing, and this sometimes led to divided views on important issues and prevented the party from developing a clear parliamentary platform, forcing it instead to balance competing political interests and differing interpretations of its Islamist agenda. The party has been both a supporter and an opponent of the government over the years. It was initially a junior member of the government's coalition, assisting in an effort to marginalize the Yemeni Socialist Party, the former ruling party of South Yemen. Subsequently, in 1997, Islah joined the opposition, and since that time has given somewhat less attention to an explicitly Islamist agenda and attached higher priority to political, economic, and social reform. Like Islamist opposition parties elsewhere in the region, the party calls for greater democratization and insists that democracy and Islam are compatible.[68]

In Kuwait, Islamic political movements have long been an important part of the political scene. Kuwait gained independence from Britain in 1961 and set up the first elected parliament in the Arab Gulf region in 1963. Moreover, although Kuwait's ruler, the emir, has the final say in political matters, the parliament was nonetheless given important powers, including responsibility for approving the state budget and all key laws and the right to question government ministers. Political parties are not permitted in Kuwait, but the Kuwaiti wing of the Muslim Brotherhood, the Islamic Constitutional Movement, Hadas, has long been one of several political factions that contest elections and participate actively in parliamentary affairs. Integrated in this way into the Kuwaiti political mainstream, Hadas has regularly challenged both the emir and the liberals in parliament on various issues. Its deputies called for a constitutional amendment that would strengthen the country's commitment to Islamic law, for example, and opposed such measures as women voting and men and women studying together at the university.

The emir suspended the parliament for several years in the 1970s and 1980s, but parliamentary life resumed in 1992, a year after Kuwait's liberation from Iraqi occupation, and Hadas continued to play an important role. Interestingly, in part because Kuwait's open political system has not required different Islamic tendency movements to unite against the regime, two additional Islamic political groupings emerged in the 1990s, including, in addition to Hadas, the more radical Popular Islamic Alignment and the National Islamic Coalition, representing Shi'i Islamists.[69] In the election of 1999, Islamist candidates won twenty of the parliament's fifty seats, with sixteen going to liberals and the remaining fourteen going to pro-government candidates.

In the 1970s, the official position of the Palestine Liberation Organization (PLO) was that the conflict with Israel should be resolved by establishing a single democratic and secular state in all of Palestine. Nevertheless, as elsewhere, there was an Islamic reawakening in Palestinian society during this period. A wide variety of Islamic cultural, educational, and religious institutions emerged in the 1970s and 1980s, and toward the end of the former decade Islamic movements also began to organize politically. The Palestinian Muslim Brotherhood was the most important of these movements, although it was not the only group to mobilize in the name of Islam.[70]

Given Israeli restrictions on Palestinian political activity in the West Bank and Gaza, Islamists devoted much of their energy to building support on university campuses, where, during the 1980s, they increasingly prevailed in student elections.[71] Islamic political movements also had some success in organizing more broadly, in part because some space was provided by Israel. Both Israel and Jordan sought to counter PLO influence among ordinary Palestinians in the 1980s, and so Jordan provided funds, often of Saudi origin, that Israel permitted to flow to Islamist movements in the occupied territories, and the groups themselves were granted a measure of latitude to organize.[72] Early in 1988, a few weeks after the outbreak of the intifada, the Palestinian uprising against the Israeli occupation, leaders of the Muslim Brotherhood in Palestine established the Islamic Resistance Movement, Hamas, which gradually extended its political influence. Leaflets distributed by Hamas played a role in giving direction to the intifada, along with those of mainstream nationalists; and, after the signing of the Israeli-Palestinian accord in 1993, Hamas represented and gained strength among Palestinians opposed to peace with Israel. Public opinion polls toward the end of the decade showed that Hamas was the preferred faction of about 20 percent of West Bank and Gaza Palestinians, roughly half the proportion favoring Fatah, the dominant faction in the PLO. During the first decade of the twenty-first century, after the collapse of the Israeli-Palestinian peace process, support for Hamas continued to grow, and the party defeated the previously dominant Fatah faction in the parliamentary elections of 2006.

Democracy and Political Islam

During the earlier stages of the Islamic resurgence, in the 1970s and 1980s, some observers predicted that political Islam would turn out to be a transient phenomenon; it would remain politically important in some countries but, more generally, it would ultimately prove to be only a temporary digression from the more powerful historical trends of modernization and secular nationalism that had predominated during the post–World War II period. Clearly such predictions were not correct. As indicated by the incomplete but nonetheless broadly representative sample of national experiences described above, parties and movements committed to a significant role for Islam in government and political affairs had become important political actors by the end of the twentieth century. Although not equally important everywhere, and not always important to the same degree or in precisely the same way, the organizational strength and popular appeal of advocates of political Islam were having a significant impact on political life across the Middle East and North Africa.

At the same time, the Middle East and North Africa have in recent years been marked not only by the rise of political Islam but also by the currents of democratization that have swept over much of the developing and post-Communist world, what is sometimes called the "third wave" of democratization. This third wave often includes the view that political space for Islamists is required but, more than that, that solutions to society's problems are not to be found in an embrace of the "correct" political ideology, be it socialist, Islamist, or other, but rather in political pluralism and the kind of genuine political contestation through which ordinary citizens can express their views, have meaningful choices, and hold autocratic rulers accountable.

Arab intellectuals, political activists, and civil society leaders, as well as many ordinary citizens, not only lament the autocratic character of the political systems by which their countries are governed but insist as well that democratization must be a central component of any strategy for addressing the problems faced by their societies. Such sentiments were clearly in evidence by the mid-1980s and became increasingly widespread in the years that followed. A Jordanian journalist wrote in 1990, for example, that there are everywhere "signs of a profound desire for change—for democracy and human rights, for social equity . . . for accountability of public officials."[73] According to another analyst writing at the time, "the demand for human rights, participation and democracy comes from across the political spectrum. . . . The call for democracy is the subject of meetings, conferences and academic studies."[74] One such meeting was a pan-Arab conference, held in Amman, Jordan, in 1991, and attended by prominent intellectuals. Participants called for a "new Arab order" and declared in their final communiqué that "democracy should take priority in the pan-Arab national project. It should not be sacrificed for any other value or cause—including Arab unity itself."[75]

Democracy is also central to the views that ordinary men and women hold about the way their countries should be governed.[76] Public opinion research in the Middle East and North Africa, including forty surveys carried out in fifteen different countries between 2000 and 2011, makes clear that vast majorities want their countries to be governed by a political system that is democratic. Among the nearly 65,000 respondents in all of these surveys taken together, 85.6 percent of those interviewed expressed the view that democracy, whatever its drawbacks, is the best form of government; and among respondents in the most recent surveys, conducted in 2010 and 2011, 82.2 percent agreed with this statement.[77] These data, together with those from several surveys carried out before 2000, are used in later chapters to test hypotheses about determinants of the attitudes held by ordinary citizens about the role that Islam should play in government and political affairs. But while there are important divisions of opinion about Islam's place in political life, giving importance to research that seeks to account for this variance, with respect to democracy, by contrast, there is far more agreement than disagreement. Not only do more than 80 percent of the respondents in the forty surveys believe that democracy is the best political system, 90 percent say that democracy would be a good or very good system of government for the country in which they live.

Other analyses of these data show that some respondents have only a limited understanding of democracy, seeing it primarily as a mechanism for increasing government responsiveness to ordinary citizens but not necessarily thinking about minority rights, the protection of controversial speech, and other considerations that define a genuinely democratic political system. Nevertheless, the data make clear that the ability of ordinary citizens to hold rulers accountable is central to the way people want their country to be governed, and to this extent, at the very least, their views align with those of the more sophisticated Arab advocates of democracy. Interestingly, perhaps because of the persistence of authoritarianism across the region, cross-regional data from the World Values Survey indicate that public support for democracy in the Arab world is as high as or higher than in any other world region.[78]

Arab regimes have not responded to these calls for democracy. Indeed, some have retreated from political openings that for a short time in the 1990s gave a measure of hope to advocates of democracy. The discontent that gave rise to protests and disturbances a decade or two earlier thus remained as widespread as ever during the last years of the twentieth century and the first years of the new millennium. The 2005 Arab Human Development Report, prepared by a cross-section of Arab scholars and intellectuals under the auspices of the United Nations Development Programme, described "growing winds of protest against governments and the intensifying demands for radical reform around the Arab world."[79] A similar point was made in 2005 by a U.S. task force, based on meetings with Arab scholars and public officials drawn from seven countries:

> Across the Arab world, political activists are challenging the status quo. Egyptians are demanding an end to the state of emergency that has been in place almost continuously since the 1950s; Syrians have petitioned their government for political freedoms; Jordanians are seizing new economic opportunities; women in the traditionally conservative Gulf states are seeking wider political and economic participation; even Saudi Arabia is experimenting with elections at the municipal level.[80]

And, of course, anger at rulers and a profound desire for political change were reflected most dramatically in the popular uprisings that swept the Arab world in 2011. The protests that began in Tunisia in December 2010 and quickly spread to Egypt and other countries left little doubt, despite uncertainty about the outcome, regarding the desire of Arab publics to be governed in accordance with democratic principles.

Democracy and political Islam are not incompatible and are not necessarily in competition with one another. Many Islamist leaders and movements express support for pluralism and democracy and claim to want no more than an opportunity to participate in a competitive political process that enables them to seek support for their ideas and bargain about them inside the legitimate institutions of government. Advocates of democracy vary in their response to this claim. Some, possibly most, acknowledge that Islamists represent a significant and legitimate current of political opinion. Indeed, since Islam is central to the identity and culture of these countries, meaningful democracy would be impossible if movements that derive their platform from the religion were excluded from legitimate politics, or if those who wish to support these movements in free and fair elections were denied the opportunity to do so. Otherwise, democracy would be seriously compromised and the political system would not in reality be democratic at all.

Others assess the situation differently. While perhaps agreeing with this reasoning in the abstract, they contend that Islamists, or at least those in their countries, are not sincerely committed to democracy and will thus use any influence or power they acquire to support policies that would actually subvert democracy, such as denying equal rights to women or imposing a strict interpretation of Islamic law in other areas. "One man, one vote, one time" is the slogan used by some who believe that democracy would be in danger should Islamist movements and parties gain a substantial measure of power, even if that power were acquired through the democratic process. This phrase first emerged in relation to the elections in Algeria in the early 1990s, where it expressed a fear that the Islamist party that won the country's first free and fair election might not permit electoral competition in the future. Not all who make this argument are necessarily sincere. Some may be motivated by a desire to eliminate an important political competitor, rather than by a genuine commitment to the preservation of democracy, and they thus find in this allegation a convenient justification for their position. Nevertheless, while some believe that meaningful democracy is impossible *without* the inclusion of Islamist parties and movements, others believe, or claim to believe, that it very well may be impossible *with* their inclusion.[81]

The remaining part of the emerging picture concerns the response of rulers in the Muslim-majority countries of the Middle East and North Africa, and particularly in the Arab world since the question of Islamist political participation does not arise, although for very different reasons, in either Turkey or Iran. In some Arab countries, such as Lebanon, Kuwait, and Palestine, parties and groupings that advance an Islamist platform have achieved an apparently secure place in the political arena, and one that, opposition notwithstanding, will almost certainly permit them to continue to exert political influence. But in many other Arab countries, the ruling regime has sought to limit, and has usually succeeded in limiting, the political space available to Islamists.

In some countries, this has involved a clamp down on all political dissent; and this includes countries that had previously taken halting steps toward democratization, or in a few cases even bold steps, in response to popular unrest or the currents of political reform that were bringing dramatic changes in post-Communist and other late-developing countries. As one scholar wrote in 1999 when describing the fate of democratic experiments initiated during the preceding decade, the situation is "exceptionally bleak . . . from the spectacular crash and burn of Algeria's liberalization to Tunisia's more subtle but no less profound transformation into a police state, from Egypt's backsliding into electoral manipulation [and repression of Islamic political movements] to the obvious reluctance of Palestinian authorities to embrace human rights."[82]

Students of the region thus talked about the persistence, or robustness, of authoritarianism, pointing out that in numerous instances the state has acted to suppress any opponents posing a challenge it believes too serious to tolerate.[83] Assessing the situation in 2005, one analyst wrote that authoritarianism has persisted in the Middle East and North Africa "because the coercive apparatus in many states has proven exceptionally able and willing to crush reform initiatives from below."[84] Nor did the situation subsequently improve. Looking back in 2010 over the history of Arab politics, another analyst pointed out that "among the sixteen independent Arab states of the Middle East and coastal North Africa, Lebanon is the only one to have *ever* been a democracy."[85]

But if regime unwillingness to tolerate significant challenges from any quarter structures the political environment within which Islamist parties and movements operate, these groups have also been affected by state actions for which they are the specific target. Moreover, given their independent organizational strength and relative success in elections, they have usually represented the challenge to regime hegemony about which rulers have been most concerned and against which these rulers have most frequently taken action. In Egypt, for example, the government escalated its campaign against the Brotherhood in 2006 and 2007, arresting thousands of its members and pushing through numerous constitutional amendments that, according to Amnesty International, constituted the greatest erosion of human rights since the rule of Anwar Sadat. In Jordan, the government moved against the charity arm of the Muslim Brotherhood in 2006, replacing its board with more acceptable members, and, in 2007, it interfered in the municipal and parliamentary elections in order to ensure an outcome it favored. Noting that there have been comparable developments in a number of other countries, a study published in 2010 by the Brookings Institution Center in Doha concluded that "Arab regimes have come to the conclusion that repression of Islamic groups is an effective strategy, largely because it is." And in some cases at least, "the political exclusion of Islamists appears to have 'tamed' them, pushing them away from electoral contestation toward less threatening social activities."[86]

Such actions have not only constrained the political activities of Islamist groups, they have also led to intense and sometimes acrimonious debates within the groups themselves. The division is usually between those who believe the best strategy is to boycott elections and otherwise withdraw from the state-sanctioned political process and those who believe it would be better to seek an accommodation with the regime. The former argue that state actions make political and electoral participation meaningless, whereas the latter believe that more will be accomplished if the movement seeks an accommodation with the regime. As a result, as noted in the study mentioned above, "some of the Middle East's most prominent Islamist groups are in a state of crisis, racked by internal divisions and struggling to respond to regime repression." Nor is this something of which regimes are unaware. On the contrary, according to the same study, Arab regimes have come to see repression not only as a way to hamper the political activity of Islamist groups and reduce their political gains, but also as "an effective tool with which to encourage internal divisions within Islamist movements, particularly between those who advocate a confrontational stance—through street protests, for example—and those who see it as their responsibility to protect members of the group from mass arrests."[87]

National Variations

This brief historical overview of political developments and ideological currents in the Middle East and North Africa during the second half of the twentieth century reveals several region-wide trends. One is a steady resurgence of Islam, both among ordinary citizens and in the political arena. In the latter connection, even though developments were not everywhere the same, the period was marked by growth in the importance of political movements that organized and campaigned under the banner of Islam. As a result, again despite some cross-national variation, the proposition that Islam should play an important role in government and political affairs, indeed the leading role, had strong advocates. Over the course of this period, political Islam became an essential component in public discourse about political formulae—in the way that people, many of whom were deeply discontent with the political and economic status quo, thought about and argued about the way their country should be governed.

A second trend is that political Islam, despite its salience, has not been uncontested. Leftist ideologies lost much of their former appeal, but in their place emerged, both among intellectuals and activists and in the arena of public opinion, broad support for a democratic political formula that emphasizes pluralism, assigns responsibility for legislation and policy-making to leaders accountable to the people, and sees political Islam as only one among a variety of platforms that compete for support within a democratic framework accepted by all participants. Some, perhaps even many, support both democracy and an important political role for Islam, insisting that there is no contradiction or inconsistency in this. But while this position rejects any suggestion that Islam and democracy are incompatible, it places the former within the framework of the later and stands in contrast to the call of Islamists for society to be governed exclusively by Islamic law as interpreted by men of Islamic learning.

A final trend is that neither political Islam nor democracy has emerged as the defining characteristic of the political system by which most Muslim-majority countries of the Middle East and North Africa are governed. To be sure, there are several cases where Islam does indeed occupy a central place in political affairs, or where, at the very least, those who believe their country should be governed by Islamic institutions and Islamic law have disproportionate political power. Iran and Saudi Arabia are the best examples, although in both there are segments of the population that would prefer a different political arrangement. There are also a few countries where the political system is essentially democratic. Turkey is the best example, although there remain some limitations on political freedom and these limitations appear to be growing. A few others may be characterized as partly free, or perhaps quasi-democratic, meaning that citizens have some freedom to criticize the government and that elections are competitive, albeit not always free from government interference. More common, however, are situations where political life is dominated by an autocratic ruler and a small political elite, with opposition to the prevailing order expressed both by advocates of political Islam and by advocates of democracy.

These trends shaping the region's political history from the 1950s through the first decade of the present century show how and why Islam became a central concern in political discourse and in debates about the most appropriate political formula. They have given rise to a pattern that is broadly generalizable across the Middle East and North Africa: in the context of an ongoing search for an appropriate and agreed-upon political formula, and with large segments of the population dissatisfied with the prevailing political and economic order, the view that Islam should play a leading role in government and political affairs, or at least a very important role, is widely and vigorously advanced but also widely and vigorously contested. Nor is this likely to change in the foreseeable future, despite the important shocks that some countries have experienced in the wake of the Arab Spring.

The existence of region-wide historical trends and a broadly applicable political configuration does not mean that there is no cross-country variation with respect to political systems. Indeed, quite the opposite is the case. Some countries are governed by monarchs, and some are republics with a strong president or prime minister. More relevant to the present discussion is that some countries are not free but others are at least partly free, with elections that are competitive, even if they sometimes are for seats in assemblies with only limited power. Islamist opposition movements are important political actors in some countries, less so in others, and are virtually absent, or only underground, in still others.

The political system that has emerged in each Muslim-majority country of the Middle East and North Africa is a product not only of the broad political and ideological currents that have marked the region as a whole but also of each country's own unique historical experience and its particular political, economic, demographic, and cultural characteristics. The following summary outline of differences between the political systems of Turkey, Syria, Tunisia, Algeria, Iran, Saudi Arabia, Qatar, Jordan, Morocco, Kuwait, Lebanon, Iraq, and Bahrain as they existed at the end of the first decade of the present century, around 2010, illustrates the very diverse ways in which region-wide trends have played out in individual countries, their impact having been shaped and given tangible expression in each case by country-specific circumstances.

- The Turkish political system is competitive and was for many years avowedly secular, but the country's most important political party has Islamist origins, and it sometimes works to implement an Islamist social agenda.
- The regimes in Syria and Tunisia are secular; Islamist political movements are suppressed and meaningful political competition is not permitted.
- The Algerian regime is secular but permits some Islamist parties and candidates to participate in elections that sometimes are and sometimes are not relatively free and fair.
- There is political competition in Iran, but the system is essentially theocratic, and only candidates approved by religious authorities can participate in elections.
- The monarchical Saudi Arabian political system is also theocratic, and there are no state-approved mechanisms for legitimate political competition.
- There is no organized political competition in Qatar, where Islamic law is applied in matters of personal status, but the rulers reject the kind of theocracy that exists in Iran and Saudi Arabia.
- Jordan and Morocco are both ruled by monarchies that claim religious legitimacy, and in both countries Islamist opposition parties compete in elections that sometimes have and sometimes have not been free of government interference.
- There are no political parties in Kuwait, but Islamists are well organized and have free rein to participate in political life and compete with others in elections for a parliament that enjoys a measure of political influence.
- In both Lebanon and Iraq the most important Islamist parties have a sectarian character and seek not only to advance the cause of political Islam but also to protect or improve the position of a particular confessional group.
- There is some, albeit limited, political contestation in Bahrain, with both Sunni and Shi'i Islamist parties competing in elections.

It is important to keep this variation in mind as the focus of the present inquiry shifts to the attitudes toward political Islam held by ordinary men and women. Although the question of Islam's place in government and political affairs figures prominently on the agenda of the region as a whole, the nature and determinants of people's views about this question may vary from country to country. The extent to which people believe that Islamic institutions, officials, and laws should play a leading role, or at least a very important role, in government and political affairs is unlikely to be the same in every Muslim-majority country of the Middle East and North Africa. Equally important, the *reasons* that some men and women support political Islam while others do not may also differ from country to country. Thus, if more than a description of this individual-level variation is to be offered, meaning that if questions are to be asked not only about whether and how but also about why citizen attitudes and the factors that shape them differ across the countries of the region, it will be necessary to consider the potential conditioning impact, and hence the explanatory power, of particular national circumstances. More specifically, it will be necessary to undertake analyses that investigate the degree to which cross-national variation in individual-level, within-country findings about the nature and determinants of citizen attitudes is accounted for by differences in country-level attributes and experiences.

Explanatory power may be found in temporal as well as cross-national variation since the circumstances of many countries have themselves varied over time. In many countries, for example, Islamist movements have been stronger and more important political actors during some periods and weaker and less important actors during others. Similarly, the political system in many countries has been more open at some points in time and less open at others to political contestation. The mapping of this temporal variation is not necessary for the purposes of this introduction, which are to indicate how and why political Islam came to occupy a central place on the political agenda of the Middle East and North Africa and to point out that discussions and debates about Islam's political role take place in, and are shaped by, the national as well as the regional context. But the importance of temporal variation does make it necessary to investigate the political conceptions and judgments of ordinary citizens in relation to the situation in their countries at the time these views were measured.

Against this background, the chapters to follow lay a foundation for, and then undertake, a two-level analysis aimed at identifying the country-level or time-sensitive attributes and experiences that encourage the emergence of particular attitudes among ordinary citizens and, even more, that constitute conditions under which particular individual-level attributes and experiences make citizens disproportionately likely to possess a given attitude toward Islam's political role. For example, should economic dissatisfaction foster support for political Islam among individuals in some countries but not others, or in the same country at some points in time but not others, it will be important to ask why this difference occurs. The data and methodology with which such questions will be investigated are presented in chapter 1. For the present, the points to be retained, in addition to those describing broad regional trends and their evolution during the last half-century, are that the nature and determinants of citizen attitudes toward Islam's political role may vary across countries and/or over time and that the goal is not only to map, or describe, these differences but also learn as much as possible about why they occur. To do this it is necessary to identify attributes and experiences that define the national or temporal conditions under which particular patterns relating to the nature, distribution, and determinants of citizen attitudes are disproportionately likely to be found.

With these objectives in mind, chapter 1 describes the public opinion data that have been brought together for this study and discusses issues of methodology associated with their analysis. Chapter 2 then draws upon these data to provide a description of the degree to which, and the ways in which, Islam is part of the daily lives of ordinary men and women in Muslim-majority countries of the Middle East and North Africa. This description focuses on personal religiosity and religious attachment, rather than attitudes toward *political* Islam, in order to provide a better understanding of the normative context within which attitudes are formed and debates about political Islam take place. In this connection, chapter 2 also focuses on the different ways that ordinary men and women think about how Islamic codes should be interpreted and applied in the organization of society and the conduct of people's lives. Accounting for variance in citizen attitudes toward political Islam is the focus of the individual-level analysis reported in chapter 3. Hypotheses about factors that predispose an individual toward either support for or opposition to the proposition that Islam should play a significant role in government and political affairs are introduced and tested. Chapter 4 builds on the individual-level findings reported in chapter 3 and proceeds to a survey-level analysis, the second level of the two-level analysis. More specifically, this chapter investigates and seeks to identify the time-specific characteristics of countries in which particular individual-level determinants of attitudes toward political Islam are disproportionately likely to have explanatory power. Finally, a short concluding chapter summarizes major findings and identifies avenues for future research.

1 A Two-Level Study of Attitudes toward Political Islam

Data and Methods

Until a decade or so ago, the investigation of individual attitudes, values, and behavior patterns was the "missing dimension" in political science research dealing with the Arab and Muslim Middle East.[1] Such research, although not completely absent, was limited to a very small number of American, Arab, and Turkish political scientists. It was also limited with respect to the countries where systematic survey research could be conducted, the degree to which representative national samples could be drawn, and the extent to which sensitive questions about politics could be asked.[2]

There are complaints about the paucity of research in this area going back to the 1970s. A major review of the scholarship on Arab society, published in 1976, called attention to the absence of systematic research on political attitudes and behavior patterns. The author of this review, I. William Zartman, stated that "the critical mass of research [in the field of political behavior] has been done outside the Middle East" and "data generation and analysis in the region remain to be done."[3] Malcolm Kerr, another leading student of Arab politics, offered a similar assessment a few years later. Writing in the foreword to *Political Behavior in the Arab States*, Kerr stated that there is a need for much more research in which the individual is the unit of analysis in order "to bring a healthier perspective to our understanding of Arab politics . . . and so that we may see it less as a reflection of formal cultural norms or contemporary world ideological currents and more as [the behavior] of ordinary individuals."[4]

Political scientist Michael Hudson echoed these concerns in the mid-1990s. In his contribution to a 1995 volume, *Liberalization and Democratization in the Arab World,* Hudson observed that "compared to other regions, empirical survey work on the Arab world is meager." Like Kerr, Hudson also noted that this encourages a "reductionist" approach to inquiry, one in which grand generalizations are advanced in the mistaken belief that citizen orientations can be explained and predicted from a knowledge of the "essential" attributes of Islamic or Arab culture.[5] William Quandt, yet another prominent scholar who studies the Middle East, similarly wrote about the danger of accounts that are not based on systematic and objective empirical research and that, therefore, can easily lead to misconceptions and stereotypes. In a discussion of the extensive civil violence that plagued Algeria during the 1990s, Quandt noted that people, including some Arabs, often ask, "why does Algeria have this deep crisis?" and they then answer their own question with statements like "the Algerians are violent people; they live in mountains. That is the way they have always been." Emphasizing the problematic nature of such explanations, Quandt wrote: "It is too easy to explain any country's problems by 'that's just the way they are.'"[6]

Essentialist explanations are problematic not only because they assert that people hold certain views or behave in certain ways *because* they are Arabs and/or Muslims but also, and even more fundamentally, because they mistakenly assume that there *are* clear and uncontested definitions of what constitute "Arab" and "Muslim" orientations. This approach ignores the significant differences that exist between Arab and Muslim countries, as well as the equally important individual-level variation that exists within countries. Important differences associated with age, education, class, gender, ethnicity, and residence are, in effect, defined out of existence by essentialist characterizations, or they are at least deemed to have so little explanatory power as to be unworthy of attention. The antidote to such flawed reasoning resides in rigorous survey research, which offers an objective, empirical basis not only for determining the aggregate views held by Arab and Muslim populations but also for mapping the normative and behavioral variation that exists both across and within countries.

Beyond contributing to misinformation, and perhaps even to myths and stereotypes, the absence of valid and reliable survey data has significantly limited the degree to which insights about the Arab and Muslim world can contribute to the less descriptive and more theoretical research agenda of contemporary political science. For example, the initiation of democratic transitions in many developing and post-Communist countries in the 1980s and 1990s brought increased interest in the political attitudes and values of ordinary citizens. But while important generalizable insights emerged from survey research in Latin America, sub-Saharan Africa, East Asia, and Eastern Europe, little was known about the extent to which patterns observed elsewhere might apply to Arab countries or whether evidence from the Arab world might itself contribute to the refinement of generalizable explanatory models.

Writing in this connection in 1999, political scientist Lisa Anderson discussed some of the ways in which research on the Arab world might inform, as well as be informed by, approaches and theories within the discipline of political science. Among the examples she discussed in connection with a broader analytical contribution are studies that account for individual-level variance in support of Islamist political movements and in conceptions of national identity, subjects that relate, in part, to the focus of the present study. Further, although Anderson also complained about the paucity of rigorous survey research in Arab countries, she went on to observe that "the limited survey research done in the Arab world has had disproportionately high payoffs, as both transient attitude shifts and more profound changes in conceptions of national identity have been revealed and verified."[7]

The most important reason for the dearth of survey research dealing with political issues is not a lack of interest on the part of political scientists or an absence of the training necessary to carry out such research. Nor is it, as is sometimes alleged, that ordinary citizens in the Arab and Muslim world are overly deferential to political authority and hence do not have clear and independent views on salient political issues. The explanation lies, first and foremost, in the undemocratic character of most Muslim-majority countries in the Middle East and North Africa. This made survey research impossible in many places, or at least required investigators to accept very severe limitations on the questions they could investigate, and this in turn discouraged scholars and students with an interest in Arab and Muslim politics from selecting topics that require this kind of research. As explained in 1987 by political scientist Iliya Harik, political attitude surveys are possible "only under conditions of political freedom," and the most important explanation for the paucity of such surveys in the Arab world is that the "political climate for this type of research does not exist."[8] Another prominent Arab social scientist, Saad Eddin Ibrahim, made the same point. Basing his conclusion on surveys carried out under the auspices of the Center for Arab Unity Studies, Ibrahim reported that "the Arab political environment is extremely hostile to scientific field research and deeply suspicious of the motives of serious and objective inquiry."[9]

Harik and Ibrahim offered these observations in the 1980s, and to a great extent they characterize the 1990s and the first few years of the twenty-first century as well. The situation has changed to a significant degree during the last decade, however. The Middle East still lags far behind other world regions with respect to freedom and civil liberties. But even before the Arab uprisings of 2011 there had been notable progress in some countries, at least to the point where official approval for survey research either was not needed or could be obtained; and so at present there are approximately a dozen Arab countries, as well as Turkey, in which it is possible to carry out systematic and objective political attitude surveys.

This situation has made possible a significant increase in political surveys of Muslim populations in the Middle East and North Africa. The number of opinion surveys dealing with political subjects does remain low, not only in comparison with regions where democratic political systems are more common but also in absolute terms. Nevertheless, the difference between the present and the period through the end of the twentieth century is striking.

One factor that differentiates the present from the preceding period is the growing number of local scholars with the interest and training needed to carry out valid, reliable, and representative political attitude studies. Important, too, is the growing number of academic institutions that conduct public opinion research, including research on political attitudes and behavior. A good example is the Center for Strategic Studies at the University of Jordan, which conducts surveys not only in Jordan but also, occasionally, in other countries as well. In 2005, the center presented findings from political attitude surveys in five Arab countries in a volume entitled *Revisiting the Arab Street: Research from Within.*[10] Another important example is the Ramallah-based Palestine Center for Policy and Survey Research, which began its work in the mid-1990s and has now carried out several hundred polls among Palestinians in the West Bank and Gaza Strip. A more recent example is the Social and Economic Survey Research Institute at Qatar University in Doha. Established in 2008, the institute has included political attitude questions on a number of its recent surveys of Qatari citizens and the country's expatriate and migrant worker populations. An even more recent example is the Arab Center for Research and Policy Studies, which is also based in Doha. Established in 2010, the Arab Center works with partners in a number of Arab countries to conduct surveys on political, economic, and social issues.

The increasingly hospitable political climate is also reflected in the growing number of marketing and media research firms that study public opinion. Although not academic in character and only occasionally investigating topics of direct political relevance, these polling agencies are increasingly in evidence in Egypt, Tunisia, Lebanon, Morocco, Kuwait, and the United Arab Emirates. Some, like Tunisia's Sigma Conseil, operate in a single country, although Sigma plans to open branches in other North African countries. Others, like the Pan Arab Research Center, which is based in Dubai, have branch offices in many Arab countries. The presence of these firms and the broadening scope of the topics about which they do surveys reflect both an increase in the ability to ask sensitive questions and greater recognition that the views of ordinary citizens matter.

Greater freedom to conduct public opinion research has led some individuals and institutions in the Middle East and North Africa to seek opportunities to benefit from the experience and expertise of established survey methodology programs in the United States, and this has contributed further to the frequency and quality of survey research in the region. The institute at Qatar University has a multiyear partnership with the University of Michigan's Institute for Social Research, for example. More generally, since 2003 the University of Michigan has brought roughly one hundred social scientists from seven different Arab countries to Ann Arbor for survey methodology training, while its faculty and graduate students have conducted survey research workshops and seminars in six Arab countries. More than 500 local scholars, analysts, and graduate students have participated in these workshops.

American scholars and doctoral students in political science are also conducting surveys in the Middle East and North Africa much more frequently than in the past. For example, with partial funding from the U.S. National Science Foundation, I conducted one or more surveys of political attitudes and values in seven Arab countries between 2003 and 2006. Local scholars collaborated in much of this work. Prominent among the growing number of other examples that could be cited are Amaney Jamal of Princeton University and Shibley Telhami of the University of Maryland. Both have gained visibility for their research on Arab political attitudes and both have recently presented their findings in very well-reviewed books.[11] Jamal's first book was awarded the American Political Science Association's prize for the best book in comparative politics in 2008.

Among political science doctoral students who study the Middle East and North Africa, dissertation research that includes a survey component is no longer the rarity that it was a few years ago. This reflects not only the opportunities that have emerged in the region in recent years but also the increasing likelihood that these students will have received training not only in Middle East politics but also in the theory and research methodology of the discipline. At the University of Michigan, recent political science dissertations focused on the Middle East have been based, at least in part, on surveys conducted in Morocco, Algeria, Lebanon, Palestine, Jordan, Yemen, Bahrain, and Qatar; and three these dissertations have won American Political Science Association "best dissertation" awards.[12] In all of these examples, the University of Michigan had until recently been something of an outlier, but in fact the pattern is increasingly similar among scholars and students of Middle East politics at other major research universities in the United States.

A related development, further illustrating the changing regional climate for politically focused survey research, is the degree to which there is collaboration between local and foreign scholars. An important example, perhaps the most important, is the multicountry Arab Barometer,[13] which was established in 2005. The Arab Barometer is governed by a steering committee composed of both Arab and American scholars and works with local scholars and researchers in the participating Arab countries. It is one of the six autonomous regional units that make up the Global Barometer Surveys network.[14] Between 2006 and 2013, the Arab Barometer carried out three waves of surveys dealing with governance and political affairs. The first wave, conducted between 2006 and 2009, included Morocco, Algeria, Palestine, Jordan, Lebanon, Yemen, and Bahrain. The second and third waves, conducted in 2010–2011 and 2012–2013, respectively, added Egypt, Tunisia, Iraq, Sudan, Saudi Arabia, and Libya. All of the surveys are based on face-to-face interviews with large and nationally representative samples of ordinary men and women. Following a short embargo, the data are placed in the public domain and may be obtained for secondary analysis from either the Arab Barometer website or the Inter-University Consortium for Political and Social Research at the University of Michigan.

It is also notable that the World Values Survey (WVS) has been extended to the Muslim Middle East. The WVS is a global network of social scientists who have been surveying the social, cultural, and political orientations of ordinary men and women at five-year intervals since 1990.[15] Hundreds of scholarly articles and policy papers have been written using WVS data, and, during the fourth wave of surveys in 2005–2006, the WVS questionnaire was administered to national samples in more than eighty societies. The WVS was not carried out in a single Arab country during the first two waves of surveys, but, beginning with the third wave in 2000, the WVS has been conducted at least once, and in many cases twice, in Egypt, Morocco, Jordan, Algeria, Iraq, Saudi Arabia, Lebanon, Tunisia, Libya, and Qatar, as well as the non-Arab Muslim-majority countries of Turkey and Iran. Moreover, directors of the WVS, working in collaboration with Arab and Muslim partners, have added to the standard WVS survey instrument a number of questions pertaining to religion and other topics that increase the survey's relevance for Arab and Muslim publics. The addition of these questions is particularly important for the present study.

Various other U.S. and international organizations are also now conducting politically focused survey research in the Middle East and North Africa with increasing frequency. Motivated in part by the terrorist attacks of September 11, 2001, and the U.S.-led wars in Afghanistan and Iraq that followed, the research of these organizations has given particular attention to attitudes toward the United States, terrorism, and international relations more generally.

An important recent study ably describes much of this research in considerable detail.[16] It draws in part on nationally representative surveys conducted by the World Public Opinion organization, which is managed by the Program on International Policy Attitudes at the University of Maryland, and reports on polls conducted between 2006 and 2009 in Egypt, Morocco, Iraq, Iran, Jordan, Palestine, and Turkey, as well as those in Muslim-majority countries in other world regions. It also summarizes findings from other prominent organizations that are carrying out surveys in the Middle East and North Africa. Among these are the Pew Research Center, the Gallup World Poll, and Zogby International. Between them, in addition to most of the countries where the Program on International Policy Attitudes has conducted surveys, they have in the last few years carried out one or more polls in Tunisia, Lebanon, Kuwait, the United Arab Emirates, and Saudi Arabia. Some of these data have been analyzed and presented in valuable "Arab Public Opinion Poll" reports by Shibley Telhami.[17]

Looking toward the future, the revolutions and uprisings that took place in many Arab countries beginning in 2011, or in late 2010 in Tunisia, may further expand opportunities for political attitude research. From Morocco to Yemen, beginning in January 2011 and then over the remainder of the year and beyond, the nebulous collective known simply as "the people" (*al-sha'ab*) took to the streets to demand increased accountability, fundamental reform, and a democratic alternative to the prevailing political and economic order. The events of this period, popularly known as the "Arab Spring," offered unambiguous evidence that the views of ordinary citizens matter—that men and women in the Muslim Middle East think about and often have strong views about the way their societies should be governed.

Whether and to what extent these uprisings would bring meaningful transitions to democracy was in most instances unclear, and this uncertainty has for the most part persisted. On the one hand, some authoritarian regimes forcefully and aggressively pushed back, as in Bahrain, for example, and most notably in the case of Syria. In other instances, as in Jordan, Morocco, and Saudi Arabia, leaders undertook modest reforms or distributed resources in an effort to diffuse public discontent without fundamentally altering the status quo, and in the short-term at least these efforts appear to have achieved their objective. On the other hand, where the old regime fell, the persistence of ideological, sectarian, or regional divisions, as well as economic and other problems, made progress toward the establishment of a legitimate and viable governing structure difficult and uncertain. This was the case in Tunisia, Yemen, Libya, and Iraq; and in Egypt these challenges led to the collapse of the first democratically elected government in 2013. Nevertheless, the Arab Spring not only increased awareness of the importance of studying mass political attitudes, values, and behavior, it also raised the possibility that politically focused public opinion research would become possible in still more countries of the Middle East and North Africa and, equally important, that in more countries of the region there would emerge the institutional foundation needed for this type of research to be initiated and led by indigenous scholars.

Uncertainty about the future notwithstanding, the result of these various and interrelated trends is that information about the political attitudes, values, and behavior patterns of ordinary men and women can be gathered in a growing number of Muslim-majority countries in the Middle East and North Africa, and to a substantial degree relevant information is already available. I have myself been conducting political attitude surveys in the region for more than four decades. I have sought not only to discover what people think or how they behave but also, first, to identify the factors and causal mechanisms that shape individual orientations and account for variance and, second, to discover and specify in conceptual terms the system-level conditions under which these causal stories obtain.[18]

The present study builds on the experience and insight developed during these four decades. It also builds on the substantially increased quantity and scope of the politically focused survey research, including both my own work and that of others, that the trends described above have made possible. This has enabled me to create a dataset that brings together surveys conducted in a wide range of

Muslim-majority countries in the Middle East and North Africa over a time span of more than a decade. It would have been impossible to construct such a cross-national and longitudinal dataset ten years ago.

The Data

The Carnegie Middle East Governance and Islam Dataset constructed for this study, hereafter the Carnegie dataset, integrates forty-four surveys carried out in fifteen different countries.[19] All of these surveys include questions about Islam's role in government and political affairs. They also include questions about religious practice and belief, about the interpretation of Islamic laws and prescriptions, and about a wide range of other political and social attitudes and behaviors. This integrated dataset contains the responses of 67,680 ordinary men and women over the age of eighteen. Table 1.1 lists the surveys included in the dataset, grouped by country and ordered by year, as well as the number of respondents in each survey. As the table shows, four of the surveys were carried out before 2000; the rest are distributed fairly evenly between 2000 and 2011.

Taken together, these surveys constitute an extremely strong, indeed an unprecedented, foundation for understanding the views about political Islam held by Muslim publics in the Middle East and North Africa. There are at least three ways in which the integrated data file constructed from these surveys is unique. The first is the degree to which it is comprehensive and captures the diversity of the Middle East and North Africa. Although the datatset does not include surveys from all countries in the region, it is nonetheless based on a broadly representative sample of countries. This sample includes societies in every geographic region: three Maghrib countries in the west, Morocco, Algeria, and Tunisia; Egypt and the central Mashreq states of Lebanon, Palestine, and Jordan; Turkey in the north; Iraq and Iran in the east; and, finally, two large states, Saudi Arabi and Yemen, and three small states, Kuwait, Bahrain, and Qatar, in the Arabian Gulf area to the south. The dataset includes surveys conducted in both monarchies and republics, in countries that are more free and countries that are less free, in some of the richest and some of the poorest countries in the Middle East and North Africa, and in societies that vary significantly in the extent to which their populations are heterogeneous. Further, the forty-four surveys from which the dataset has been constructed range across a time period that stretches from before the terrorist attacks on the United States on September 11, 2001, through the second Palestinian intifada, the war in Iraq, and the Arab uprisings that began in Tunisia in the final days of 2010. The dataset thus provides a unique foundation for deriving analytical insights about the Middle East and North Africa during the first decade of the twenty-first century.

The representative character of the forty-four surveys means that Christians and other non-Muslims were also surveyed and are included in the dataset. Spe-

Table 1.1. Surveys and Sample Sizes Organized by Country and Date

Country and year	N	Country and year	N	Country and year	N
Algeria 2002	1,282	Jordan 2003	1,000	Palestine 2003	1,320
Algeria 2004	1,446	Jordan 2006	1,143	Palestine 2006	1,270
Algeria 2006	1,300	Jordan 2007	1,200	Palestine 2008	3,430
Algeria 2011	1,216	Jordan 2008	967	Palestine 2010	1,200
Bahrain 2009	436	Jordan 2010	1,188	Qatar 2010	1,060
Egypt 1988[a]	292	Kuwait 1988	300	S. Arabia 2003	1,502
Egypt 2000	3,000	Kuwait 2005	750	S. Arabia 2011	1,405
Egypt 2008[b]	3,051	Lebanon 2007	1,195	Sudan 2011	1,538
Egypt 2011	1,220	Lebanon 2010	1,387	Tunisia 2011	1,196
Iran 2000[b]	2,532	Morocco 2001	2,264	Turkey 2001	4,607
Iran 2005	2,667	Morocco 2005	1,083	Turkey 2007	1,346
Iraq 2004	2,325	Morocco 2006	1,277	Yemen 2006	1,440
Iraq 2006	2,701	Morocco 2007	1,200	Yemen 2007[c]	717
Iraq 2011	1,236	Palestine 1995	2,368	Yemen 2011	1,200
Jordan 2001	1,223	Palestine 1999	1,200		
				Total observations	67,680
				Total surveys	44
				Total countries	15

[a] The 1988 Egypt survey was only carried out in Cairo.
[b] The 2008 Egypt survey and the 2000 Iran survey do not contain items pertaining to political Islam. They are included in the integrated multisurvey dataset for purposes unrelated to the present study but do not provide data for the present investigation of attitudes relating to Islam's political role. Without these two countries, the number of observations is 62,097 and the number of surveys is 42. The number of countries remains 15.
[c] The 2007 Yemen survey was found to have a number of respondent duplicates. Only one respondent in the set of duplicates was retained, thereby reducing the size and representativeness of the sample.

cifically, 3.4 percent of the 67,680 respondents, or 2,330 men and women, are neither Sunni nor Shi'i Muslims. The vast majority of these individuals are either Lebanese or Egyptian Christians, with the former constituting 48.1 percent of all non-Muslims and the latter constituting another 18.5 percent. Smaller percentages of Christians and other non-Muslim respondents are present in other surveys, primarily those in Jordan and Palestine. Although these non-Muslim respondents are excluded from the analyses reported in the present study, they have been retained in the Carnegie dataset for possible use in other investigations.

A second way in which the dataset constructed for the present study is distinctive concerns the thoroughness of the information it provides about public attitudes and behavior pertaining to governance and political affairs and, of particular relevance for the present investigation, about conceptions, preferences, and practices relating to Islam. Overall, the data file contains responses to 235 questions, tapping into a wide range of normative and behavioral orientations. Not every question was asked in every survey, but many were asked in most surveys, and a number of key questions were asked in all but a few surveys. Among the substantive foci of these items are political system preferences; regime evaluation; civic engagement; political culture orientations such as political knowledge, political interest, political and interpersonal trust, and political and social tolerance; personal and communal identity; and women's status and gender equality.

With respect to Islam, the dataset includes multiple questions on three key dimensions: personal piety, views about Islam's place in government and political affairs, and judgments about the way that Islamic codes and prescriptions should be interpreted. Accordingly, with its central focus on the views that ordinary citizens hold about their society and the way it should be organized and governed, and with an even deeper focus on what people think about the political and societal role of Islam, the data brought together for analysis make it possible to undertake an investigation of unusual strength and sophistication.

A third distinctive attribute of the dataset is the inclusion of a substantial number of country-level variables. There are measures of thirty-four national attributes, including such political characteristics as degree of political freedom, religious freedom, civil liberties, and corruption; such economic attributes as per capita GDP, unemployment level, degree of income inequality, and percent of GDP from natural resource rents; such social and human development attributes as adult literacy, school enrollment ratios, life expectancy, percentage of women in the labor force, and score on the the United Nations Human Development Index; and such demographic characteristics as population, percentage of the population living in urban areas, percentage of the population under the age of fifteen, and ethnic and linguisitc fractionalization. These measures characterize each country at the time of each survey. In addition, however, in order to permit the investigation of temporally sequenced explanatory relationships, there are also measures of many of these national attributes at a time five years and/or ten years prior to conducting the survey. Finally, there are twelve additional country-level variables based on the means or medians and on the standard deviations or ranges of selected individual-level measures.

The inclusion of these time-sensitive national attributes makes it possible to undertake analyses in which both individual-level and country-level factors can be treated as determinants of attitudes toward political Islam and in which interaction between the two categories of explanatory factors can be examined. In the "two-level" analyses that the dataset permits, country-level attributes are treated as conditionalities for the purpose of specifying the characteristics of a country's politcal, economic, and/or social environment that determine the extent to which, and by extension why, an individual's personal circumstances and experience play a role in shaping his or her attitudes toward Islam's place in political affairs. Important indivudal-level variable relationships are thus mapped cross-nationally and over time in terms of conceptually defined properties, thereby significantly increasing the specificity and explanatory power of the resulting analytical insights. Given the very substantial data collection requirements, this kind of two-level analysis is rare even in research on developed democratic countries. Additional information about the logic and design by which it will be guided in the present study is provided later in this chapter.

Sources

Most of the surveys listed in table 1.1 come from one of three sources: (1) the Arab Barometer; (2) a series of surveys that I designed and conducted with support from the U.S. National Science Foundation (NSF) and others; and (3) the World Values Survey (WVS).

The dataset includes nineteen surveys from the Arab Barometer, of which I am codirector. Nine of these surveys were conducted between 2006 and 2009 in the first wave of Barometer surveys. These include two surveys in Jordan and Palestine and one each in Morocco, Algeria, Lebanon, Bahrain, and Yemen. The remaining ten surveys were conducted in 2010 and 2011 in the Barometer's second wave. These include surveys in Algeria, Tunisia, Egypt, Sudan, Palestine, Lebanon, Jordan, Saudi Arabia, Yemen, and Iraq.

The dataset also includes six surveys that were conducted as part of a project I directed on the Nature and Determinants of Regime Preference and Political Values in the Middle East and North Africa. These surveys were carried out between 2003 and 2006, with the cooperation of local scholars and institutions, in Morocco, Algeria, Palestine, Jordan, Kuwait, and Yemen. The project was supported, in part, by the U.S. National Science Foundation. The survey in Morocco was also supported, in part, by the American Institute for Maghrib Studies.

The datatset includes fifteen surveys from the World Values Survey. For three of these surveys I had (or shared) responsibility for data collection. Eight of these fifteen surveys come from the WVS's third wave, which was carried out between 2000 and 2004 and was the first to include countries in the Middle East and North Africa. These surveys were conducted in Morocco, Algeria, Egypt, Jordan, Saudi Arabia, Iraq, Iran, and Turkey. Six surveys come from the fourth WVS wave, which was carried out between 2006 and 2007 in Morocco, Egypt, Jordan, Iraq, Iran, and Turkey. The remaining survey, conducted in Qatar in 2010, was part of the fifth WVS wave.

The four remaining surveys do not come from any of the three sources described above. These surveys were conducted in Egypt and Kuwait in 1988, and in Palestine in 1995 and 1999. The Egypt and Kuwait surveys were directed by Dr. Jamal al-Suwaidi, who currently directs the Emirates Center for Strategic Studies and Research in Abu Dhabi. Dr. al-Suwaidi and I designed the survey instrument, and he then supervised the data collection, including the training and supervision of interviewers. The 1995 Palestinian survey was carried out by the Palestine Center for Policy and Survey Research, which at the time was based in Nablus and called the Center for Palestine Studies and Research. The 1999 Palestinian survey was carried out by the Jerusalem Media and Communications Centre.

Data from various subsets of these surveys have been analyzed and presented in numerous publications, most of which focus on issues associated with governance and/or international relations and some of which also give attention to Islam. A representative subset of my own relevant publications based on many of these surveys has been reprinted in my book *Public Opinion in the Middle East,* mentioned earlier. These publications provide additional information about sampling procedures, as well as interviewer training, validity, and reliability in measurement, and other important methodological considerations.

Sampling

All of the surveys listed in table 1.1 are based on face-to-face interviews and all but two are based on representative, probability-based national samples. The exceptions are the early surveys in Egypt and Kuwait, both of which were conducted in 1988 and used quota sampling. The Egyptian sample was limited to Cairo. A few of the surveys are based on national probability samples developed by or with assistance from government statistical agencies. This is the case for several of the surveys in Morocco and for the survey in Qatar. The rest of the surveys used mutlistage area probability sampling, or cluster sampling, to select respondents. In a few cases, most notably in three of the four surveys in Algeria, interviewing was done in localities (communes) that were randomly selected, but quota sampling based on the most recent census data was then used to select respondents within each commune.

The various ways in which area probability/cluster sampling was carried out in the vast majority of surveys are illustrated by the following descriptions of procedures used in Palestine and Jordan in 2003, in Iraq in 2006, and in Egypt and Tunisia in 2011. The 2003 Palestinian survey, and all but one of the other surveys in Palestine, was carried out by the Palestine Center for Policy and Survey Research. The 2003 survey in Jordan, and all of the others surveys in Jordan, was carried out by the Center for Strategic Studies at the University of Jordan. Both of these 2003 surveys were part of the NSF-funded project described above. The 2006 survey in Iraq, as well as all of the the other Iraqi surveys, was conducted by the Baghdad- and Amman-based Independent Institute for Administration and Civil Society

Studies. The 2006 Iraq survey was part of the third wave of the WVS. The 2011 Egyptian survey was carried out by the the Al-Ahram Center for Political and Strategic Studies in Cairo, and the 2011 Tunisian survey was carried out, with academic oversight provided by an Arab Barometer team, by Sigma Conseil, a commercial market-research firm based in Tunis. Both of these surveys were part of the second wave of the Arab Barometer. The information about sampling procedures presented below has been provided by the units and individuals who designed and carried out the surveys.

PALESTINE 2003

The Palestinian survey used three-stage cluster sampling based on the 1997 national census. Palestine was divided into several strata, with each stratum representing the towns, cities, villages, and refugee camps in the sixteen governorates (*muhafazat*). Palestine was also divided into "counting areas," or clusters, with each containing a number of families. The number of families in each cluster, which ranged from 80 to 110, determined the size of that cluster, and the total number of sampling clusters in Palestine was 3,200. The 1997 census provided detailed data on the families as well as detailed maps showing every house in each cluster.

A sample of 120 clusters was randomly selected using probability proportionate to size. Clusters were organized according to size (number of families) and geographic location (West Bank or Gaza Strip) in order to ensure representation of all strata and clusters of all sizes. After selecting the clusters in the West Bank and the Gaza Strip, eleven homes were selected in each cluster using systemic sampling. The total size of the sample was 1,320 adults. The third stage in the sampling process occurred inside the home. Using a Kish table, fieldworkers selected a household member over eighteen years of age for the interview.

JORDAN 2003

The Jordanian survey used three-stage cluster sampling based on the 1994 national census. Jordan was divided into several strata representing the rural and urban populations in each governorate (*muhafaza*). In addition, each of Jordan's five main cities (Amman, Wadi al Sir, al Zarqa, Irbid, and al Rusaifeh) was treated as an independent stratum. Jordan was also divided into blocs, or clusters, with each containing an average of eighty families. There were 800 sampling clusters, and detailed information about the families in each was available through the national census.

A sample of one hundred clusters was randomly selected using probability proportionate to size. Clusters were organized according to size (number of families) and geographic location in order to ensure representation of all strata and clusters of all sizes. After selecting the sampling clusters, ten households were selected in each cluster using systemic sampling. Total size of the sample was therefore 1,000 adults. The third stage in the sampling process occurred inside the household. Using a Kish table, fieldworkers selected a household member over eighteen years of age for the interview.

IRAQ 2006

The Iraqi sample covered all eighteen of the country's governorates. A multistage, probability-based sample was drawn to select respondents, beginning with census districts (*qada*), followed by subdistricts (*nahia*), and then blocks. Blocks were regarded as the primary sampling units, with ninety-six ultimately selected, and the number of individuals to be interviewed in each block was determined by its relative population according to the 1997 census. Given that residential information provided by the census was frequently out of date, fieldworkers were instructed to "spot map" the selected blocks in urban areas and the block-equivalent units in rural areas and then to randomly select the required number of households in each. Similar procedures were employed to select households in Kurdistan, which was not covered by the 1997 census. Finally, within each selected household, one respondent age eighteen or older was randomly selected using the last birthday method. A list of random birthdays was carried by every interviewer, and birthdays were assigned to household members who did know them, as was sometimes the case among older individuals.

EGYPT 2011

The survey in Egypt used a self-weighted multistage stratified cluster sample that was provided by the Egyptian Central Bureau of Statistics. The population was divided into twenty-one strata representing the country's twenty-one governorates, and each of the twenty-one strata was divided into a rural stratum and an urban stratum. A total of 120 clusters were then randomly selected from these 42 strata, with the number of clusters in each proportional to its population. As a result, 58 percent of the clusters were from rural areas and 42 percent were from urban ones. Thereafter, ten households were randomly chosen from each cluster and a Kish table was used to select the individual to be interviewed in each, thereby producing a sample of 1,200 respondents.

TUNISIA 2001

Area probability sampling was used in the Tunisian survey. The smallest administrative unit in Tunisia is the *'amada,* and, since a sampling frame was not available from the Central Bureau of Statistics, all of the *'amadas* in each governorate were listed and classified according to the number of the households and the proportion of their urban and rural populations. Smaller *'amadas* were treated as sampling clusters, whereas larger ones were divided into several clusters, each containing about 700 to 800 households. Very small *'amadas* (usually small villages) were combined so that these clusters would also have about the same number of households. In making decisions about dividing or combining *'amadas*, local council maps and Google earth maps were consulted. When necessary, fieldworkers made site visits to gather the necessary information. After identifying the clusters, 120 were randomly selected, with the number from each governorate based on the ratio of that governorate's population to the country's population. Using maps, ten households were then randomly selected from each cluster and, taking gender into consideration, one person in each household was selected for the interview.

Variables and Measures

All but two of the surveys listed in table 1.1 include one or more questions pertaining to the role of Islam in government and political affairs, as well as questions pertaining to normative and situational factors that may play a role in shaping the way people think about Islam's place in political life. Since almost all of these forty-two surveys were carried out as part of multicountry projects, and also since I was personally involved in the design and/or direction of more than two-thirds of these surveys, many key questions were included on a large number of the interview schedules. Not every question pertaining to political Islam or other salient topics was asked in every survey, however, and so it has been important not only to establish that items are reliable and valid measures but also to establish cross-survey conceptual equivalence whenever different items must be used to measure views about political Islam or any other key concern.

Table 1.2 lists the ten items in the dataset that will be used to measure attitudes toward Islam's role in government and political affairs. Among these are questions that ask about the place in political life that should be occupied by, or the political influence that should be exercised by, Islamic officials, laws, or institutions. Most of these questions begin with a statement about Islam's political role and then ask respondents whether (and how strongly) they agree or disagree with that statement. For example, one of the items states: "Men of religion should have no influence over the decisions of government." The response options to this item are: "strongly agree," "agree," "neither agree nor disagree," "disagree," and "strongly disagree." Other items ask about the importance of a particular government policy or action, stating, for example: "The government should implement only the laws of the Shari'a." The response options in this case are: "very important," "important," "somewhat important," "not important," and "not important at all." Table 1.2 also reports the number of surveys that included each of the ten questions. As the table shows, many questions were asked in a very

Table 1.2. Items Used to Measure Attitudes toward Islam's Role in Government and Political Affairs

Item	Number of surveys containing item	Percent of surveys containing item[a]
Government should implement only the laws of the Shari'a	36	83.7
Men of religion should not influence how people vote in elections	36	83.7
It would be better for our country if more people with strong religious beliefs held public office	35	81.4
Men of religion should have no influence over the decisions of government	35	81.4
Religious practice is a private matter and should be separated from sociopolitical life	30	69.8
Our country should be governed by Islamic law and a political system in which there are no political parties or elections	28	65.1
A candidate's religiosity would be an important consideration in my attitude toward a person running for political office	25	58.1
Politicians who do not believe in God are unfit for public office	15	34.9
Religious leaders should not interfere in politics	2	4.6
Islamic values should play a larger role in government policy	1	2.3

[a] Percent is based on the forty-two surveys that included at least one item pertaining to political Islam.

high proportion of the forty-two surveys. Some others were asked in fewer surveys, or in one case only one.

In order to select the particular items with which to construct a measure of attitudes toward Islam's place in political affairs for each the forty-two surveys, I employed factor analysis when the survey asked three or more of the items listed in the table, and correlation analysis when the survey asked only two of the items pertaining to political Islam. In addition to guiding item selection, these procedures permitted the assessment of reliability and validity and provided an empirical basis for inferring conceptual equivalence in cross-survey analyses.

Factor analysis assesses the degree to which each item or variable in a set is associated with an underlying concept or construct, described as a *factor,* which in this case is a continuum ranging from opposition to support for Islam having a role in government. Associations are expressed in terms of *loadings,* which, like correlations, vary from –1 to 1, and an item with a strong loading (well above or below 0) may be presumed to be a reliable measure of the underlying concept. Consistency across independent measures demonstrates reliability, and a strong loading provides such a demonstration, since it indicates that responses to an item are consistent with responses to other items that also have strong loadings on the same factor. This would not be the case if something other than the content of the question were influencing responses, in which case, whatever the reason, the item would not be reliable.

Consistency, or inter-item agreement, also offers evidence of validity, since all items with strong loadings necessarily measure the same underlying concept or construct, which is defined by whatever the items with strong loadings have in common—views about political Islam in this case. Accordingly, although validity cannot be proved but must rather be inferred, there is not likely to be very much uncertainty about the shared content of a battery of internally consistent items, and by extension about what each individual item is measuring. This is particularly clear in the present study, since all of the items explicitly ask about Islam's political role and have substantial face validity. Each item with a strong factor loading may therefore be assumed to measure what it purports to measure, which is the definition of validity.

For illustrative purposes, table 1.3 presents the factor analyses that have been carried out with data from five of the surveys: Palestine 2003, Algeria 2004, Iraq 2006, Yemen 2006, and Morocco 2007. For each survey, the table shows the items that have strong loadings on an underlying concept, which in this case is a continuum of views about whether or not Islam should have an important place in political affairs. The strong loadings, as discussed, offer evidence that the items are reliable and valid.

Another advantage of factor analysis is that it permits items to be combined into indices, expressed as factor *scores,* thereby providing a multi-indicator measure that captures more of the variance associated with attitudes toward political Islam than would any single item by itself. In the present study, an index of this type, created by generating factor scores from items with strong loadings on the same factor, has been constructed for each survey having at least three items that ask about Islam's political role. Items with low factor loadings in a particular survey, and which therefore are either unreliable or invalid measures of the underlying concept, were excluded from the battery of items used to generate factor scores. In the analysis to be taken up in later chapters, the indices generated in this way will be treated as the dependent variable in tests of hypotheses

Table 1.3. Factor Loadings of Items Measuring Attitudes toward Political Islam in Five Surveys

	Palestine 2003	Algeria 2004	Iraq 2006	Yemen 2006	Morocco 2007
Government should implement only the laws of the Shari'a		.747	.791	.555	
Men of religion should not influence how people vote in elections	−.628				−.843
Men of religion should have no influence over the decisions of government	−.719			−.468	−.880
Religious practice is a private matter and should be separated from sociopolitical life	−.683	−.623			
It would be better for [country] if more people with strong religious beliefs held public office	.463		.829	.684	
Politicians who do not believe in God are unfit for public office		.610		.528	.505
Religious leaders should not interfere in politics			−.705		
A system governed by Islamic law in which there are no political parties or elections would be good for [country]				.609	

that seek to account for variance in people's views about the role Islam should play in government and politics.

Conceptual equivalence, as well as reliability and validity, is important, and particularly so in the present study. Since the analysis to be undertaken will compare findings about the determinants of variance in attitudes toward political Islam across multiple surveys, it is essential that the concept being measured in each survey be the same—that it actually *be* views about Islam's political role that is measured. Otherwise, the comparison would be meaningless. If the measure in each survey is valid, as explained above, it is probable that the same concept is in fact being measured in the different surveys. On the other hand, since the items with high loadings used to construct the index measuring attitudes toward political Islam in one survey may not be identical to the items with high loadings used to construct the index in a different survey, validity by itself does not establish conceptual equivalence. Although unlikely, it is possible that different kinds of attitudes about Islam's political role are being measured in the different surveys. In this case, the measures may all be valid, but they are not equivalent. They are not measuring the same underlying concept, or at least not the same dimension of that concept.

The present study addresses this problem through the use of *bridging* items. If factor scores in different surveys are based on some identical items and some different items, all of which have strong factor loadings, the identical items play a bridging role. They demonstrate that the different items are in fact measuring the same underlying concept since they measure the same concept that the identical items measure.

The factor loadings for the five surveys presented in table 1.3 illustrate this point. The pattern of factor loadings in the 2003 Palestinian survey shows, for example, that the item asking whether religion and politics should be separated is associated with the same underlying concept as are the item that asks about religious leaders exercising political influence and the item that asks about having more men of Islamic learning hold public office. And in the Algerian 2004 survey, the item asking about a separation of religion and politics is associated with the same underlying concept as are the items asking about the Shari'a and about the fitness for public office of politicians who do not believe in God. The item asking about the separation of religion and politics is thus a bridging item, linking patterns found in the two surveys. It provides strong evidence that the other three items in the 2003 Palestinian survey and the other two items in the 2004 Algerian survey are all associated with the same underlying concept, the concept with which the item asking about a separation of religion and politics is associated. Accordingly, it may be concluded that the index constructed from the questions asked in Palestine in 2003 and the index constructed from the questions asked in Algeria in 2004 are conceptually equivalent.

The same logic applies not only to pairs of surveys but to all of the surveys that provide data for the present study. In the 2006 Iraq survey, for example, the item asking about the Shari'a and the item asking about people with strong religious beliefs holding public office are bridges to the 2006 Yemeni survey. The former question is also a bridge to the 2004 Algerian survey and the latter is also a bridge to the 2003 Palestinian survey. There is no item in the 2006 Iraqi survey that provides a bridge to the 2007 Moroccan survey, but all of the items are in fact indirect bridges, since each is associated with an underlying concept with which, in other surveys, the questions asked in Morocco in 2007 are also associated. For example, factor analysis of the 2006 Yemeni data shows that two items from the 2006 Iraqi survey (those that ask about Shari'a and about people with strong religious beliefs holding public office) and two different items from the 2007 Moroccan survey (those that ask about men of religion having influence in government decisions and about the fitness for public office of people who do not believe in God) are all associated with the same underlying dimension. Similarly, factor analyses of the 2003 Palestinian data and the 2004 Algerian data show that at least one item in the 2006 Iraqi survey and one different item in the 2007 Moroccan survey are, again, associated with the same underlying dimension. The index measuring attitudes toward political Islam constructed from the 2006 Iraqi data and the one constructed from 2007 Moroccan data may thus be considered conceptually equivalent.

A small number of surveys included fewer than three items pertaining to political Islam. In six surveys, only two relevant questions were asked, or at least only two that proved to be reliable and valid when asked in those surveys. And in two other surveys, Saudi Arabia in 2003 and Qatar in 2010, the interview schedule included only one relevant item. Nevertheless, since all the items, with the exception of the one item asked in Qatar, had been asked and had strong factor loadings in a large number of the other surveys, there is no reason to assume that they are not reliable and valid measures of the same concept that is measured in the other instances—attitudes toward Islam's political role. Moreover, in all six instances where only two items were available, these items are highly correlated and have strong loadings when subjected to factor analysis; and thus, as elsewhere, they have been combined to form multi-item indices. Accordingly, for these surveys, like those discussed above, the items and indices constitute measures that are not only reliable and valid but also conceptually equivalent to those derived from the data in other surveys.

The views that ordinary men and women hold about Islam's political role are the central focus of the present inquiry. Accordingly, the dependent variable in this study, constructed using the procedures described above, is an index that measures attitudes toward political Islam for each individual in the dataset. In chapters 3 and 4, we present and test hypotheses about some of the individual-level and country-level determinants of these attitudes. As noted earlier, the dataset contains responses to many questions beyond those pertaining to political Islam, and some of these items are used to operationalize the independent variables in the hypotheses and the control variables included in the analysis when testing these propositions. Nondependent variables in the analysis include measures of religiosity and other personal attributes and of views about a number of political and societal concerns.

Questions about personal religiosity are also of interest for the light they shed on people's thinking about Islam beyond the realm of politics, for the information they provide about the broader normative context of Muslim-majority countries in the Middle East and North Africa and about the place of Islam in the

Table 1.4. Questions and Response Options Used to Measure Personal Religiosity

How often do you read the Quran?   Every day or almost every day, Several times a week, Sometimes, Rarely, or Never

How often do you pray?   Very often (several times a day), Often (every day), Sometimes (once or twice a week), Rarely (one or two times a month or only on religious holidays), Never

Independently of whether you go to religious services or not, would you say you are: Religious, Somewhat religious, Not religious

When you consider what would make a suitable spouse for your son or daughter, would you say that each of the following is Very important, Somewhat important, A little important, or Not important at all: S/he doesn't pray

Which of the following best describes you?   Above all I am [nationality of country], Above all I am a Muslim, Above all I am an Arab, Other

How often do you pray/perform in the mosque?   Very often (several times a day), Often (every day), Sometimes (once or twice a week), Rarely (one or two times a month or only on religious holidays), Never

Do you refer to religious teachings when taking decisions about your life?   Always, Sometimes, Rarely, Never

Are you member of a religious organization?   Not a member, Inactive member, Active member, Leader

When you need advice about a personal problem, how often do you consult each of the following?   An imam or *fakih:* Often, Sometimes, Rarely, Never

lives of the Muslim men and women who reside in these countries. Table 1.4 lists the relevant items—those pertaining to religious practice and belief—that were included on the interview schedule administered in at least one of the surveys. Almost all were asked in a large number of the surveys. Drawing upon these items and using the factor analytic procedures described above, a multi-item index of personal religiosity has been constructed for each survey. As with the index of attitudes toward political Islam, each survey's measure of personal religiosity may be considered reliable, valid, and conceptually equivalent to those of other surveys. A number of these items are also used in chapter 2 to provide a picture of the extent to which Islam is present in the everyday lives and identities of ordinary men and women in the Muslim societies of the Middle East and North Africa.

Beyond providing information about the broader normative environment within which Middle Eastern and North Africa Muslim publics reside, the personal religiosity index is of interest because, at the individual level of analysis, it measures an orientation that is a particularly important determinant of the

Table 1.5. Questions and Response Options Used to Measure Attitudes toward Gender Equality and Evaluation of the Governing Regime

Attitudes toward gender equality

On the whole, men make better political leaders than women do.   Strongly agree, Agree, Neither agree nor disagree, Disagree, Strongly disagree

A university education is more important for a boy than a girl.   Strongly agree, Agree, Neither agree nor disagree, Disagree, Strongly disagree

Men and women should have equal job opportunities and wages.   Strongly agree, Agree, Neither agree nor disagree, Disagree, Strongly disagree

Men make better business executives than women do.   Strongly agree, Agree, Neither agree nor disagree, Disagree, Strongly disagree

Regime/government evaluation

I'm going to name a number of institutions. For each one, please tell me how much trust you have in it. Is it a great deal of trust, quite a lot of trust, not very much trust, or none at all?

—The prime minister

—The courts/judicial system

—Parliament

—The police

—Military

—The civil service

How satisfied you are with the performance of the current [country] government?   Very Satisfied, Somewhat satisfied, Not very satisfied, Not at all satisfied

Our political leaders care about ordinary citizens.   Strongly agree, Agree, Neither agree nor disagree, Disagree, Strongly disagree

Public officials pursue their own interests.   Strongly agree, Agree, Neither agree nor disagree, Disagree, Strongly disagree

judgments people make about Islam's political role, as is shown in the analysis reported in chapter 3. Accordingly, personal religiosity will be included as an essential control variable when testing hypotheses about the explanatory power of other factors that may account for variance in the views held by ordinary citizens about the place Islam should occupy in government and political affairs.

Independent variables in the hypotheses to be tested are: conservatism-liberalism in cultural values, operationalized in terms of attitudes toward gender equality; evaluation of the governing regime; personal economic circumstances and economic satisfaction; and education. Attitudes toward gender equality and regime evaluation are measured with multi-item indices generated in the same way as attitudes toward political Islam and personal religiosity. Table 1.5 lists the items that, in survey-specific combinations, have been used to construct each index.

Analysis

The dataset created for this project contains both individual-level and country-level variables. This makes it possible both to test hypotheses about micro-level determinants of attitudes toward political Islam and to identify macro-level factors that account for variance in the explanatory power of these micro-level determinants. The macro-level factors that will be used to identify conditioning effects are the country-level attributes listed in table 1.6.

Individual-Level Analysis

Individual-level analysis, or "within-system" analysis, involves testing hypotheses that specify relationships in which an individual-level independent variable purports to account for variance on an individual-level dependent variable. In the present study, as noted, individual-level attitudes toward Islam's political role serve as the dependent variable, and individual-level attributes and normative orientations are independent variables. Here, as elsewhere in the present study, the analysis uses all of the forty-two surveys in the dataset that include one or more questions about political Islam and for which, accordingly, a measure of views about Islam's political role has been generated. Hypotheses proposing individual-level explanatory relationships, and findings from the individual-level analyses by which these hypotheses are tested, are presented in chapter 3.

Although it might be tempting to test individual-level hypotheses separately for each of the forty-two surveys, this would be extremely unwieldy. It would also yield little more than country-specific and time-specific insights. Thus, while those interested in a particular country at a particular point in time would probably find a separate analysis of the relevant survey data to be instructive, the present study's goal of deriving broader insights and defining in conceptual terms the conditions under which these insights apply are better served by pooling the data from the forty-two surveys for the individual-level analysis. The pooled analysis, presented in chapter 3, assesses whether the causal stories set forth in individual-level hypotheses are generally operative in the Middle East and North Africa, even if they do not apply in every country or at every point in time. This should not be understood as seeking one-size-fits-all explanations, however. An examination of whether, when, how, and, by extension, why findings differ across the forty-two surveys, why, in other words, data from some surveys provide support for a particular individual-level hypothesis while data from other surveys do not, will be undertaken through the two-level analysis, which is presented in chapter 4.

Weighting

An important question that arises when pooling data from multiple surveys for individual-level analysis is whether and how the surveys should be weighted. One option, which at first glance would seem to be appropriate, would be to weight the surveys on the basis of the country's population. This would correct for the fact that surveys conducted in small countries, such as Kuwait, Bahrain, and Qatar, each of which has no more than two or three million people, many of whom are not even citizens, are treated the same as countries with seventy or even eighty million men and women, as in the case in Turkey, Iran, and Egypt.

Another plausible option would be to weight surveys on the basis of the country's influence in regional or international affairs. Since the goal is to identify factors that play a role in shaping views about political Islam broadly across the region, surveys from countries with greater regional influence should perhaps be given greater weight than surveys from countries that have little impact on trends beyond their own borders. Weighting on this basis would require deriving a measure of regional influence, which might be possible by considering such factors as a country's size, geographic position, historical role, ideology, wealth, industrial base, and media reach. Building such a measure would be challenging, however. Moreover, regional influence probably is not unidimensional, and in any event subjective decisions would have to be made about which factors to include and how much importance to attach to each.

Although there is a degree of logic supporting each of these weighting options, neither is appropriate for the present study. Weighting by population would have almost the same effect as eliminating the data from all but the seven or eight most populous countries. With this weighting, Egypt, Iran, and Turkey, along with Algeria, Iraq, Morocco, and Sudan, would provide more than 75 percent of the data points, and what characterizes the citizens of these countries would thus be found to be characteristic of the region as a whole. In effect, findings from a test of hypotheses with the data from these seven countries would be only slightly different than findings from a test with the data from all of the forty-two surveys. And while countries that are only somewhat less populous, like Saudi Arabia and Yemen, would have at least some impact on the findings, the six or seven least populous countries, those with no more than six million citizens, and in some cases two million or less, would have no impact at all on the results. It would be as if there had been no surveys in these latter countries.

Weighting on the basis of regional influence would involve some of the same problems, in addition to the methodological difficulties mentioned above. While some countries do play a greater role than others in shaping region-wide trends, it is almost certain that domestic circumstances are more important, and in all probability considerably more important, in determining the factors that predispose men and women toward one position or another in their thinking about Islam's place in government and politics. It is thus important that each of the national contexts in which Middle Eastern and North African Muslims reside be given equal weight, regardless of whether some have greater region-wide visibility and resonance than others. For purposes of the present study, in other words, the goal of shedding light on broader trends is not served by giving disproportionate attention to a few highly "influential" countries, even if these countries could be identified; it is rather served by looking for patterns that are likely to apply in most, or at least very many, of the highly diverse domestic environments that are found in the Middle East and North Africa.

The preceding discussion does not mean that pooled analyses should be carried out with no weighting at all. On the contrary, two weights need to be introduced. The first is straightforward and corrects for the fact that sample sizes vary across the surveys included in the dataset. Without such a correction, surveys based on larger samples would contribute disproportionately to the results of the analysis; and this would be problematic since, as discussed, the project regards the experience of every population surveyed as equally salient since its goal is to uncover region-wide patterns. To correct for differences in sample size, a variable using the formula of $1/N$, where N is the number of respondents in the survey, has been computed and introduced as a weight in analyses based on pooled data. The inclusion of this weight eliminates sample size differences.

A second weight is also needed, and this is because surveys conducted in the same country at different points in time may not be entirely independent. Indeed, if the time that has elapsed between two surveys in the same country is very small, the populations from which the samples are drawn will be almost identical. Alternatively, the greater the time span between surveys conducted in the same country, the more different are the populations, and not only because some citizens will have died while others will have reached adulthood, thereby changing the demographic composition and overall aggregate character of the population. Equally important, or probably even more important for present purposes, the greater the time span the more likely it is that intervening events and/or changes in economic, social, or political conditions will have modified the circumstances of the country, thereby making the environment in which its population resides significantly different and reducing the degree to which the different samples have in fact been drawn from a truly identical population.

In order to address this issue, a second weight has been created. There is an unavoidable element of subjectivity in creating this weight since it requires a determination of the relative overlap and independence of partially identical populations surveyed at different points in time. Such determinations need not be arbitrary, however; plausible guidelines can be adopted and these can be informed by knowledge of the national, regional, and international environment. In the present study, surveys that were conducted in the same country at an interval of four or more years are considered to have provided essentially independent observations. These surveys are given a weight of 1.0. If the interval between surveys is less than four years, the surveys are given a weight of less than 1.0. More specifically, two surveys that are one year apart are each assigned a weight of .65, so that the two together count for 1.3 times as much as would one of the surveys had the other not been conducted. Surveys that are two years apart are each given a weight of .80, and surveys that are three years apart are each given a weight of .90.

Additionally, when a survey is both preceded and followed by surveys in the same country at intervals of less than four years, that particular survey is given a slightly lower weight than it would have received had one of the other two surveys not been conducted. This is illustrated by the weights given to the four surveys in Palestine between 2003 and 2010: 2003 (weight = .90); 2006 (weight = .75); 2008 (weight = .65); and 2010 (weight = .80). The 2003 survey received its full weight of .90 because its overlap involves only one other survey that is three years away, the survey conducted in 2006. Similarly, the 2010 survey received its full weight of .80 because its overlap involves only one other survey that is two years away, the survey conducted in 2008. By contrast, the 2006 and 2008 surveys were given lower weights because each overlaps with two other surveys. The 2006 survey overlaps with one survey three years away and one survey two years away, and hence it received a weight of .75. The 2008 survey overlaps with two other surveys that are each two years away, and hence, at .65, its weight is slightly lower.

Survey-Level Analysis

In addition to the direct effect of individual-level factors, the present study is particularly interested in whether and how individual-level, within-country relationships vary as a function of country-level contextual factors. The pooled analysis in chapter 3 ignores the possibility that the strength and significance of individual-level relationships might vary across the forty-two surveys. In fact, however, this is exactly the case; and so in chapter 4 the study undertakes survey-level analyses in order to assess the degree to which, and the ways in which, the applicability and explanatory power of individual-level within-system relationships differ as a function of country-level circumstances and experiences. Although not as elaborate as the multilevel modeling undertaken in some particularly sophisticated studies, this approach follows an analytical strategy that others have shown to be productive in exploring the connection between individual-level and country-level explanatory factors.[20]

The first step in this approach consists of estimating the strength and significance of relevant individual-level relationships *within* each macro-level unit. Therefore, to begin, the pooled individual-level analyses reported in chapter 3 are replicated in each of the forty-two surveys in the dataset that contain items pertaining to political Islam. Following this, for each survey, two measures based on these findings are generated for the survey-level analysis. The first is a measure of whether or not the test of each individual-level hypothesis found the proposed relationship to be statistically significant. The second is the coefficient that expresses the strength of the hypothesized relationship between the individual-level independent variable and support for political Islam. Finally, with these measures treated as dependent variables, bivariate and multivariate analyses are carried out in which some of the time-specific country-level political, economic, and demographic characteristics mentioned in the description of the dataset presented above are the independent variables. The previously discussed weights developed to adjust for population overlap are included in these analyses.

It may be that the strength and significance of an individual-level determinant of attitudes toward political Islam are not the same in all of the surveys for which data are available, that the relationship it specifies is sometimes found and sometimes not found or that the analysis sometimes reveals a significant relationship that is different than the one proposed by the hypothesis. If so, the simplest way to deal with these dissimilar findings might be to provide a descriptive catalog that lists the countries and years of all the surveys and then indicates whether in each case the analysis supports the hypothesis, does not support it, or indicates the existence of a relationship other than the one proposed. Thus, for example, it might be reported that higher levels of economic dissatisfaction tended to foster support for political Islam in Iraq in 2004 and in Algeria in 2006 but not in Morocco in 2005 or Jordan in 2011. Or, it might turn out that in Kuwait in 1988 and Saudi Arabia in 2003 it was greater economic *satisfaction* that increased the likelihood of supporting political Islam. This kind of catalog is likely to be unwieldy, however, and most important, it would be useful primarily to those who are interested in the particular situation in one or only some of these countries at the time the survey was conducted.

But, while this type of catalog of findings would be valuable to those concerned with the political dynamics of particular places and/or time periods, it does not shed any light on the reasons for the differences between Iraq in 2004 and, say, Morocco in 2005. It does not by itself provide any information about what it is about Iraq in 2004 and about Morocco in 2005 that makes economic dissatisfaction an important determinant of views about political Islam in one society but not the other. Nor, as a result, does it offer any generalizable insights. Those with deep knowledge of the two countries can address this question, of course; but while this can be instructive, perhaps very instructive, the insights remain speculative rather than informed by systematic comparative research. Further, such assessments become both more difficult and much less useful, at least to a broader audience, as the places and/or points in time for which data are available become more numerous and more heterogeneous. In this case, and especially if the goal is to explain rather than merely describe the variation in findings over space and/or time, the kind of conceptually focused analysis described above, which is undertaken in chapter 4, will be much more instructive.

A cross-national and over-time comparative analysis that explores such possibilities is frequently described as "substituting variable names for proper names." Instead of asking whether there is a strong and significant relationship between economic dissatisfaction and attitudes toward political Islam among Iraqis in 2004, among Moroccans in 2005, and among all of the other populations that have been surveyed, the analysis investigates whether or not the relationship between the two individual-level variables is significantly more likely to be of a specified character in countries or time periods possessing particular attributes. Thus, again, the within-system, individual-level relationship is treated as a dependent variable, and attributes of place and time—the variables that have been substituted for country names and years—are treated as independent variables in an analysis that seeks to account for, rather than merely describe, cross-survey variance in the individual-level within-system relationship.

This kind of survey-level analysis thus has the potential to enrich very significantly our understanding of why some people are more supportive while others are less supportive of a political role for Islam. Building on the first step of analysis, which identifies individual-level attributes and experiences that account for individual-level variance, the survey-level analysis undertakes to specify, in terms of conceptual properties, and thus in terms that also make findings relevant to those interested in countries and world regions beyond the Middle East and North Africa, the national attributes and time-period characteristics that are important conditionalities. The analysis in this way helps to account for cross-survey variance in the relationship between individual-level variables.

As discussed, the dataset constructed for the present study contains thirty-four different country-level and time-adjusted variables whose potential conditioning impact may be considered. Among these, as mentioned earlier, are indices of political freedom and civil liberties; GDP per capita; the UN's Human Development Index; and other political, economic, and demographic variables compiled by the World Bank, UNESCO, and other international agencies and research projects. The dataset also includes measures lagged by five or ten years for many of these characteristics. Table 1.6 lists the thirty-four country-level and time-adjusted variables included in the dataset.

Causal Inference

In concluding this discussion of data and methodology, it should be pointed out that although statistical significance provides a foundation for *inferring* that relationships that purport to be causal are indeed causal, causation can only be

Table 1.6. Country-Level Variables Included in the Dataset

Political characteristics

Year of independence

Colonial heritage

Years under colonialism

Civil Liberties Index (Freedom House, 1–7 scale)

Political Rights Index (Freedom House, 1–7 scale)

Status of freedom (Freedom House, 1–3 scale)

Corruption Perception Index (Transparency International, 0–10 scale)

Percentage of women in the lower house of Parliament

Legal Protection of Religion Index (Association of Religion Data Archives, 0–3 scale)

Freedom of Religion in Practice Index (Association of Religion Data Archives, 0–2 scale)

Government Funding of Religion Index (Association of Religion Data Archives, 0–12 scale)

Government Regulation of Religion Index (Association of Religion Data Archives, 0–10 scale)

Economic characteristics

GDP (in millions of U.S. dollars)

GDP per capita (in current U.S. dollars)

Per capita national income (in current U.S. dollars)

GINI coefficient

Percent unemployed (age 15 and older)

Percent of women in labor force

Percentage of GDP from natural resource rents (oil, natural gas, and minerals)

Per capita natural resource rents (oil, natural gas, and minerals)

Social and demographic characteristics

Population (in millions)

Area (in square kilometers)

Percentage of urban population

Percent of population under age 14

Percent of non-Muslim population

United Nations Human Development Index

Life expectancy (in years)

Adult literacy rate (age 15 and older)

Female literacy rate (age 15 and older)

Gross secondary school enrollment rate

Female secondary school enrollment rate

Linguistic fractionalization

Religious fractionalization

Ethnic fractionalization

inferred. This limitation is present throughout non-experimental social science research and must be acknowledged and accepted. The case for causal inference can nonetheless be strengthened by incorporating relevant control variables into the analysis, and this has been done in the individual-level, within-survey regression analyses reported in chapter 3. It is also necessary to consider and assess whether relationships that are statistically significant make sense—both theoretically and substantively, and the present study gives attention to this as well. Indeed, chapter 3 makes explicit the pathways and causal stories from which hypotheses have been derived and that make the proposed hypotheses plausible. Thus, although caution is always in order, a causal connection can be attributed with a reasonable degree of confidence, at least provisionally and in anticipation of further research, to the individual-level relationships that the analyses presented in chapter 3 find to be statistically significant.

The survey-level analyses presented in chapter 3 are also concerned with causality. Given the limited number of surveys, however, and particularly given the very large number of country-level attributes that might plausibly be treated as either independent variables or control variables, chapter 4 addresses the issue in a different manner. First, the individual-level analyses undertaken in chapter 3 are replicated for each survey in the multisurvey dataset, and the resulting survey-specific significance levels and coefficients are treated as dependent variables. Second, referring to the attributes listed in Table 1.6, the analysis identifies any country-level characteristics that are related to one or both of these dependent variables to a statistically significant degree and then describes the structure of each significant relationship. Finally, the potential explanatory power of each statistically significant relationship is considered and, going beyond the findings themselves, the discussion offers insights, or more accurately, perhaps, informed speculation, about the attitude-shaping dynamics suggested by these relationships linking country-level attributes and individual-level explanations.

Although these insights may be persuasive, or at least plausible, they remain unavoidably subjective. They are based on conditional associations rather than demonstrated causal connections. At the same time, they make a necessary start at identifying causal stories that tell why, rather than merely whether, individual-level attributes and circumstances have the greatest impact in particular political, economic, and/or social environments on the views held by ordinary citizens about the role Islam should play in political affairs. Thus, hopefully, this informed speculation will provide both an instructive point of departure for further reflection and a stimulus to additional research aimed at a fuller understanding of the attitude-shaping mechanisms at work.

The dataset constructed for this project, together with the analytical procedures described in this chapter, allow for an unusually thorough description of what Muslim citizens in the Middle East and North Africa think about political

Islam, and about Islam's place in their lives more generally. Even more significant, however, and largely unprecedented, it allows for a rigorous, nuanced, and conceptually focused investigation of the pathways that lead these men and women either toward or away from the view that Islam should play an important role in government and political affairs. It proceeds by first testing hypotheses that purport to identify individual-level attributes and experiences that increase the likelihood that a person will have a favorable or unfavorable attitude toward political Islam. Thereafter, to the extent that an individual-level independent variable sometimes has explanatory power and sometimes does not, the investigation proceeds to a second level of analysis in which the conditioning effects of various country-level and time-adjusted attributes are examined. The result is a two-tiered explanation of the variance associated with views about Islam's political role, an explanation that identifies both the individual-level factors that predispose individuals toward a particular viewpoint and the conditioning national and/or temporal circumstances that specify when these factors have such an impact. The present study will only make a start in deriving instructive causal stories from its findings. Without this empirical foundation, however, the quest for understanding would result in assessments that would almost certainly be much less precise, much more fragmented, and much less useful to those seeking explanatory insights of broader applicability.

2 Islam in the Lives of Ordinary Muslims

In order to fully understand the way that ordinary citizens think about Islam's place in government and political affairs, it is important to understand as well the degree to which, and the ways in which, Islam plays a broader role in people's lives. The extent and scope of Islamic practice, involvement in Islamic study groups, and other personal religious activities have varied over time in the same way that the strength of Islamist movements and the interest in political formulae with an Islamic dimension have varied. Moreover, religion is by no means absent from the lives of men and women who do not believe that Islam should play an important role in government and politics. On the contrary, Islam is one of the most important factors shaping the overall character of Middle Eastern Muslim societies. Even many Christians in the region say that the civilization of which they are a part, and with which they identify, cannot be understood without reference to Islam. The way that Islam has shaped, and continues to shape, society and culture in the Middle East and North Africa and elsewhere in the Muslim world is nicely described by Bernard Lewis in *The Shaping of the Modern Middle East*:

> Religion means different things to different peoples. In the West it principally means a system of belief and worship ... but for Muslims, it conveys a great deal more than that. Islam is a civilization, a term that corresponds to Christendom as well as Christianity in the West. No doubt, many local, national, and regional traditions and characteristics have survived and have gained greatly in importance in modern times, but on all the peoples that have accepted them, the faith and law of Islam have pressed a stamp of common identity, which remains even when the faith is lost and the law has been abandoned.[1]

At the same time, it would be a mistake to reify Islam's preeminent role in the shaping of society and culture and, especially, to lose sight of the fact that there is considerable variation in the lives people lead in Muslim-majority countries. The degree to which people make the religion a reference point in the conduct of their personal and collective affairs is not unchanging; it has been much more pronounced during some time periods and much less pronounced during others. Variation across and even within societies is no less important. As Hopkins and Ibrahim point out in their important study of Arab society, "while Islam constitutes the backbone of the Arab value system, there are several subsystems of values, some predating and others subsequent to Islam. The mix among all these has produced varying configurations of values, norms, and behavior patterns in different Arab [and other Muslim] countries and in different subcommunities within the same country."[2] Emphasizing family life but also writing about society and culture more broadly, Bowen and Early make the same point in their introduction to *Everyday Life in the Muslim Middle East:*

> Muslim Middle Easterners from a myriad of backgrounds do not all describe their experiences, raise their children, or practice rituals in the same way. The ideal or typical "Muslim family" may not really exist, given that some Muslims live in extended families in the villages and others in nuclear families in cities. A "Muslim state" or "Muslim society" is difficult to define. Middle Eastern Muslims differ in geography, ethnicity, religion, class, gender and local customs . . . Upper class Muslims may feel they have more in common with members of their class (including Christians) in another country than they do with lower class fellow nationals.[3]

Against this background, and recalling that a major goal of the present study is to shed light on the context in which are embedded both citizen attitudes about political Islam and the societal dynamics that shape these attitudes, the data described in the preceding chapter may be interrogated in order to discern the extent and character of Islam's broader salience for Muslim publics in the Middle East and North Africa. The surveys did not include questions about all relevant normative orientations, and not every question asked in some surveys was asked in all of the others. Nevertheless, the data provide information across countries and over time about the nature and distribution of important orientations pertaining to Islam. These orientations include personal religiosity and the interpretation of Islamic codes in areas of public life that do not have a direct connection to politics.

Personal Religiosity

Table 2.1 presents aggregate responses to the five items pertaining to personal religiosity listed below. The number of surveys in which a question was asked is shown in parentheses. Response distributions were determined by pooling data from all of the surveys in which the question was asked with, as explained in chapter 1, the data weighted to correct for sample size differences and for the fact that populations surveyed in a country at different points in time may not be entirely independent. The non-Muslims in the dataset, who are few in number, are not included in Table 2.1 or the other tables in this chapter.

> Independently of whether you go to religious services or not, would you say you are religious? Yes, religious; In between/somewhat religious; No, not religious (32 surveys)
> How often do you pray? Regularly (every day); Sometimes (once or twice a week); Rarely or never (28 surveys)

Table 2.1. Aggregate Distribution of Personal Religiosity Levels

Item/Response	Percent	Cumulative percent
Independently of whether you go to religious services or not, would you say you are religious?		
Yes, religious	60	60
In between/somewhat religious	27	87
No, not religious	13	100
How often do you pray?		
Regularly (every day)	86	86
Sometimes (once or twice a week)	6	92
Rarely or never	8	100
How often do you read the Quran?		
Every day or almost every day	29	29
Several times a week	34	63
Sometimes	24	87
Rarely or Never	13	100
When you consider who would be a suitable spouse for your son or daughter, would you say that each of the following attributes is very important, somewhat important, a little important, or not important: that s/he prays [the question also asks about attributes unrelated to religion that are not listed here]		
Very important	57	57
Somewhat important	20	77
A little important	10	87
Not important	13	100
Which of the following best describes you?		
Above all I am [nationality of country]	22	28
Above all I am a Muslim	69	91
Above all I am an Arab	5	96
Other	4	100

How often do you read the Quran? Every day or almost every day; Several times
a week; Sometimes; Rarely; Never (25 surveys)

When you consider who would be a suitable spouse for your son or daughter, would you say that each of the following attributes is very important,
somewhat important, a little important, or not important: that s/he prays
(17 surveys) [the question also asks about attributes unrelated to religion
that are not listed here]

Which of the following best describes you? Above all I am [nationality of coun-
try]; Above all I am a Muslim; Above all I am an Arab; Other (17 surveys)

Although none of the items included in table 2.1 was asked in all of the surveys, items asked in the same surveys are highly correlated, and response distributions are for the most part very consistent, which increases confidence that the
findings reported in the table are accurate. Further, as discussed more fully in
chapter 1, there is additional evidence that the items are reliable and valid and may,
with confidence, either be combined to form a multi-item index or, as in the present discussion, examined separately.

The item that asks respondents whether or not they consider themselves to
be religious, which was asked in the largest number of the surveys, provides a good
overall picture of the aggregate distribution of personal religiosity. It shows that
three-fifths of the respondents consider themselves to be religious, and only
13 percent report that they are not religious. The distribution of responses related
to prayer suggests that even individuals who describe themselves as "somewhat
religious," as opposed to "religious," tend to pray regularly. Moreover, in those
surveys that included both "every day" and "several times a day" as possible responses, praying several times a day was usually chosen by a majority of the
respondents. The proportion of respondents who read the Quran regularly is smaller
than the proportion of respondents who pray regularly. Nevertheless, 63 percent
of those interviewed report reading the Quran at least several times a week, and
only 13 percent say they rarely or never read it. The remaining two items were asked
in fewer surveys, but response distributions nonetheless suggest similar conclusions about the extent of personal religiosity. Fifty-seven percent deem it very important that their son or daughter marry someone who prays, and 20 percent deem
it at least somewhat important. Finally, when asked about their personal identity,
69 percent reported "above all I am a Muslim," which is more than three times as
many as those that selected the nationality of their country as the most important component of their identity (22 percent).[4]

The five response distributions shown in table 2.1 are very consistent, which
inspires confidence in the accuracy of the picture that emerges, since different
questions were asked in different countries or in the same country at different
points in time. On average, 60 to 65 percent of a country's Muslim citizens are

religious, praying regularly, reading the Quran frequently, insisting that their children marry persons who pray, and considering the religion to be the most important component of their identity. The other end of the personal religiosity spectrum is occupied by 10 to 15 percent of the Muslim population. These individuals do not pray, or pray only rarely; they rarely if ever read the Quran; they are indifferent to the religiosity of their children's marriage partners; and they identify themselves first and foremost in terms of nationality. In between is approximately a quarter of the Muslim population. Most of these somewhat religious individuals pray regularly, a practice that is common not only among the most religious, but otherwise they tend to be less observant and attach less importance to religion.

Cross-National Variation

While table 2.1 makes it clear that religion is an important factor in people's lives and an important characteristic of the social environment within which they reside, the table offers only a region-wide picture of the situation. It is possible that under this broad normative umbrella there exists significant variation across societies and/or over time. It may be the case, in other words, that the degree to which a population is religious is determined, in part, by the character and circumstances of the country in which it resides, or perhaps by the ideological and cultural climate that predominates during particular time periods.

To explore some of these possibilities, response distributions on the items pertaining to personal religiosity can be compared across countries, grouped according to various attributes. Table 2.2 presents two such comparisons, focusing on demographic attributes that may play a role in shaping normative orientations. The first of these compares the response distributions of individuals in countries that differ with respect to the presence or absence of a significant Shi'i population, in effect comparing the aggregate religiosity levels of the citizens of Iran, Iraq, Bahrain, Lebanon, Yemen, and Kuwait to the aggregate religiosity levels of the citizens of the nine other countries where surveys have been conducted. In each of the former countries, at least one quarter of the population is Shi'i, the lowest proportion being in Kuwait, where about one-quarter of its population is Shi'i. This is followed by Yemen, where 35 to 40 percent of the population is Shi'i.[5]

The second comparison in table 2.2 is between the response distributions of individuals in countries that are, respectively, lower and higher in the proportion of the population living in cities. Ratings are based on proportions at the time the surveys were conducted, although in fact these are very consistent over the present study's time span. Less urbanized countries are here defined as those in which no more than 68 percent of the population lives in cities, 68 percent being the median for the countries included in the present study. Among these are Yemen, Sudan, Morocco, Algeria, Egypt, Iraq, Iran, and Turkey in 2001. More urbanized

Table 2.2. Personal Religiosity Levels by Country Population Attributes

Item/Response	Significant Shi'i population		Proportion of population living in cities	
	Yes (%)	No (%)	Lower (%)	Higher (%)
Independently of whether you go to religious services or not, would you say you are religious?				
Yes, religious	57	61	59	61
In between/somewhat religious	30	27	29	26
No, not religious	13	12	12	13
How often do you pray?				
Regularly (every day)	90	84	87	86
Sometimes (once or twice a week)	5	6	6	5
Rarely or never	5	10	7	9
How often do you read the Quran?				
Every day or almost every day	26	31	26	32
Several times a week	39	32	33	36
Sometimes	25	23	26	21
Rarely or Never	10	14	15	11
When you consider who would be a suitable spouse for your son or daughter, would you say that each of the following attributes is very important, somewhat important, a little important, or not important: that s/he prays [the question also asks about attributes unrelated to religion that are not listed here]				
Very important	61	55	53	62
Somewhat important	18	21	21	19
A little important	11	10	12	7
Not important	10	14	14	12
Which of the following best describes you?				
Above all I am [nationality of country]	22	19	21	18
Above all I am a Muslim	67	72	71	72
Above all I am an Arab	5	5	3	7
Other	6	4	5	3

countries, those above the median, include Saudi Arabia, Jordan, Lebanon, Palestine, and Turkey in 2007, with the highest proportions found in the small Arab Gulf states of Kuwait, Bahrain, and Qatar.

Table 2.2 suggests that countries with a significant Shi'i population and countries without a significant Shi'i population differ very little in the degree to which their citizens are personally religious. There are a few minor differences between the distributions of personal religiosity in the two categories of countries, but these are never very large. The five response distributions in the table permit eighteen comparisons between countries with and countries without a significant proportion of Shi'a, but in only one case is there a difference as large as seven percentage points and in only two other cases is there a difference of six percentage points. Differences are even smaller in all of the other cases. For example, men and women who describe themselves as religious are 57 percent and 61 percent, respectively, of the respondents in the two groups of countries; and the proportions who report that they are not religious at all are 12 percent and 13 percent, respectively. Response distributions on the four other items pertaining to personal religiosity are also nearly identical in the two groups of countries. The findings presented in table 2.2 thus strongly point to the absence of any significant difference in either the extent or the distribution of personal religiosity levels in Muslim-majority countries that have and that do not have a substantial Shi'i population.

The comparison of personal religiosity levels in countries that have, respectively, smaller and larger proportions of their populations living in cities yields a similar conclusion. There is a nine-point difference in one instance: 62 percent of the respondents living in the more urbanized countries consider it very important that the spouse of their son or daughter be someone who prays, whereas this view is expressed by only 53 percent of the respondents living in the less urbanized countries. But in only one other case is there a difference of even six percentage points. Thus, again, the findings presented in table 2.2 suggest that both the extent and the distribution of personal religiosity levels are very nearly identical in the more urbanized countries and in the less urbanized countries of the Middle East and North Africa.

The proportion on a country's population that is Shi'i and the extent to which its population lives in cities are only two among many demographic attributes that play a role in shaping a country's character. Nevertheless, among Muslim populations, at least in the Middle East and North Africa, findings about these two attributes, taken together, point to a broader conclusion about the relationship between a country's demographic characteristics and the degree to which its population is personally religious—and this is that there is not much of a connection. Proportion of Shi'a and extent of urbanization are qualitatively very different, with one having to do with religion and culture and the other having to do with lifestyle, and this indicates that the finding of no relationship to aggregate levels of personal religiosity applies to quite dissimilar kinds of national demographic environments. Accordingly, although additional research might identify some exceptions, or possibly even indicate that the attributes examined in the present analysis are themselves the exceptions, the findings presented in table 2.2 make much more likely the broader conclusion that national demographic characteristics do not by themselves constitute conditions that either increase or decrease the likelihood that men and women in a Muslim-majority country in the Middle East or North Africa will be religious.

Table 2.3 presents two additional comparisons. It compares aggregate personal religiosity levels in countries grouped according to levels of economic development and social development. Per capita Gross Domestic Product (GDP) is used to measure economic development, and ratings on the United Nations Human Development Index are used to measure social, or human, development. The two measures are correlated, but they nonetheless provide information about very distinct dimensions of development.[6] While per capita GDP measures the overall wealth in a country, it does not by itself provide any information about the distribution of that wealth or about the well-being of most ordinary citizens. The UN Human Development Index, by contrast, is based on indicators of overall well-being, indicators that would not yield a high rating if relatively few citizens were benefitting from such things as education and health care. The dissimilar character of these two measures of development, as is the case with national demographic attributes, increases the possibility that the findings presented in table 2.3 will suggest broader conclusions.

The first two columns in table 2.3 compare the aggregate personal religiosity levels of respondents in countries that, respectively, at the time they were surveyed, had a per capita GDP either below or above the median of all of the countries in the dataset, that median being $1,952. The comparisons show that levels of personal religiosity are nearly identical on three items, those asking about prayer, reading the Quran, and a respondent's identity. In these cases, the pattern is very similar to that observed in the comparisons based on national demographic characteristics. The response distributions are somewhat different on the two remaining items, although these differences are neither extremely large nor entirely consistent. By a magnitude of nine percentage points, men and women in countries with a lower per capita GDP are more likely than those in countries with a higher per capita GDP to consider it very important that their son or daughter marry a person who prays. Beyond this, however, the response distributions are very similar. By contrast, aggregate personal religiosity as measured by self-definitions differs between the two groups of countries not in central tendency but rather in dispersion; respondents in countries with a higher per capita GDP are more likely than are respondents in countries with a lower per capita GDP to describe themselves as either religious or not religious but not, by a magnitude of twelve percentage points, to describe themselves as in-between or somewhat religious.

Table 2.3. Personal Religiosity Levels by Country Development Indices

Item/Response	Per capita Gross Domestic Product		Human Development Index	
	Lower (%)	Higher (%)	Lower (%)	Higher (%)
Independently of whether you go to religious services or not, would you say you are religious?				
Yes, religious	57	62	53	68
In between/somewhat religious	34	22	37	17
No, not religious	9	16	10	15
How often do you pray?				
Regularly (every day)	85	88	87	89
Sometimes (once or twice a week)	6	4	6	4
Rarely or never	9	8	7	7
How often do you read the Quran?				
Every day or almost every day	31	27	29	30
Several times a week	37	32	33	37
Sometimes	23	25	24	22
Rarely or never	9	16	14	11
When you consider who would be a suitable spouse for your son or daughter, would you say that each of the following attributes is very important, somewhat important, a little important, or not important: that s/he prays [the question also asks about attributes unrelated to religion that are not listed here]				
Very important	62	53	51	64
Somewhat important	19	21	22	18
A little important	10	10	12	7
Not important	9	16	15	11
Which of the following best describes you?				
Above all I am [nationality of country]	19	21	20	20
Above all I am a Muslim	72	68	71	71
Above all I am an Arab	3	7	3	6
Other	6	4	6	3

The last two columns in table 2.3 compare the aggregate personal religiosity levels of respondents in countries that, respectively, at the time they were surveyed, had either a higher or a lower rating on the UN Human Development Index. The index, which annually assigns countries a rating between 0 and 1, measures general well-being and is based on adult literacy, school enrollment ratios, life expectancy at birth, and standard-of-living indicators. The time-adjusted ratings in the dataset range from a low of .38 for Sudan in 2011 to a high of .91 for Kuwait in 2005, with a median of .72 for Iran in 2000.

Comparisons based the Human Development Index show patterns very similar to those based on per capita GDP: the distributions are again almost identical on the items pertaining to prayer, reading the Quran, and identity; there is again more dispersion in self-definitions of religiosity among men and women in countries with a higher Human Development Index score; and there is again a substantial difference, of fifteen percentage points, in the proportion of respondents who deem it very important that their son or daughter marry someone who prays. The latter finding, however, is the one instance in which the pattern clearly deviates from that based on per capita GDP comparisons. In this case, the view that it is very important for one's son or daughter to marry someone who prays is more widespread among respondents in countries with a *higher* rating on the Human Development Index, whereas in the comparisons based on per capita GDP this view is more widespread among respondents in countries with a *lower* per capita GDP.

There is no immediately apparent explanation for the finding that in the comparison based on levels of *social* development respondents in countries with a *higher* level of development are more likely to deem it important that their child marry someone who prays, whereas in the comparison based on levels of *economic* development this view is more likely to be held by respondents in countries with a *lower* level of development. This may reflect the fact that some countries had dissimilar ratings on the two measures of development at the time they were surveyed. This is the case for Palestine and, at the time of some of the surveys, for Jordan, Morocco, Iran, Tunisia, and Algeria. In these instances, a more religious response is usually more frequent when economic development is higher and social development is lower and, correspondingly, a religious response is usually less frequent when economic development is lower and social development is higher. If this is correct, since it is very unlikely that economic development by itself pushes toward greater religiosity, this suggests that social development may carry some explanatory power and, more specifically, that a higher level of social development, even in countries with a lower level of economic development, may involve forces that tend to push the populations of those countries away from religiosity. This is only the case for the question about the marriage partner of one's son or daughter, however, and so, even if correct, it does not suggest a more general conclusion about the relationship between a country's level of development and the aggregate personal religiosity of its population.

The other finding in table 2.3 that deserves comment is the greater dispersion in self-reported religiosity among respondents in countries that were high in economic and/or social development at the time they were surveyed. This suggests that development in the Middle East and North Africa, either economic development or social development, gives rise to an environment in which Muslim men and women are disproportionately likely to perceive themselves as being near one pole or the other of a personal religiosity continuum. But while this may say something instructive about the impact of development on the religious outlook of ordinary citizens, greater dispersion pertains only to perceptions and self-descriptions and is not present in responses to questions, such as those pertaining to prayer and reading the Quran, that ask about actual religious behavior.

The findings presented in tables 2.2 and 2.3, taken together, suggest that there is not a significant or consistent relationship between a country's demographic character or level of development and the aggregate personal religiosity of its population. Two very limited exceptions to this generalization, associated with national variations in level of development, were discussed above. Overall, however, even with these exceptions considered, the distributions presented in tables 2.2 and 2.3 resemble very much those presented in table 2.1. Accordingly, the data strongly suggest that the general pattern derived from table 2.1 is broadly applicable across the very diverse national environments in which Muslim populations in the Middle East and North Africa reside: 60 to 65 percent are religious, 10 to 15 percent are not religious, and the remaining 25 percent or so are in-between, or somewhat religious.

Temporal Variation

While there may not be any systematic and significant cross-country variation with respect to aggregate personal religiosity, as suggested by tables 2.2 and 2.3, it remains possible that there has been some notable variation over time. Indeed, the historical survey presented in the introduction makes clear that there has been variation over time in the extent of religious observance and attachment to Islam among ordinary citizens in the Middle East and North Africa. It remains to be determined, however, whether any such variation characterizes the decade or so encompassed by the present study—whether the pattern reported in table 2.1 characterizes the whole of this period or whether, alternatively, personal religiosity is either higher or lower during the earlier and later years during which surveys have been conducted.

To investigate this possibility, table 2.4 presents responses to the five items pertaining to personal religiosity using data from surveys grouped into two

Table 2.4. Personal Religiosity Levels by Time Period

Item/Response	Through 2006 (%)	After 2006 (%)
Independently of whether you go to religious services or not, would you say you are religious?		
Yes, religious	71	52
In between/somewhat religious	14	38
No, not religious	15	10
How often do you pray?		
Regularly (every day)	82	91
Sometimes (once or twice a week)	7	4
Rarely or never	11	5
How often do you read the Quran?		
Every day or almost every day	26	32
Several times a week	38	31
Sometimes	23	25
Rarely or Never	13	12
When you consider who would be a suitable spouse for your son or daughter, would you say that each of the following attributes is very important, somewhat important, a little important, or not important: that s/he prays [the question also asks about attributes unrelated to religion that are not listed here]		
Very important	57	56
Somewhat important	19	21
A little important	9	10
Not important	15	13
Which of the following best describes you?		
Above all I am [nationality of country]	18	32
Above all I am a Muslim	72	59
Above all I am an Arab	4	8
Other	6	1

temporal categories: surveys conducted in 2006 or earlier and surveys conducted in 2007 or later. These time periods have been selected, in part, because they yield groups that each contain about one-half of the surveys in the dataset, although the exact proportions vary from item to item, since not all items were asked in every survey. At the same time, the two periods are demarcated by significant regional developments, which may help to account for differences between them, should any be found. For example, important developments during 2007, the first year in which the second group of surveys was conducted, include a significant evolution of the U.S.-led war in Iraq; elections in Algeria, Morocco, Egypt, Jordan, Lebanon, and Turkey; and armed conflict between Fatah and Hamas in Palestine.

Table 2.4 shows that there are some important differences in the aggregate personal religiosity of respondents surveyed in 2006 or earlier and that of respondents surveyed in 2007 or later. These differences are not always in the same direction, but for the most part they indicate that personal religiosity was higher during the earlier time period. The most striking differences are in self-definitions of religiosity and in identity. With respect to the first, 71 percent of the men and women interviewed in 2006 or earlier describe themselves as religious, whereas only 52 percent of those interviewed in 2007 or later describe themselves as religious. With respect to identity, 72 percent of those interviewed earlier stated that "above all I am a Muslim," whereas only 59 percent of those interviewed later described their identity in this way. Nearly one-third of those in the later surveys listed their country as the primary focus of their identity. Beyond these two items, response distributions for the two time periods are somewhat but not entirely similar, and the differences that do exist are not in the same direction as those based on self-definitions of religiosity and identity. With respect to religious practice, including both prayer and reading the Quran, respondents in the earlier surveys actually report being less observant than respondents in later surveys, by a difference of nine percentage points in the case of prayer.

Differences between the two time periods in frequency of prayer and reading the Quran may not be large enough to require much attention. It may be sufficient to report that there is a difference between the earlier and later time periods but that this is limited to perceptions and self-descriptions and does not involve behavior or religious observance. Nevertheless, it is worth asking how to interpret the finding that respondents surveyed in the later period are less likely to describe themselves as religious and to report that their primary identification is with Islam, even though in practice, in terms of religious observance, they are actually, in the aggregate, somewhat more religious. To the extent that this is the best way to think about the pattern of response distributions presented in table 2.4, a plausible explanation may be that perceptions of others inform judgments about oneself, and, as a result, individuals are less likely to consider themselves very religious if they live in a country or during a time period in which religious observance is more widespread. In this context, perhaps, men and women may be inclined to see themselves as no more religious, or possibly even less religious, than most other members of their society.

Differences between the two time periods in aggregate personal religiosity might be the result of country factors rather than, or as well as, temporal factors. This is not a serious concern in the present study, however, since most countries were surveyed in both the earlier and later time periods. These countries include Jordan, Palestine, Iraq, Morocco, Yemen, Algeria, Egypt, Saudi Arabia, and Turkey. Further, to the extent that additional countries were surveyed during the latter time period, this includes both countries in which the population is somewhat less religious, such as Lebanon and Tunisia, and some countries in which the population is somewhat more religious, such as Sudan and Qatar. Thus, to the extent that there is a difference in aggregate personal religiosity between the two time periods, it is almost certainly not because some countries were surveyed in 2006 or earlier and other countries were surveyed in 2007 or later.

Taken in their entirety, comparisons based on national attributes and time periods suggest that personal religiosity is distributed in a fairly consistent manner over the space and time encompassed by the forty-two surveys in the dataset that contain questions about political Islam. The following pattern, also reported above, continues to offer the best overall description of the religious environment in which most individuals reside, a few exceptions notwithstanding: more than half but less than two-thirds of the population is religious; a much smaller proportion of the population, not less than 10 percent but probably not more than 15 percent, is not religious; and the rest of the population, at least 20 percent and sometimes closer to or even slightly above 30 percent, is somewhat religious. At the same time, while this distribution offers the best overall picture of the distribution of personal religiosity among Muslims in the Middle East and North Africa during the last ten to fifteen years, our data also show that there has been a modest increase in religious observance during the last few years, and also, perhaps because perceptions of others influence judgments about one's own level of religiosity, a notable increase in the proportion of men and women who describe themselves as "somewhat religious" rather than "religious" and who report that their primary identification is not with Islam.

Individual-Level Variation

Although aggregate personal religiosity does not vary significantly or systematically as a function of country or temporal conditions, it is possible that men and women whose individual circumstances are dissimilar, who differ with respect to sex, economic circumstance, education, or age, for example, are not equally likely to be personally religious. This possibility is explored by comparing respondents grouped on the basis of these individual-level attributes. Findings are presented in tables 2.5, 2.6, 2.7, and 2.8, which, respectively, present comparisons between men and women, between individuals whose economic situation is more favorable and less favorable, between better educated and less well-educated individuals, and between older and younger individuals.

Table 2.5 compares the response of men and women to the five survey items pertaining to personal religiosity. Interestingly, it shows that there are only a few very modest gender-related differences. The largest differences concern self-described religiosity and prayer. In the first case, women describe themselves as religious more frequently than men by a margin of six percentage points. In the second case, women report praying regularly more frequently than men by a margin of seven percentage points. Beyond this, however, the overall response distributions on these two items, as well as the response distributions on the three other items, show that preferences and practices relating to Islam are very similar for women and men. Thus, while self-assessments of religiosity and reports about prayer might suggest that women are somewhat more likely than men to be observant, gender-linked differences are small and do not provide a basis for inferring that women are significantly more likely than men to be religious. The conclusion to be drawn from table 2.5, taken in its entirety, is rather that levels of personal religiosity among both men and women are very similar to the pattern of aggregate personal religiosity reported in table 2.1.

These findings may be unexpected, particularly to those who assume that Islamic attachments are weaker or less widespread among women than among men. Although interpretations and practice vary widely, Islamic law grants different rights to women and men, and women frequently, or at least sometimes, complain that the Shari'a does not accord them equal rights in the areas of marriage, divorce, inheritance, and other matters pertaining to personal status and family affairs. Women's groups in some countries, with support from some men, have therefore been active in pressing their governments for reforms that would reduce the degree to which personal status and family law are based on the Shari'a, or that would at least change the way that Islamic law is usually interpreted and applied in this area. For example, in Morocco in 2004 and in Algeria in 2005, women's groups played a leading role in persuading political leaders to adopt reforms in the area of family law.[7]

Yet it would be incorrect to conclude that this has led most Muslim women to turn away from Islam or to be any less likely than men to be observant and to identify with Islam. Indeed, while some women have been active in urging and mobilizing support for the reform of family law, other women, apparently many others, have opposed such reform. In the debates about women and family law in Morocco, for example, many women demonstrated in support of reform, but even

Table 2.5. Personal Religiosity Levels by Sex

Item/Response	Men (%)	Women (%)
Independently of whether you go to religious services or not, would you say you are religious?		
Yes, religious	57	63
In between/somewhat religious	27	27
No, not religious	16	10
How often do you pray?		
Regularly (every day)	83	90
Sometimes (once or twice a week)	6	5
Rarely or never	11	5
How often do you read the Quran?		
Every day or almost every day	28	31
Several times a week	33	35
Sometimes	26	22
Rarely or Never	13	12
When you consider who would be a suitable spouse for your son or daughter, would you say that each of the following attributes is very important, somewhat important, a little important, or not important: that s/he prays [the question also asks about attributes unrelated to religion that are not listed here]		
Very important	56	57
Somewhat important	20	20
A little important	10	10
Not important	14	13
Which of the following best describes you?		
Above all I am [nationality of country]	21	18
Above all I am a Muslim	70	73
Above all I am an Arab	5	5
Other	4	4

larger numbers of women turned out in opposition demonstrations.[8] Against this background, and given the findings reported above, it is likely not only that women are guided by Islam in their own lives no less than are men, but also that women, on the whole, have views similar to those of men regarding Islam's societal role. In any event, whatever the implications for questions of legal reform and other societal issues, the extensive survey data brought together in the present study leave little doubt that in the Middle East and North Africa Muslim women and Muslim men differ little on key dimensions of religiosity and attachment to Islam.

Table 2.6 compares responses of individuals with differing economic circumstances to the five items pertaining to personal religiosity. Specifically, it compares the response distributions of individuals whose economic situation is, respectively, either "satisfactory," "neither satisfactory nor unsatisfactory," or "unsatisfactory." Economic satisfaction is measured by monthly income and an item that asks respondents how satisfied they are with the financial situation of their household. The item asking people about their financial situation provides five response possibilities, ranging from "very satisfied" to "very dissatisfied." Monthly income is expressed in terms of quintiles. The three categories in table 2.6 are based on the two measures taken together, or on one of them in the few instances where one item but not the other was included in the survey instrument.

The table shows that there are differences associated with economic circumstances on some of the items but not on others. On two of the items, those involving self-descriptions of religiosity and frequency of prayer, individuals who are satisfied with their economic situation are less likely than are individuals whose economic situation is neither satisfactory nor unsatisfactory, by a margin of eight percentage points in each case, to give the most religious response. Sixty-seven percent of the respondents in the latter category, those who are less than fully satisfied with their economic situation, describe themselves as religious, and 91 percent of these same men and women report praying every day. Among respondents who are satisfied with their economic circumstances, by contrast, only 59 percent describe themselves as religious and only 83 percent say they pray every day.

Although these are not very substantial differences, they nonetheless suggest that personal religiosity may be inversely related to economic satisfaction. This is not consistently the case, however. Respondents who are dissatisfied with their economic situation are not more likely to describe themselves as religious or to pray every day than are respondents who are neither satisfied nor dissatisfied with their economic situation. In fact, on the question that asks about prayer, these dissatisfied men and women are in actually somewhat *less* likely than those who are neither dissatisfied nor satisfied with their economic circumstances to report that they pray every day. Accordingly, the tendency for the individuals who are satisfied with their economic situation to be somewhat less religious notwithstanding,

Table 2.6. Personal Religiosity Levels by Economic Satisfaction

Item/Response	Satisfied (%)	Neutral (%)	Dissatisfied (%)
Independently of whether you go to religious services or not, would you say you are religious?			
Yes, religious	59	67	66
In between/somewhat religious	29	21	19
No, not religious	12	12	15
How often do you pray?			
Regularly (every day)	83	91	86
Sometimes (once or twice a week)	7	4	5
Rarely or never	10	5	9
How often do you read the Quran?			
Every day or almost every day	29	34	29
Several times a week	35	33	36
Sometimes	23	24	23
Rarely or Never	13	9	12
When you consider who would be a suitable spouse for your son or daughter, would you say that each of the following attributes is very important, somewhat important, a little important, or not important: that s/he prays [the question also asks about attributes unrelated to religion that are not listed here]			
Very important	54	58	60
Somewhat important	21	23	19
A little important	11	8	8
Not important	14	11	13
Which of the following best describes you?			
Above all I am [nationality of country]	18	21	21
Above all I am a Muslim	73	69	70
Above all I am an Arab	4	4	5
Other	5	6	4

the data do not provide unambiguous evidence of an inverse relationship between economic well-being and personal religiosity.

Responses to the other three items offer further evidence that economic satisfaction and personal religiosity are not very strongly related. Table 2.6 permits thirty-six comparisons based on the twelve response options offered by the three items taken together. Comparisons can be made between respondents who are satisfied and those who are neither satisfied nor dissatisfied, between respondents who are neither satisfied nor dissatisfied and those who are dissatisfied, and between respondents who are satisfied and those who are dissatisfied. These comparisons yield only one six-point difference: 60 percent of the respondents who are dissatisfied with their economic situation say that it is very important for their son or daughter to marry someone who prays, whereas 54 percent of those whose economic situation is satisfactory hold this view. All of the thirty-five other comparisons yield smaller differences. As a result, comparisons based on response distributions, as well as those based on separate response options, show that the extent of personal religiosity is very similar among ordinary citizens who are satisfied, those who are neither satisfied nor dissatisfied, and those who are dissatisfied with their economic situation.

In sum, while table 2.6 shows that individuals who are satisfied with their economic situation are somewhat less likely than others to be religious, the degree to which they differ from others in this respect is never very large and there is almost no difference at all on some of the attitudes and behavior patterns pertaining to religion. Coupled with the absence of any substantial difference in the aggregate personal religiosity of individuals who are dissatisfied with their economic situation and those who are not dissatisfied but also not satisfied, the major conclusion to be taken from table 2.6 is that personal religiosity varies to some extent, but not to a very great extent, as a function of economic satisfaction.

As with the findings about sex and religiosity, one might have expected the data to reveal a much more robust association between religiosity and economic satisfaction. With the exception of some small Arab Gulf states, there are significant gaps of wealth and opportunity in the Muslim-majority countries of the Middle East and North Africa. The discussion in the introduction gives a sense of these gaps, describing how they have contributed to widespread protests on a number of occasions and helped to fuel the popular uprisings that swept much of the Arab world in 2011. Given these circumstances, one might have expected that the least fortunate members of society would be disproportionately likely to embrace their religion, seeking to find comfort in the midst of economic distress and, perhaps, to show the Creator that they are worthy of something better. Alternatively, high levels of personal religiosity might be more common among men and women in advantageous economic situations, the rationale in this case being that religiosity reflects, at least in part, an expression of appreciation and a way of giving thanks for one's relative comfort. In fact, however, neither of these possibilities, nor any other that might be thought to foster a connection between economic circumstance and personal religiosity, describes a social or personal dynamic that characterizes the Middle East and North Africa. The most that can be said is that men and women who are satisfied with their economic situation tend, in some respects and to a limited extent, to be less religious than individuals who are not satisfied.

Table 2.7 compares the responses of individuals with differing levels of education to the five survey items pertaining to personal religiosity. Specifically, it compares the response distributions of individuals who have had only a primary school education or less, those who have completed high school, and those with a postsecondary education. Some of the findings in the table suggest that levels of personal religiosity do not vary as a function of this important demographic attribute. For example, the proportion of respondents who pray regularly is the same, 87 percent, in all three of the categories based on level of education. In addition, there is only a two-point difference between the proportions of better educated and less well-educated respondents who read the Quran every day, or between those who rarely or never read it, and there is also only a two-point difference between the respective proportions of better educated and less well-educated respondents whose primary identification is with Islam.

Other findings in table 2.7 suggest a different conclusion; they show that the degree to which ordinary citizens are religious does sometimes differ from one level of education to another. For example, respondents with a primary school education or less are more likely to describe themselves as religious, by a margin of ten percentage points, than are respondents with a secondary education; and by a margin of nine percentage points they are less likely than respondents with a postsecondary education to describe themselves as not religious at all. Also, by margins of nine and ten percentage points, respectively, these poorly educated men and women are less likely than those who have received a secondary or postsecondary education to consider it very important that their son or daughter marry someone who prays. The implication of these latter findings is not fully clear, however, since in one instance respondents with primary schooling or less are more religious than others and in the other instance these men and women are less religious than those who have had more education.

Taken together, some minor variation notwithstanding, the findings presented in table 2.7 show that personal religiosity is not significantly or consistently related to level of education. This is at least somewhat unexpected. In particular, it might have been expected that the least well-educated men and women would be disproportionately likely to be personally religious, presumably because, following the logic of social mobilization, they are less exposed to diverse perspectives and more reliant on traditional sources of information and authority for

Table 2.7. Personal Religiosity Levels by Education

Item/Response	Primary or less (%)	Secondary (%)	Postsecondary (%)
Independently of whether you go to religious services or not, would you say you are religious?			
Yes, religious	64	54	60
In between/somewhat religious	27	33	22
No, not religious	9	13	18
How often do you pray?			
Regularly (every day)	87	87	87
Sometimes (once or twice a week)	4	6	5
Rarely or never	9	7	8
How often do you read the Quran?			
Every day or almost every day	28	30	30
Several times a week	39	36	37
Sometimes	23	25	25
Rarely or Never	10	9	8
When you consider who would be a suitable spouse for your son or daughter, would you say that each of the following attributes is very important, somewhat important, a little important, or not important: that s/he prays [the question also asks about attributes unrelated to religion that are not listed here]			
Very important	51	60	61
Somewhat important	20	21	20
A little important	11	9	8
Not important	18	10	11
Which of the following best describes you?			
Above all I am [nationality of country]	23	21	18
Above all I am a Muslim	69	70	71
Above all I am an Arab	3	5	6
Other	5	4	5

normative guidance. A curvilinear relationship between education and personal religiosity is another plausible possibility. The logic here is that the *traditional* piety of the least well-educated individuals is accompanied by an inclination toward religiosity among the best-educated individuals resulting from the stresses, uncertainties, and frustrations associated with modern lifestyles. But while these possibilities remain subjects for reflection and future research, neither is supported by responses to more than one of the items included in the table. Accordingly, the immediate conclusion to be drawn from the findings presented in table 2.7 is that personal religiosity does not vary significantly or systematically as a function of education.

Table 2.8 compares levels of religiosity across three different age cohorts: men and women between ages eighteen and twenty-four, those between ages twenty-five and thirty-four, and those ages thirty-five and older. Reflecting the age distribution in most of the Middle East and North Africa, the first two age categories contain 22 percent and 29 percent, respectively, of the respondents in the multisurvey dataset constructed for the present study. The three categories used to explore age differences thus permit comparing the personal religiosity levels not only of relatively older and relatively younger individuals but also of both those who had only recently reached young adulthood and those who had been young adults, or simply adults, for a number of years when interviewed. As discussed below, this distinction turns out to be instructive.

The findings presented in table 2.8 are somewhat different than those presented in tables 2.5, 2.6, and 2.7. Whereas differences in personal religiosity associated with sex, economic satisfaction, and education were quite limited, the differences associated with age are more consistent. For one thing, on three of the items, those involving self-described religiosity, frequency of prayer, and frequency of reading the Quran, respondents ages twenty-four or younger are substantially less religious than respondents ages thirty-five or older. Specifically, 55 percent of the youngest respondents describe themselves as religious, compared to 63 percent of the oldest respondents; 81 percent of the youngest respondents report praying regularly, compared to 90 percent of the oldest respondents; and 23 percent of the youngest respondents report reading the Quran very often, compared to 34 percent of the oldest respondents. Furthermore, demonstrating systematic variation, the table also shows that respondents ages twenty-five to thirty-four are more religious than younger individuals and less religious than older individuals on all three of these items.

A question that arises in connection with these differences pertaining to age is whether or not younger people will "mature" as they grow older and thus, in the future, come to possess the views and orientations that characterize older people today, or whether, alternatively, early socialization has led today's young people to embrace a worldview that is likely to change little during their lifetime.[9]

Table 2.8. Personal Religiosity Levels by Age

Item/Response	24 and under (%)	25–34 (%)	35 and over (%)
Independently of whether you go to religious services or not, would you say you are religious?			
Yes, religious	55	58	63
In between/somewhat religious	27	28	27
No, not religious	18	14	10
How often do you pray?			
Regularly (every day)	81	84	90
Sometimes (once or twice a week)	7	7	4
Rarely or never	12	9	6
How often do you read the Quran?			
Every day or almost every day	23	26	34
Several times a week	35	38	32
Sometimes	28	25	21
Rarely or Never	14	11	13
When you consider who would be a suitable spouse for your son or daughter, would you say that each of the following attributes is very important, somewhat important, a little important, or not important: that s/he prays [the question also asks about attributes unrelated to religion that are not listed here]			
Very important	56	59	55
Somewhat important	20	21	20
A little important	12	9	10
Not important	12	11	15
Which of the following best describes you?			
Above all I am [nationality of country]	21	17	22
Above all I am a Muslim	70	74	70
Above all I am an Arab	5	5	4
Other	4	4	4

Although the available data do not permit a precise answer to this question, the fact that the present study draws upon surveys conducted over more than a decade, and also since, as shown in table 2.4, there do not appear to be important time-period differences in the regional climate relating to personal religiosity, the best guess is that the circumstances under which younger people and older people experienced early socialization are not very different and, therefore, the differences seen in table 2.8 do not represent "embedded" perspectives that may be resistant to change as people grow older. In any event, whether or not those who were younger when surveyed will hold different views when they are older, table 2.8 does indicate that younger individuals in the Middle East and North Africa are somewhat less religious and older individuals in the region are somewhat more religious.

The conclusion that younger men and women are less likely to be religious should nonetheless be accepted with a measure of caution. On the one hand, the differences reported above are not so great as to suggest that large numbers of young people are turning away from Islam or that religious observance is the exception rather than the norm among men and women under twenty-five years of age. On the other hand, response distributions are nearly identical across age cohorts on the item asking about the spouse of the respondent's son or daughter and on the item asking about identity. This suggests that broader Islamic values and attachments are no less pronounced among younger individuals than they are among older individuals, and that differences in personal religiosity associated with age, to the extent they exist, are in the area of religious observance and not in the relevance of Islam to people's lives more generally.

The findings reported in tables 2.2 through 2.8 show that variation across countries, within countries, and over time sometimes is, but more often is not, associated with differences in aggregate levels of personal religiosity and attachment to Islam. The fifteen countries from which the present study draws data differ very significantly in size, wealth, ethnic composition, urbanization, literacy, and much more. Algeria and Bahrain differ greatly in size and population; Yemen and Qatar differ greatly in wealth; Lebanon and Tunisia differ greatly in ethnic diversity; Kuwait and Morocco differ greatly in urbanization; and Jordan and Sudan differ greatly in literacy. Yet, comparisons of groups of countries located at dissimilar points along these continua find more similarities than differences in the degree of personal religiosity and attachment to Islam among their populations. It is surprising, and instructive, that variations in the circumstances of a country, variations reflecting important differences in demographic character and level of development, do not account for more variance in personal religiosity.

Respondents in countries surveyed at different points in time differ at least somewhat in aggregate personal religiosity. This is not particularly surprising, since the surveys brought together in the present study cover a period marked by events that might well have changed the regional and domestic environments in ways that impact the way people think about Islam. The first decade of the twenty-first century witnessed, for example, the U.S. invasion and occupation of Iraq, new Arab-Israeli confrontations, domestic unrest and even violence in some countries, important elections in a number of countries, and debates and sometimes reforms in some countries regarding the place of the Shari'a in national legal systems. But while there are differences in personal religiosity between the citizens of countries surveyed during the first years of this period and the citizens of countries surveyed later, these differences are not all in the same direction. Men and women in countries surveyed before 2007 are more likely to describe themselves as religious and to report that their primary identification is with Islam, whereas men and women in countries surveyed later have higher levels of religious observance. Connecting these dissimilar temporal differences to particular events, or kinds of events, merits further investigation and offers a promising avenue for future research.

Finally, there are some differences in personal religiosity associated with individual-level attributes, but the data show that these differences are relatively few and rarely very substantial. The positive relationship between age and religiosity is a notable exception, even though the magnitude of the differences across age categories is not particularly large. Another exception, or partial exception, is the occasionally lower religiosity level of individuals whose economic situation is satisfactory. Beyond this, however, individual-level attributes have very limited explanatory power. Given the importance of sex, education, and economic circumstance in shaping the environment within which people lead their daily lives, it is surprising that personal religiosity and attachment to Islam do not vary to a greater extent as a function of these individual-level attributes.

Taking these findings together, and acknowledging that this is not the whole story, the broad overall conclusion to be drawn is that the pattern first depicted in table 2.1, which presents averages of the response distributions in all of the surveys included in this analysis, describes a pattern that with considerable consistency applies across countries, within countries, and over the last decade in the Middle East and North Africa. Roughly 60 to 65 percent of the population is religious; another 25 percent or so is somewhat religious, although most of these individuals pray regularly; and 10 to 15 percent say they are not religious, do not pray or read the Quran, and do not attach importance to Islam in family matters or in the definition of their identity.

Interpreting Islam

While religious observance and guidance in personal affairs are the most fundamental ways that Islam touches the lives of individual Muslims, the understandings and judgments these ordinary men and women make about Islam's prescriptions regarding public affairs are also relevant and important. The Shari'a presents itself as the moral and legal basis for the organization of the Muslim community and for the public behavior of its members, and it is accepted as such by many of the faithful.

There is, however, as with any body of law, room for disagreement about the intent that lies behind the text and about which provisions apply, and how they apply, in particular public policy arenas. With respect to the rights and status of women, for example, debates are not limited to the question of whether or not Islamic law should be followed. These debates are also, and may be primarily, about what Islamic law requires of a society that chooses to be guided by Islam. Does it require that a woman be veiled, for example, or only that she dress modestly?

Differing interpretations pertaining to polygamy are frequently presented to illustrate this point. Although the practice of polygamy is rare and has few advocates, it is sanctioned by Islamic law and so defended as permissible by those who argue for a strict and literal interpretation of the Shari'a. This is the position not only of conservative Muslim jurists but also of many ordinary citizens who, even if they disapprove of the practice itself, accept that Islamic law gives a Muslim man the option of taking up to four wives. Yet other jurists, although their numbers are more limited, offer a different interpretation of the Islamic position on polygamy. They point out that polygamy is conditional on a husband's ability to treat all of his wives equally, that this is by definition impossible, and that, as a consequence, Islamic law as properly understood does not support polygamy.

The issue of polygamy, while a contentious and perhaps controversial example, is helpful in thinking about what is a central concept in Islamic jurisprudence, the concept of *ijtihad*, meaning "interpretation" and understood more fully as the exercise of creative, independent legal reasoning that stands in contrast to the acceptance of legal authority established by earlier jurists.[10] *Ijtihad* has been central to the Muslim community since its earliest days, with both classical and modern scholars of Islam pointing out that it enshrines a pluralism of opinion, the so-called *ijtihadic* pluralism, that was a significant contributor both to the community's early accomplishments and to the development and enrichment of Islamic law. As Hallaq observes, it was through the diversity fostered by *ijtihad* that the law "found the flexibility to accommodate, through variant legal norms, different situations that would otherwise have come under the same codified rule."[11]

The questions to which this leads in present-day Muslim society, although not new, are: Who is qualified to engage in *ijtihad* (to be a *mujtahid*, an "interpreter of the law")? And, to what extent do changing circumstances justify new interpretations? With respect to the first question, as a study focused on women and family law notes, "most of the *ulama* and their followers claim that only the *ulama* themselves possess the traditionally accepted qualifications and expertise to be a *mujtahid*," while reformers and modernists argue that since there is no ordained clergy in Islam one must simply be a learned person and, accordingly, "all Muslims may qualify" to be a *mujtahid*. The reformers add, providing part of their answer to the second question, that the demands of modern society are such that, beyond traditional religious knowledge, a *mujtahid* should possess "expertise in modern disciplines, such as medicine, economics, psychology and sociology."[12]

With respect to the second question more specifically, conservatives have sometimes argued that the "Gate of *Ijtihad*" is closed, meaning that the important matters of legal interpretation have been settled. More common is the view that legal interpretation remains important but that it must be guided solely by knowledge of the Quran and the *hadith* (corpus of reports of the teachings, deeds, and sayings of the Prophet), supplemented by familiarity with the verses that have been previously abrogated and interrogated through the art of legal reasoning.[13] In other words, for conservatives and traditionalists, there is no special concern for the needs of modern society and completing or enriching the law is not a specific objective. Reformers, by contrast, as suggested above, emphasize not only the importance of knowledge that is relevant for living in modern society but also see modernization of the law as a goal in and of itself, a goal that is essential for the construction of a society that is Islamic as well as modern. As poetically expressed by a leading Muslim reformist scholar, "[t]he Quran is like a rose that develops a new petal every passing day. In order to discover its depths and discover its jewels in its deeper layer, a new interpretation should be made every twenty-five years."[14]

This discussion provides some background for the analysis of an additional set of questions pertaining to Islam that were asked in some of the surveys in the dataset created for the present study. Most ordinary men and women do not think of themselves as *mujtahids*, of course, and there certainly are also limits to their familiarity with the finer points of Islamic law. But many ordinary men and women have had at least some religious education, the foundation of which is the Quran, and so the concept of *ijtihad* is not unfamiliar. Equally important, they are frequently exposed to the competing interpretations offered by scholars and jurists on present-day issues, and their assessment of these interpretations presumably influences both their own behavior and their broader understanding of how to think about what Islam permits and requires.

To explore this dimension of popular thinking about Islam, thirty-one of the surveys in the dataset include questions that seek to determine the degree to which respondents are predisposed either toward a more conservative and narrow interpretation of Islamic prescriptions or toward a more progressive and contextualized interpretation of Islamic prescriptions. The surveys, identified in table 2.9 and described more fully in chapter 1, are those that are part of the Arab Barometer and those conducted by the author with National Science Foundation funding. All of these surveys contained a battery of items that began with the following statement: "Today as in the past, Muslim scholars and jurists sometimes disagree about the proper interpretation of Islam in response to present-day issues." There-

Table 2.9. Surveys with Items about Interpretation of Islamic Law

Country and year	Country and year	Country and year	Country and year
Algeria 2002	Iraq 2006	Lebanon 2007	Palestine 2010
Algeria 2004	Iraq 2011	Lebanon 2010	S. Arabia 2011
Algeria 2006	Jordan 2003	Morocco 2005	Sudan 2011
Algeria 2011	Jordan 2006	Morocco 2006	Tunisia 2011
Bahrain 2009	Jordan 2008	Palestine 1995	Yemen 2006
Egypt 1988	Jordan 2010	Palestine 2003	Yemen 2007
Egypt 2011	Kuwait 1988	Palestine 2006	Yemen 2011
Iraq 2004	Kuwait 2005	Palestine 2008	

Note: Information about these surveys is given in chapter 1, with sample sizes shown in table 1.1.

after, respondents were given a number of statements and asked to indicate in each case whether they agreed strongly, agreed, disagreed, or disagreed strongly with the interpretation of Islam presented. Three of these statements capture the diversity of the thinking reflected in responses:

Islam requires that in a Muslim country the political rights of non-Muslims should be inferior to those of Muslims.

Banks in Muslim countries must be forbidden from charging even modest interest on loans because this is forbidden by Islam.

It is a violation in Islam for male and female university students to attend classes together.

Responses to these three items are presented in table 2.10.[15] In one case, that pertaining to the political rights of non-Muslim citizens in a Muslim country, the traditional Islamic position that non-Muslims, while protected in the case of Christians and Jews, do not enjoy the same rights as Muslims is rejected by roughly 70 percent of the respondents. With regard to the second item, pertaining to interest charged by banks, more than three-quarters of respondents favor a more narrow interpretation and endorse the position that interest is prohibited in Islam. On the third item, that pertaining to men and women studying together, respondents are somewhat divided between those who support a conservative interpretation of Islam that calls for separation of the sexes in public and those who favor a more liberal interpretation of what Islam requires, although a majority rejects the proposition that it is a violation in Islam for male and female university students to attend classes together.

The findings presented in table 2.10 indicate not only that there is disagreement among respondents about the proper interpretation of Islamic prescriptions as they apply to the issues of present-day society but also that the degree to which individuals are inclined toward a more conservative interpretation or a more

Table 2.10. Aggregate Distribution of Views about Islamic Interpretation

Item/Response		Percent
Islam requires that in a Muslim country the political rights of non-Muslims should be inferior to those of Muslims		
	Strongly agree/Agree	30
	Disagree/Strongly disagree	70
Banks in Muslim countries must be forbidden from charging even modest interest on loans because this is forbidden by Islam		
	Strongly agree/Agree	79
	Disagree/Strongly disagree	21
It is a violation in Islam for male and female university students to attend classes together		
	Strongly agree/Agree	42
	Disagree/Strongly disagree	58

Table 2.11. Responses to Item about Rights of Non-Muslims and Item about Banks Charging Interest Taken Together

		Banks in Muslim countries must be forbidden from charging even modest interest on loans because this is forbidden by Islam	
		Strongly agree/Agree	Strongly disagree/Disagree
Islam requires that in a Muslim country the political rights of non-Muslims should be inferior to those of Muslims	Strongly agree/ Agree	25.7%	4.6%
	Strongly disagree/ Disagree	55.1%	14.5%

progressive interpretation varies as a function of the issue involved. In other words, many individuals are not consistently conservative or consistently liberal on issues pertaining to the interpretation and application of Islamic law. Some undoubtedly *are* consistent, but, as the table suggests, there are many who are more conservative on the issue of banks charging interest but more liberal on the issue of equal rights for non-Muslims. Indeed, as shown in table 2.11, which con-

Table 2.12. Views about Islamic Interpretation by Country Population Attributes

Item/Response	Significant Shi'i population		Proportion of population living in cities	
	Yes (%)	No (%)	Lower (%)	Higher (%)
Islam requires that in a Muslim country the political rights of non-Muslims should be inferior to those of Muslims				
Strongly agree/Agree	26	32	30	31
Disagree/Strongly disagree	74	68	70	69
Banks in Muslim countries must be forbidden from charging even modest interest on loans because this is forbidden by Islam				
Strongly agree/Agree	75	80	74	83
Disagree/Strongly disagree	25	20	26	17
It is a violation in Islam for male and female university students to attend classes together				
Strongly agree/Agree	40	43	36	49
Disagree/Strongly disagree	60	57	64	51

siders views on the two issues taken together, this is the position of more than half of the respondents to whom these questions were asked. The table thus provides another indication that judgments about Islam's position on social, economic, and political issues are in many cases made independently of one another, without reference to a preexisting mindset that consistently pushes in the same direction on all matters involving the interpretation and application of Islamic law. This pattern is described as "ideological constraint" in the social science literature,[16] meaning that an individual does not have a coherent and integrated normative perspective that shapes his or her views on a wide variety of dissimilar social and policy issues.

Cross-National Variation

Tables 2.12 and 2.13 compare views about Islamic interpretation across the same country-level attributes that were considered when exploring variation associated with personal religiosity in the previous section of this chapter. As in table 2.2, table 2.12 focuses on two demographic attributes that may shape the national environment in ways that influence the thinking of a country's citizens about

Table 2.13. Views about Islamic Interpretation by Country Development Indices

Item/Response	Per capita Gross Domestic Product		Human Development Index	
	Lower (%)	Higher (%)	Lower (%)	Higher (%)
Islam requires that in a Muslim country the political rights of non-Muslims should be inferior to those of Muslims				
Strongly agree/Agree	31	30	30	31
Disagree/Strongly disagree	69	70	70	69
Banks in Muslim countries must be forbidden from charging even modest interest on loans because this is forbidden by Islam				
Strongly agree/Agree	75	82	74	83
Disagree/Strongly disagree	25	18	26	17
It is a violation in Islam for male and female university students to attend classes together				
Strongly agree/Agree	45	38	36	49
Disagree/Strongly disagree	55	62	64	51

the application of Islamic prescriptions to present-day issues. The first comparison in the table is between the views of individuals in countries that, respectively, have and do not have a significant Shi'i population. The questions about Islamic interpretation were not asked in the surveys in Iran, and so for this comparison, the countries with a significant Shi'i population are Iraq, Bahrain, Lebanon, Yemen, and Kuwait.[17]

On all three of the items pertaining to Islamic interpretation, the table shows only small differences between the response distributions for countries with a significant Shi'i population and those for countries without a significant Shi'i population. Accordingly, the three sets of response distributions are broadly in line with those based on all of the surveys and shown in table 2.10. Most respondents in both sets of countries take a more conservative position on the issue of banks charging interest, a more liberal position on the issue of the rights of non-Muslims, and are at least somewhat divided on the question of men and women studying together at universities.

Table 2.12 does reveal modest differences between respondents in the two sets of countries on two of the items, that pertaining to rights of non-Muslims and that pertaining to men and women studying together. In both instances, individuals in countries with a sizeable Shi'i population are, on average, less likely to take a traditional and conservative position. The differences are only five and six percentage points, however, which is not enough to support a conclusion that men and women in countries with a significant Shi'i population are less likely than men and women in other Muslim-majority countries of the Middle East and North Africa to believe that Islam requires a strict and literal interpretation of its codes. Rather, as in the case of personal religiosity, similarities between the two sets of countries are much more striking than differences with respect to the interpretation and application of Islamic law.

Table 2.12 also presents response distributions based on surveys in countries with a smaller proportion of their populations living in cities and those based on surveys in countries with a larger urban population. As in table 2.2, which looked at differences associated with personal religiosity, level of urbanization is divided at the median for all of the surveys in the dataset, and this means that less urbanized countries are here defined as those in which no more than 68 percent of the population was living in cities at the time the survey was conducted.

Taken in their entirety, the three response distributions for more urbanized countries and less urbanized countries are fairly similar and, as a result, each is also generally consistent with the distribution based on all respondents shown in table 2.10. Respondents in each group of countries most often support a liberal interpretation of Islam on the question of non-Muslim rights, most often support a conservative interpretation on the question of banks charging interest, and are divided more evenly on the question of male and female university students studying together. In addition, on one of the items about Islamic interpretation, that pertaining to the rights of non-Muslims, the response distributions for the two categories of countries are almost identical, being separated by only one percentage point.

At the same time, there are also some notable differences in the responses to questions about Islamic interpretation given by individuals in more urbanized countries and less urbanized countries. On two of the questions, those pertaining to banks charging interest and men and women studying together at university, individuals surveyed in countries with a larger urban population are, on average, more likely than those in less urbanized countries to support a more conservative interpretation of Islam. Eighty-three percent of the respondents in more urbanized countries believe banks in Muslim countries should be prohibited from charging interest, compared to 74 percent of the respondents in less urbanized countries who take this position. The difference is even larger on the question of male and female university students studying together. Forty-nine percent of the respondents in more urbanized countries judge this to be a violation of Islam, compared to 36 percent of those from less urbanized countries. These differences might be surprising. Since the proportion of men and women living in the traditional sectors of society is greater in countries that are less urbanized, it might have been expected that conservative interpretations of Islam would be more common in these countries. The findings presented in table 2.12 show that this is not the case. On the contrary, the table shows that conservative Islamic interpretations are at least somewhat more likely to find support in urban environments.

Two somewhat different conclusions can thus be drawn from table 2.12. The most important of these is that public predispositions about Islamic interpretation are broadly similar in Muslim-majority countries of the Middle East and North Africa that differ significantly in population attributes and demographic character. In countries both with and without a significant Shi'i population, and also in countries that are more urbanized and less urbanized, more conservative and strict interpretations of Islam are endorsed by large majorities of ordinary citizens on the question of banks charging interest, more liberal and progressive interpretations of Islam are endorsed by large majorities of ordinary citizens on the question of the political rights of non-Muslims, and ordinary citizens are divided more evenly, at least in relative terms, on the question of coeducation at universities. This distribution of views about what Islam requires and permits—about how the religion should be interpreted and applied, thus offers a description of public assessments that appears to be broadly applicable across the diverse demographic environments that characterize the Middle East and North Africa.

The second conclusion is that demographic attributes are not totally lacking in explanatory power. Countries with a lower proportion of the population living in cities at the time they were surveyed include Morocco, Egypt, Yemen, and Iraq, among others. Countries with a higher proportion of the population living in cities at the time they were surveyed include Jordan, Palestine, Lebanon, and Saudi Arabia, among others. The data presented in table 2.12 show that citizens in one of these groups of countries, that with higher levels of urbanization, are more likely than citizens in the other group of countries to support more conservative interpretations of Islam on several important questions. The difference is particularly notable on the question of coeducation, about which publics in more urbanized countries are very evenly divided while publics in less urbanized countries are skewed in favor of a more liberal interpretation of religious prescriptions.

This latter conclusion does not call into question the finding that views about Islamic interpretation are distributed in broadly similar ways in countries characterized by quite different demographic attributes. It does indicate, however, that these broad similarities do not imply a complete identity of views. Nor do they imply that the overall demographic environment in which a Muslim population resides plays no role at all in predisposing the public toward one position or another on matters of Islamic interpretation. Whether the differences between more and less urbanized countries imply causal relationships, with differences persisting when separate comparisons are made between city dwellers and residents of nonurban areas in the two sets of countries, and whether other demographic attributes also have some influence on views about the proper interpretation of Islam, are questions to which future research might productively devote attention.

Table 2.13 compares views about Islamic interpretation among individuals in countries grouped according to level of economic development and level of social and human development. There are vast socioeconomic differences between countries in the Middle East and North Africa, raising the possibility that the populations of countries that differ in this respect will have different views about social and economic issues in general and about how these issues should be understood from an Islamic perspective in particular. Table 2.13 examines this possibility. As in the examination of personal religiosity, economic development is measured by per capita GDP, and social development is measured by the UN Human Development Index, with countries divided at the median on each variable.[18]

With respect to economic development, respondents in less developed countries and those in more developed countries have, in the aggregate, virtually identical views on the question of political rights for non-Muslim citizens. By contrast, by margins of seven percentage points in each instance, respondents in more developed countries endorse a conservative interpretation of Islam on the question of banks charging interest *more* frequently than do respondents in less developed countries, and these respondents endorse a conservative interpretation of Islam on the question of coeducation *less* frequently than do respondents in less developed countries. These differences are not especially large, although they do suggest that a country's level of economic development may have some influence on the way its citizens think about how Islam should be interpreted. What is most interesting, however, is that this influence pushes toward a more conservative interpretation on one issue and toward a more liberal interpretation on the other. This is consistent with the point made earlier, and illustrated in table 2.11, that interpretations of Islam tend to be at least somewhat issue-specific and thus at best are shaped only partly by a pre-existing mindset that consistently pushes in the same direction on all matters involving the interpretation and application of Islamic law.

The second comparison in table 2.13, involving countries with dissimilar levels of social development at the time they were surveyed, shows that once again there is virtually no aggregate difference in what respondents consider to be the proper interpretation of Islam on the question of political rights for non-Muslims. In both sets of countries, 30 or 31 percent of those interviewed believe that Islam requires the political rights of non-Muslims to be inferior to those of Muslims, and 70 or 69 percent disagree with this interpretation of Islam. By contrast, as in the comparisons involving economic development, there *are* differences between respondents in the two groups of countries on the two remaining items pertaining to Islamic interpretation. Unlike the differences associated with economic development, however, individuals in countries with higher ratings on the Human Development Index in both cases hold more conservative views about what Islam permits and requires. Among men and women in countries with a higher level of social development at the time they were surveyed, 83 percent believe that Islam forbids banks from charging interest, whereas this is the position of 74 percent of the respondents in countries that have a lower level of social development. There is an even bigger difference on the question of coeducation: a conservative interpretation is supported by 49 percent of the respondents in countries with a higher Human Development Index rating and by 36 percent of the respondents in countries with a lower Human Development Index rating.

Findings based on surveys in countries that differ in their levels of economic and social development again suggest several conclusions. First, different as the countries in each pair of comparisons may be, it is again the case that publics are heavily skewed toward a liberal interpretation of Islam on one item, heavily skewed toward a conservative interpretation on another item, and divided at least somewhat more evenly on a third item. This further demonstrates that many, and probably most, ordinary citizens do not possess a particular mindset that informs their understanding of what Islam requires and that, as a result, leads them to embrace consistently more conservative or consistently more liberal interpretations across a broad range of issues. As with the findings from the comparisons based on national demographic attributes presented in table 2.12, this strongly suggests that this description of aggregate public views about the interpretation and application of Islamic prescriptions applies across the very diverse national environments that are found in the Middle East and North Africa.

Second, on one of the items, that pertaining to the political rights of non-Muslims, aggregate responses are not only consistently in the same direction, they are in fact virtually identical. In both more developed and less developed countries, and in the case of both economic and social development, 30 or 31 percent of the respondents agreed that Islam requires that in a Muslim country the political rights of non-Muslims should be inferior to those of Muslims, and 69 or 70 percent disagreed with this interpretation. This suggests that, on at least one question about what Islam intends, and presumably on some others as well, attitudes are not influenced by national circumstances. Rather, in some instances, Muslim publics in very dissimilar demographic, economic, and social environments line up in very similar ways on questions about how Islamic prescriptions should be understood.

Finally, the findings presented in table 2.13, as do some of the findings presented in table 2.12, indicate that the distribution of public views about the proper interpretation of Islam does sometimes vary as a function of national attributes. Interestingly, this variation is most likely to occur on questions about which the public is either skewed toward a more conservative interpretation or more evenly divided. Interesting as well, and surprising, is the finding that the relationship between a country's level of economic development and the views of its population on questions of Islamic interpretation is not always in the same direction. Respondents in countries with lower levels of economic development supported a more conservative interpretation of Islam in one instance and a more liberal interpretation of Islam in another instance more frequently than did respondents in countries with higher levels of economic development.

Although the magnitude of these differences is not extremely large, ranging from seven to thirteen percentage points, it is sufficient to suggest that national circumstances and characteristics may help to explain, and at the very least help to predict, variation in the way that Muslim populations understand what Islam has to say about present-day political, economic, and social issues. Since both economic and social development involve multiple dimensions, additional research will be needed to determine whether some of these dimensions are more important than others in accounting for the observed variance. Further research will also be needed to determine the degree to which a country's level of economic or social development actually conditions the thinking of its citizens about the proper interpretation of Islam—whether the associations reported in table 2.13 involve causal connections. Nevertheless, despite the questions that must await future research, the present descriptive analysis makes clear not only that there are some similarities in the way that Muslim publics in highly dissimilar national settings think about the interpretation of Islam but also that there are some noteworthy differences in the attitudinal distributions that characterize men and women in societies that differ in level of development.

Temporal Variation

Table 2.14 compares the views about Islamic interpretation of men and women in countries surveyed prior to 2007 to those in countries surveyed in 2007 or later. On all three of the items pertaining to Islamic interpretation, the pattern first reported in table 2.10 is visible in both the earlier time period and the later time period: responses are skewed toward a more liberal interpretation with respect to the political rights of non-Muslims and toward a more conservative interpretation with respect to banks in Muslim countries charging interest. There is less of a broadly shared tendency on the issue of coeducation.

Although assessments of Islam's position on interest charged by banks are distributed in nearly identical ways in the two time periods, there are time-period differences in the way that responses to the other two items are distributed. Moreover, in both cases, the time-related difference is in the direction of increased support for a liberal interpretation of Islam. The difference is particularly large in the distribution of responses to the question about male and female students attending classes together at university. Among respondents in countries surveyed in

Table 2.14. Views about Islamic Interpretation by Time Period

Item/Response	Through 2007 (%)	After 2007 (%)
Islam requires that in a Muslim country the political rights of non-Muslims should be inferior to those of Muslims		
Strongly agree/Agree	34	28
Disagree/Strongly disagree	66	72
Banks in Muslim countries must be forbidden from charging even modest interest on loans because this is forbidden by Islam		
Strongly agree/Agree	78	79
Disagree/Strongly disagree	22	21
It is a violation in Islam for male and female university students to attend classes together		
Strongly agree/Agree	49	34
Disagree/Strongly disagree	51	66

2006 or earlier, 49 percent deemed this to be a violation of Islam. Among respondents in countries surveyed in 2007 or later, by contrast, only 34 percent endorsed the view that Islam prohibits coeducation at university. On the question pertaining to the political rights of non-Muslims, the difference between the two time periods is smaller but in the same direction, with men and women in countries surveyed later endorsing a liberal interpretation of Islam more frequently, by a margin of six percentage points, than individuals in countries surveyed earlier.

Findings about temporal variation, like those about cross-country variation, point to both continuity and change in the way that ordinary citizens think about the proper interpretation of Islamic prescriptions—in their understanding of what Islam requires and permits with respect to the political rights of non-Muslims, banks in Muslim countries charging interest, and male and female university students attending classes together. The most important continuity, which characterizes the views of Muslim populations surveyed between 2007 and 2011 just as it characterizes the views of Muslim populations surveyed earlier, concerns the overall distribution of judgments about Islamic interpretation. In both time periods, as was the case among respondents residing in countries with very different demographic profiles and levels of development, large majorities agree with a liberal interpretation of Islam on the question of political rights for non-Muslims, large majorities agree with a conservative interpretation of Islam on the question of banks charging interest, and Muslim populations are more evenly divided in their views about Islam's position on gender mixing in higher education.

The experience of the Middle East and North Africa during the years spanned by the surveys brought together for the present study give this finding particular significance. Numerous important events and developments occurred in the region during this period, many of which, singly or collectively, impacted national and regional environments and might be expected to have influenced the way Muslim men and women think about their religion. Among these are the emergence and evolution of the U.S.-led war in Iraq, major confrontations between Israelis and Palestinians and between Israel and Hezbollah, one or more elections in most of the countries in the region, continuing debates and in some cases reforms pertaining to the role and interpretation of the Shari'a in national legal systems, and finally, before one-third of the surveys conducted after 2006 were carried out, popular uprisings and in some instances a change of regime in a number of Arab countries. Many of these events played out in a way that gave ordinary citizens an opportunity to reflect on the role in society that should be played by Islam and to form, or reexamine, their judgments about public figures and movements that stand for more progressive or more restrictive interpretations of Islam. Nevertheless, while the cumulative effect of the events buffeting the Middle East and North Africa during this period presumably did, to at least some degree, influence the outlook of ordinary citizens, these events did not bring with them any fundamental change in people's understanding of what Islam requires and permits on several very salient issues.

The preceding applies to issues about which popular views are heavily skewed in one direction or the other, where substantial majorities endorse either a more liberal or a more conservative interpretation of Islam. In these areas, where there is greater agreement and perhaps even something approaching a consensus, Muslim populations surveyed later express views that differ very little from those of Muslim populations surveyed earlier. The take-away insight this suggests, which may be tested further in future research, is that to the extent an understanding about the proper interpretation and application of Islam on a particular issue is widely shared, that understanding is less likely to change in response to external events and developments.

The findings presented in table 2.14 point to variation as well as continuity, however, and this is consistent with the insight offered above. By a margin of fifteen percentage points, which is quite substantial, respondents in countries surveyed during the latter time period endorse a liberal interpretation on the question of coeducation more frequently than do respondents in countries surveyed during the earlier time period. This is consistent with the proposition offered above, since coeducation is an issue on which there was not broad agreement and a clear tendency in one direction or the other during the earlier period, and so, presumably, people's thinking about Islam's position on this issue was less resistant to modification and more likely to be influenced by changes in the regional and/or domestic environment.

Like many of the propositions and insights derived from this chapter's essentially descriptive analysis, additional research will be needed to assess both their accuracy and their explanatory power. In the case of temporal variation, this research will need to determine whether change is indeed more likely on some kinds of issues than others, and particularly whether judgments pertaining to issues about which there is broad agreement are more resistant to change than are judgments pertaining to issues about which the public is more divided. In addition, however, future research will need to do more than determine whether a multifaceted collection of region-level and country-level developments has produced observable change in some of the views about Islamic interpretation held by ordinary citizens. In order to explain as well as describe any variation that has occurred, future studies must also strive to determine, to the extent possible, the degree of explanatory power that can be attributed to particular events and experiences, or particular classes of events and experiences. In other words, to the extent that a constellation of regional or national events and experiences are found to have had an impact on public opinion, it will be necessary, in order to arrive at a fuller understanding and develop genuinely informative causal stories, to discern the pathway that links specific elements of the constellation to specific patterns of attitudinal change.

Individual-Level Variation

Tables 2.15 through 2.18 explore the possibility that explanatory power is to be found in individual-level demographic variation by comparing the views about Islamic interpretation held by individuals who differ with respect to sex, economic circumstance, education, and age.

Table 2.15 compares the responses of men and women and shows that the views of the two sexes are distributed in nearly identical ways on the question of equal political rights for non-Muslims and on the question of banks charging interest. The views of both men and women divide in the same way on these issues, with more than two-thirds of each sex believing that Islam does not require inferior political rights for non-Muslims, and more than three-quarters of each sex believing that Islam does prohibit banks in Muslim countries from charging even modest interest. Men and women do have differing views about Islam's position on coeducation, however, although the response distributions of the two sexes are not as dissimilar as might have been expected. By a margin of seven percentage points, men are more likely than women to agree or agree strongly, and correspondingly by a similar margin men are less likely than women to disagree or

Table 2.15. Views about Islamic Interpretation by Sex

Item/Response		Men (%)	Women (%)
Islam requires that in a Muslim country the political rights of non-Muslims should be inferior to those of Muslims			
	Strongly agree/Agree	31	30
	Disagree/Strongly disagree	69	70
Banks in Muslim countries must be forbidden from charging even modest interest on loans because this is forbidden by Islam			
	Strongly agree/Agree	78	79
	Disagree/Strongly disagree	22	21
It is a violation in Islam for male and female university students to attend classes together			
	Strongly agree/Agree	45	38
	Disagree/Strongly disagree	55	62

Table 2.16. Views about Islamic Interpretation by Economic Satisfaction

Item/Response		Satisfied (%)	Neutral (%)	Dissatisfied (%)
Islam requires that in a Muslim country the political rights of non-Muslims should be inferior to those of Muslims				
	Strongly agree/Agree	32	29	30
	Disagree/Strongly disagree	68	71	70
Banks in Muslim countries must be forbidden from charging even modest interest on loans because this is forbidden by Islam				
	Strongly agree/Agree	77	77	80
	Disagree/Strongly disagree	23	23	20
It is a violation in Islam for male and female university students to attend classes together				
	Strongly agree/Agree	44	43	42
	Disagree/Strongly disagree	56	57	58

Table 2.17. Views about Islamic Interpretation by Education

Item/Response	Primary or less (%)	Secondary (%)	Postsecondary (%)
Islam requires that in a Muslim country the political rights of non-Muslims should be inferior to those of Muslims			
Strongly agree/Agree	32	31	28
Disagree/Strongly disagree	68	69	72
Banks in Muslim countries must be forbidden from charging even modest interest on loans because this is forbidden by Islam			
Strongly agree/Agree	79	80	77
Disagree/Strongly disagree	21	20	23
It is a violation in Islam for male and female university students to attend classes together			
Strongly agree/Agree	43	43	37
Disagree/Strongly disagree	57	57	63

Table 2.18. Views about Islamic Interpretation by Age

Item/Response	24 and younger (%)	25–34 (%)	35 and older (%)
Islam requires that in a Muslim country the political rights of non-Muslims should be inferior to those of Muslims			
Strongly agree/Agree	32	31	30
Disagree/Strongly disagree	68	69	70
Banks in Muslim countries must be forbidden from charging even modest interest on loans because this is forbidden by Islam			
Strongly agree/Agree	78	79	79
Disagree/Strongly disagree	22	21	21
It is a violation in Islam for male and female university students to attend classes together			
Strongly agree/Agree	37	43	43
Disagree/Strongly disagree	63	57	57

disagree strongly that it is a violation in Islam for male and female university students to attend classes together. These findings indicate that a person's sex is not likely to have much influence on the way he or she thinks about what Islam permits and prohibits in general, but that it does have some influence, although only to a relatively limited degree, when the issue involved is related to gender. In this case, to the extent the issue might be understood as increasing opportunities or equality of treatment for women, women more frequently than men believe that Islam is less restrictive in what it permits.

Table 2.16 presents the response distributions of individuals who differ in the degree to which they judge their economic situation to be satisfactory. Specifically, it compares the response distributions of individuals whose economic situation is either "satisfactory," "neither satisfactory nor unsatisfactory," or "unsatisfactory." As discussed earlier in this chapter, economic satisfaction is measured by monthly income and an item that asks respondents how satisfied they are with the financial situation of their household. The ratings in table 2.16 are based on the two measures taken together, or on one of them in the few instances where one item but not the other was included in the survey instrument.

As suggested in the presentation of findings about personal religiosity, the great economic disparities in all but a very few countries in the Middle East and North Africa might have been expected to foster among individuals with dissimilar levels of personal well-being and economic satisfaction perspectives about society that vary in ways that influence their judgments about the proper interpretation of Islam. In fact, however, the response distributions in the three categories of economic satisfaction are nearly identical on all three of the items pertaining to Islamic interpretation. Accordingly, it is clear that economic circumstances, at least as perceived by the respondent, do not account for any of the variance in the way people think about Islam's position on present-day issues.

Table 2.17 compares the responses of better educated and less well-educated individuals and shows that the views of people with different levels of education are again distributed in almost identical ways on the question pertaining to the political rights of non-Muslims and the question pertaining to banks in Muslim countries charging interest. There is a difference associated with education in people's thinking about the remaining item, which asks for an assessment of Islam's position on coeducation at university. Individuals with a postsecondary education are less likely than individuals in the other two categories based on level of education, by a margin of six percentage points, to agree or agree strongly that men and women studying together at university is a violation of Islamic prescriptions.

Finally, table 2.18 compares the views of individuals across three age cohorts: individuals under the age of twenty-five, those ages twenty-five to thirty-four, and those who are thirty-five years of age or older. Differences between the oldest and youngest individuals, or between any two age cohorts, are no more than two or three percentage points on the issue pertaining to non-Muslim rights and on the issue of banks in Muslim countries charging interest. There is a difference on the remaining item, which asks about male and female university students attending classes together. The youngest cohort of individuals, those between eighteen and twenty-four years of age, are less likely, by a margin of six percentage points, to believe that coeducation at university is a violation of Islam.

Given how dissimilar are the experiences and lifestyles of men and women, of individuals with a more favorable and a less favorable economic situation, of better-educated and less well-educated individuals, and of those who are younger and those who are older, it is somewhat surprising that similarities are much more common than differences in the views about Islamic interpretation held by individuals who differ in sex, economic satisfaction, level of education, and age. Surprising or not, however, there is not a great deal of systematic individual-level variation in judgments about Islamic interpretation. This is the case in particular with respect to the questions that ask about the proper interpretation of Islam regarding the political rights on non-Muslim citizens of Muslim-majority countries and banks in Muslim countries charging interest.

This is consistent with findings from the analyses of cross-country and temporal variation. In these instances, as in the comparisons based on individual-level attributes shown in tables 2.15 through 2.18, a similar judgment about non-Muslim rights and about banks charging interest is expressed by a large majority of men and women in each of the categories into which respondents have been divided. Thus, again, there is something approaching an agreed public position on these items, even as it endorses a more conservative and restricted interpretation of Islam in one instance and a more liberal and progressive interpretation of Islam in the other. These widely accepted positions are endorsed in equal measure by very different and distinct subsets of the population.

Although the differences shown in tables 2.15 through 2.18 are neither numerous nor large, with magnitudes of only six or seven percentage points, they are characterized by some common elements that make them worthy of note. First, they all involve the question that asks about coeducation at university. This is the issue about which publics are more divided and, as noted, about which views are at least somewhat more likely to vary as a function of country-level factors and over time. Second, in each case the difference is associated with a more liberal view of what Islam requires and permits. Finally, endorsement of a liberal interpretation is more common among respondents in the demographic categories where this might be expected: among women, among individuals with a postsecondary education, and among individuals in the eighteen to twenty-four age group. Accordingly, even though the differences are not large and similarities across the individual-attribute categories is the most important takeaway, these findings do suggest the possibility that, in at least one area and presumably others about which there is less pre-existing agreement, increased education and the emergence of a new generation may bring with them a change, and a change in a progressive direction, in the judgments of Muslim men and women about how their religion should be interpreted.

The survey data presented in this chapter offer instructive insights about the nature and distribution of personal religiosity and views about the proper interpretation of Islamic prescriptions pertaining to present-day issues. In a number of instances, there is notable cross-national, temporal, or individual-level variation in the views and behavior reported by respondents. This variation sheds light on the locus of divergent citizen predispositions relating to Islam and invites reflection about the factors that shape citizen orientations. Formulating and testing hypotheses about the determinants of this variance will be a valuable avenue for future research.

But while the tables do reveal some interesting and intriguing cross-national, temporal, and individual-level differences in attitudes and behavior, the strong similarity of most of the response distributions is the more important takeaway. With respect to both personal religiosity and Islamic interpretation, the views and behavior reported by the more than 60,000 men and women who were interviewed in the surveys reveal striking consistency in the nature and distribution of citizen orientations pertaining to Islam. There is a clear pattern pertaining to personal religiosity that consistently characterizes Muslim publics in the Middle East and North Africa and another clear pattern pertaining to Islamic interpretation that also consistently characterizes these same men and women.

With respect to personal religiosity, 60 to 65 percent of the population is religious, although the proportion of individuals who say they pray every day is around 90 percent, and roughly 10 percent of the population, or perhaps a bit more, is not religious at all. With respect to Islamic interpretation, the relative frequency of assessments that ascribe greater conservatism or greater liberalism to Islam's position on present-day issues varies as a function of the issue involved, indicating that these judgments about Islam are rarely governed by a dominant and overriding conservative or liberal mindset. Thus, approximately two-thirds of the population believes that Islam does not require that in a Muslim country the political rights of non-Muslims should be inferior to those of Muslims; approximately three-fourths of the population believes that it is a violation in Islam for banks in Muslim countries to charge even modest interest; and the population is divided more evenly on the question of whether it is a violation in Islam for male and female university students to attend classes together, although the percentage saying that it is not a violation is somewhat larger.

All of these patterns characterize the attitudes and behavior of ordinary citizens in countries with and countries without a significant Shi'i population, in more urbanized and less urbanized countries, in countries with higher and lower levels of per capita GDP, and in countries with higher and lower ratings on the UN Human Development Index. They also characterize respondents in countries surveyed before 2007 and those in countries surveyed in 2007 or later. Finally, they characterize both men and women, individuals in more satisfactory economic circumstances and those in less satisfactory economic circumstances, better-educated and less well-educated individuals, and both older and younger men and women. Accordingly, as we turn our attention in the next chapter to the perceptions and judgments of ordinary citizens about Islam's role in government and political affairs, we can draw several broad conclusions about the place of Islam in the lives of ordinary Muslims. Most men and women are engaged with their religion in serious ways, but there is nonetheless variation in both their behavior and their judgments pertaining to Islam. Additionally, and significantly, the observed patterns, and the variation they incorporate, are strikingly consistent across the region, within its very diverse societies, and over at least the last decade.

3   Why Individuals Hold Different Views about Islam's Political Role

Islam in Contested Political Arenas

Debates about Islam's role in governance in the Muslim Middle East and North Africa are not new, and thinking about Islam's role in political affairs has evolved over the last half century. The experience has not been the same in every country, of course, and the distribution of attitudes about Islam's political role is not the same in every country at the present time. Overall, however, questions about the place that Islam should occupy in government and political affairs continue to be debated and contested.

This division of opinion about Islam's political role is reflected, in the aggregate, in the survey findings presented in table 3.1. Drawing upon all of the 62,097 Muslim respondents in the dataset,[1] based on forty-two surveys in fifteen countries, and with the findings weighted to correct for sample size differences and population overlap, as described in chapter 1, the table shows a wide divergence of views about three propositions concerning the relationship between religion and politics. Specifically, 51.1 percent agree or agree strongly that men of religion should have no influence over the decisions of government, whereas 43.3 percent favor or favor strongly the exercise of such influence by men of religion, and another 5.6 percent neither agree nor disagree. With regard to the statement that religion is a private matter and should be separated from sociopolitical life, 55.5 percent agree or agree strongly, whereas 39 percent disagree or disagree strongly, and another 5.5 percent neither agree nor disagree. With regard to a third statement, that it would be better for their country if more people with strong religious beliefs held public office, 52.3 percent agree or agree strongly, whereas 42 percent disagree or disagree strongly, and another 5.7 percent neither agree nor disagree.

Not every one of the items presenting these propositions to respondents was included on the interview schedule administered in every survey. Nor, when the instrument did include one of the propositions, was the response distribution necessarily almost identical to that shown in the table. But overall, especially since a majority of the countries were surveyed at several different points in time, and often with different interview schedules, thereby making aggregated responses more reliable, the table presents an unusually clear picture of the views held by ordinary citizens. And it leaves little doubt, taking the Muslim Middle East and

Table 3.1. Responses to Items about the Place of Islam in Government and Political Affairs

Item/Response	Percent
Men of religion should have no influence over the decisions of government	
Strongly agree/Agree	51.1
Neither agree nor disagree	5.6
Disagree/Strongly disagree	43.3
Religious practice is a private matter and should be separated from sociopolitical life	
Strongly agree/Agree	55.5
Neither agree nor disagree	5.5
Disagree/Strongly disagree	39.0
It would be better for [country] if more people with strong religious beliefs held public office	
Strongly agree/Agree	52.3
Neither agree nor disagree	5.7
Disagree/Strongly disagree	42.0

Note: Only six of the surveys offered the response option of "neither agree nor disagree."

North Africa in the aggregate, that the question of Islam's political role is highly contested, not only in the political arena but among ordinary citizens as well.

Accounting for Variance

Despite the clarity of the region-wide pattern shown in table 3.1, which also suggests its temporal applicability over the dozen or so years during which the surveys included in the present study were collected, there is both within-survey and cross-survey variance that should be noted. Even more important, it is necessary to account for this variance—to identify, in other words, the factors that predispose individuals toward a more supportive or a more oppositional position on the question of whether Islam should guide a government's actions and policies.

The information required to account for variance goes beyond specifying the correlations between attitudes toward political Islam and various demographic attributes, such as education, economic status, and other personal circumstances. Rather, accounting for variance requires striving for causal stories by developing hypotheses that broaden the search for factors that have explanatory power. Then, these hypotheses need to be tested through multivariate analyses that hold other things constant and reduce the likelihood of spuriousness when making causal inferences. Finally, we must uncover both the personal and broader contextual circumstances that define the locus of applicability of whatever significant explanatory relationships have been identified.

Causality can only be inferred in such analyses, and causal inference should not be mistaken for proof that a statistically significant relationship involves a causal connection. Nevertheless, an analysis that succeeds in identifying factors that are part of a plausible and presumably persuasive causal story, and that then is able to show that the hypothesized relationships have significant and independent predictive power, goes a considerable distance toward discovering not just *what* people think about Islam's political role but also *why* they hold certain views. What then remains is to identify and define in conceptual terms the circumstances and conditionalities that specify when this predictive power obtains. An analysis that achieves these objectives possesses an important measure of explanatory power.

The dependent variable in this analysis is, of course, individual judgments about the role that Islam should play in government and politics—a continuum of individual preferences ranging from strong support for to strong opposition to the proposition that Islam should occupy an important place in a country's political life. The operationalization of this dependent variable is described in detail in chapter 1. As discussed, the measure is an index composed of the items in each individual survey that pertain to the place of Islam in politics and that have been shown by factor analysis to reliably measure the same underlying dimension. The procedure not only offers evidence of reliability, additionally, since the resulting index is unidimensional, it is almost certainly valid as well. Chapter 1 also describes the basis for concluding that the measure possesses conceptual equivalence across the forty-two surveys, despite the fact that not every item was included in every survey. This is illustrated in table 1.3, which shows the "bridging" provided by partial overlap among eight different survey items, including the three in table 3.1, that have been used to construct the indices for five of the forty-two surveys.

Four hypotheses will be tested in an effort to develop causal stories that shed meaningful light on the pathways leading to differing views about Islam's political role. The independent variables in these hypotheses are: (1) cultural preferences, and more specifically attitudes toward women's status and gender equality; (2) political judgments, and in particular an evaluation of the regime governing the country in which an individual lives; (3) economic well-being, measured in most cases by both income relative to one's co-nationals and satisfaction/dissatisfaction with the economic situation of one's household; and (4) level of education. Although far from exhaustive, meaning that other factors undoubtedly also play a role in shaping views about the place that Islam should occupy in political life, these four qualitatively different independent variables constitute a deliberately diverse set of factors for which it is possible to advance a causal story that is plausible and the evaluation of which will be instructive. Findings pertaining to the four hypotheses will significantly increase our understanding of why some citizens embrace one view and other citizens embrace a different view about the degree to which Islam should play an important political role.

Cultural Preferences and Gender Equality

The circumstances of Muslim women in the Middle East and North Africa vary widely. Women are government ministers and members of parliament, corporation managers and university presidents, scientists, engineers, journalists, and physicians. In all of these categories, there are more than a small number of examples. Thus, whereas an important study noted two decades ago that Muslim women in the Middle East face "limitations on their participation in the economy, [and] their exclusion from many fields of activity in their society,"[2] this description is increasingly out of date. Further, with as many women as men attending university in most countries, and with *more* women than men attending university in some countries, the number of women in positions of influence and prominence within their societies is certain to increase.

At the same time, women continue to be underrepresented in all of these professions, usually very seriously underrepresented, and this is the case as well in many of the mid-level fields where most individuals find employment in a modern economy. The disadvantaged situation of women in the Arab world is summarized in a 2012 Gallup Country Data Set report:

> About one in three young Arab women between the ages of 23 and 29 participate in their country's labor force versus about eight in 10 young Arab men. This gender gap is generally consistent across the 22 Arab countries and territories Gallup surveyed in 2011, but young women's labor force participation is slightly higher in low-income countries than in higher income countries.

The report goes on to state that, in many Arab countries,

> chronic job shortages combined with cultural factors, such as pressure on employers to give young men jobs that enable them to marry and start families, may limit employment opportunities for young women, [and that] the World Bank recently reported that the Middle East and North Africa region continues to have the lowest female workforce participation rate of any global region.[3]

Work and professional life is not the only arena in which the picture for women is mixed. Societal codes and practice pertaining to personal status and relations within the family frequently deny to women some of the rights and opportunities enjoyed by men, and particularly relevant in this connection are issues pertaining to marriage and divorce, property rights, and veiling and seclusion. In these and other areas, Islamic family law has usually been codified in a manner that provides women with fewer rights than men,[4] and these prescriptions, or interpretations of prescriptions, are often enshrined in national legal systems. Only in Tunisia and Turkey is polygamy formally outlawed, for example, and in most of the Muslim-majority countries of the Middle East and North Africa divorce remains easier for a man than for a woman and men and women have unequal inheritance rights. The connection between Islam and gender inequality is ambiguous in some of these areas, at least from a historical perspective. The Quran does not call for women to be veiled or kept apart from the world of men, for example, and this suggests that norms and practices in this area are not of Islamic origin.[5] Nevertheless, Muslim scholars and officials usually insist that Islam requires veiling and prohibits the public mixing of men and women, and this view is accepted by many Muslims, including many Muslim women.

A focus on these inequalities, important as they are not only for individual women and their families but also for society at large,[6] provides only a partial picture of the situation of Muslim women in the Middle East and North Africa. There has also been, and continues to be, significant progress toward removing barriers to gender equality. On the one hand, women themselves, along with supportive men, have been organizing and pressing for reforms related to family law and personal status. As a study of Egypt reported a few years ago, to view "relations between men and women in the Islamic world as the interaction of sheer power and abject obedience is quite inaccurate. Women are not passive victims, and they quite actively argue their case and seek to widen their opportunities when the chance is offered."[7]

On the other hand, many governments, sometimes responding to pressure from women's groups or other progressive movements, have enacted reforms that remove, or at least reduce, some of the legal bases for gender inequality. The Supreme Constitutional Court of Egypt, for example, declared gender equality to be fully compatible with Islam and a fundamental component of a just society, and it insisted, therefore, that the state consider the promotion of gender equality to be part of its constitutional obligation.[8] In Morocco, where the personal status code had previously been established by royal decree, reforms were debated and subsequently approved by the National Assembly in 2004.[9] Among the more than one hundred ratified amendments to the code, which were substantial, although less far-reaching than some had wanted, were provisions specifying that a woman cannot be married against her will, that a man cannot take a second wife without gaining agreement from a judge that there are genuinely exceptional circumstances, and that both men and women can petition for divorce and that divorce proceedings should take place in civil rather than religious courts.[10]

These accounts, brief as they are, paint a picture of women's status that is problematic, complicated, dynamic, and, perhaps most important, contested, all

Table 3.2. Responses to Items about Gender Equality

Item/Response	Percent
A married woman can work outside the home if she wishes	
Strongly agree/Agree	82
Disagree/Strongly disagree	18
Men and women should have equal job opportunities and wages	
Strongly agree/Agree	71
Disagree/Strongly disagree	29
A university education is more important for a boy than a girl	
Strongly agree/Agree	31
Disagree/Strongly disagree	69
A woman can be president or prime minister of a Muslim country	
Strongly agree/Agree	54
Disagree/Strongly disagree	46
A woman can travel abroad by herself if she wishes	
Strongly agree/Agree	35
Disagree/Strongly disagree	65
On the whole, men make better political leaders than women do	
Strongly agree/Agree	76
Disagree/Strongly disagree	24

Note: Only six of the surveys offered the response option of "neither agree nor disagree." This option was offered for only one of the three items in the table, and it was selected by only 1 percent of all respondents. Here and after, the "neither agree nor disagree" response option is not included. Also, here and after, percentages are rounded to the nearest whole number.

at the same time. They also describe an issue about which Muslim publics are not of one mind. Table 3.2, which again presents aggregate findings from the forty-two surveys in the dataset that include questions about political Islam, illustrates the division of opinion about a cross-section of issues pertaining to gender equality. The table also shows that the central tendency and degree of dispersion of public views varies considerably from item to item. On some questions, attitudes are heavily skewed in the direction of support for gender equality. For example, 82 percent of the respondents agree or agree strongly that a married woman can work outside the home, if she wishes; 71 percent agree or agree strongly that men and women should have equal job opportunities and salaries; and 69 percent disagree or disagree strongly with the proposition that a university education is more important for a boy than a girl.

On other questions, by contrast, citizens are more divided or the distribution of attitudes is skewed against gender equality. Only 54 percent agree or agree strongly that a woman can be president or prime minister of a Muslim country; only 35 percent agree or agree strongly that a woman can travel abroad by herself, if she wishes; and only 24 percent disagree or disagree strongly with the proposition that men make better political leaders than women. These findings not only indicate that attitudes are not distributed the same way on all issues pertaining to gender equality, they also shed light on the kinds of issues with respect to which citizens are, respectively, more likely to favor and less likely to favor equality between men and women. More specifically, support for gender equality is more widespread on questions pertaining to personal opportunity and mobility and support for gender equality is less widespread on questions involving leadership and unchaperoned interaction with strangers.

Finally, recalling some of the findings about Islamic interpretation presented in chapter 2, it may be noted that Muslim publics are also divided in their views about what Islam has to say about gender equality. Respondents split somewhat evenly on the question of whether it is a violation in Islam for male and female university students to attend classes together. As shown in table 2.10, 42 percent agreed or agreed strongly and 58 percent disagreed or disagreed strongly that coeducation at university is a violation of Islam. Even among female respondents, as shown in table 2.15, 38 percent judged coeducation in higher education to be a violation of Islam. On the other hand, the findings presented in chapter 2 also suggest that attitudes have been changing. Individuals in countries surveyed after 2006 were more likely, by a margin of 15 percentage points, to believe that Islam, properly interpreted, does *not* prohibit men and women from studying together at university. And, interestingly, the difference in responses between the time periods before and after 2006 was actually slightly larger for men, being 17 percentage points for men and only 12 percentage points for women.

The dataset also includes a question that asks respondents their views about Islam's position on veiling, and the findings, which were not presented in chapter 2, but are presented here in table 3.3, show a pattern that is in some respects similar and in other respects different from that pertaining to coeducation. Sixty percent of all respondents agree or agree strongly that Islam does not require that a woman wear a veil in public, endorsing a more liberal interpretation, in other words. This is about the same as the percentage who agreed or agreed strongly that coeducation is not a violation of Islam. Thus, again, Muslim publics in the Middle East and North Africa are divided on whether Islam, properly interpreted, places restrictions on the behavior of women and their interaction with men, with views nonetheless skewed to a modest degree in support of a more liberal interpretation of what Islam prohibits and permits. In contrast to views about coeducation, however, the 60–40 division of opinion characterizes both

Table 3.3. Views about the Proper Interpretation of Islam with Respect to Women's Dress

	Surveyed in 2006 or earlier			Surveyed in 2007 or later		
	All (%)	Men (%)	Women (%)	All (%)	Men (%)	Women (%)
In Islam a woman should dress modestly, but Islam does not require that she wear a veil						
Strongly agree/Agree	61	60	61	60	59	61
Disagree/Strongly disagree	39	40	39	40	42	39

Note: This item and others pertaining to Islamic interpretation were introduced with the following statement: "The opinions of Islamic jurists and religious scholars differ with regard to their interpretations of certain issues in Islam. I want to ask to what extent you agree or disagree with the following interpretations of some of these issues."

women and men and both those surveyed in earlier years and those surveyed more recently.

Even though the way public opinion divides varies from question to question, it is clear that there is both substantial support and substantial opposition to equality between the sexes among Muslim publics in the Middle East and North Africa. There is also a substantial division of opinion regarding the proper interpretation of Islam on questions pertaining to the status and rights of women. The proposition that this division of opinion helps to account for the substantial variance that exists in attitudes toward Islam's political role, as well as the expected direction of the relationship between attitudes toward gender equality and attitudes toward political Islam, are expressed in Hypothesis 1, presented below.

> H1. Individuals who hold more conservative views on social and cultural issues and thus are less supportive of gender equality are more likely than individuals who hold more progressive views on social and cultural issues and thus are more supportive of gender equality to believe that Islam should play an important role in political affairs.

Both perceived value congruence and policy expectations offer a rationale for this hypothesis and suggest mechanisms that are probably operating if the proposition is confirmed. On the one hand, citizens who hold more traditional and conservative cultural values, particularly relating to women's status and gender equality, are likely to believe, and quite reasonably so, that persons who hold important positions in Islamic institutions or play a prominent role in Islamic social or political movements share their values in this area and in other areas that

Islam seeks to regulate. On the other hand, precisely for this reason, they are also likely to believe that these shared values and the behavior patterns they encourage and sanction will be reflected to a greater degree in the enactment and enforcement of legislation, as well as in public policy and government programs more generally, to the extent that the country is governed by a political formula that permits more individuals with religious credentials or attachments to hold public office and exercise influence in shaping government decisions and resource allocations. Thus, at the heart of the causal story to which Hypothesis 1 calls attention is the idea of normative congruence: Among men and women in Muslim-majority countries of the Middle East and North Africa, individuals will tend to view favorably those political leaders, platforms, and formulae that they believe will advance their own values and ideological commitments, and they will tend to disapprove of political leaders, platforms, and formulae that they believe will move society away from the norms and values they favor.

Despite the appeal of this logic, it is at least possible that some individuals, and perhaps even many individuals, do not actually perceive a very strong convergence between their own attitudes about gender equality and the way society would be governed were greater political influence to be exercised by persons with strong Islamic attachments. This possibility is suggested by the tendency, especially in recent years, of many Islamist leaders to endorse more liberal positions on women's rights. This reflects, at least in part, the entry of Islamist movements into the electoral arena and the desire of Islamist leaders and movements to broaden the base of their support more generally. This trend is documented in a recent longitudinal study of Islamic party platforms, which finds:

> Prior to the mid-1990s, a majority of the platforms in our collection favored the implementation of *Shari'a* and a ban on interest and made some mention of *jihad* and opposition to Israel. Since that time, half or fewer of the platforms have adopted such positions. By contrast, recent platforms are more likely to mention democracy, the rights of women, and the rights of minorities. Hence: *Islamic parties have (relative to their starting point) liberalized their stances significantly over the past several decades.*[11]

This liberalization may reflect the evolving beliefs of Islamic and Islamist leaders, among whom there are indeed debates about the interpretations and requirements of Islam, or it may be entirely tactical. Nor is it self-evident that any liberalization that has occurred will color the way ordinary citizens view Islamic leaders more generally. Nevertheless, this movement does suggest at least the possibility that many individuals will view men (and women) of religion as motivated less by sincere normative commitments and more by political expediency and thus, like all politicians, too ready to compromise. To the extent this is the case, attitudes toward gender equality will be much less of a motivating factor in pushing individuals to either support or oppose a political formula that assigns an important role to Islam. In other words, there will be less perceived ideological congruence, or at least more of a belief that whatever convergence of values exists is of little practical significance, and so attitudes toward gender equality will have less explanatory power than that proposed in Hypothesis 1.

Like other hypotheses, the relationship posited in Hypothesis 1, however persuasive the logic that supports it might seem, remains to be tested. It may or may not receive support from the empirical analysis to be undertaken. Or the analysis may show that there is support for the hypothesis among some population categories, but not among others, or in some countries or at some time periods, but not others. But the point to be noted in advance of this test is that implicit in the hypothesis, and now made explicit, is a causal story about why cultural preferences, particularly those pertaining to women's status and gender equality, may account for variance in, and may thus be an important determinant of, the preferences held by ordinary Muslim citizens in the Middle East and North Africa about the role Islam should play in government and politics.

Political Judgments and Regime Evaluation

A number of analysts, myself included,[12] have argued that support for Islamist movements, and perhaps for political Islam more generally, is in part a protest against the political and economic status quo and, more specifically, against the regimes that ordinary citizens hold responsible for the situation about which they complain. The complaints of these men and women in the Muslim-majority countries of the Middle East and North Africa, particularly, but not only, in those countries with more autocratic regimes, include: persistent poverty, a large gap between rich and poor, corruption and favoritism that promote inequality and limit economic and status mobility, and a political system that severely restricts the prospects for meaningful change and rarely tolerates even modest public criticism. Thus, in the eyes of many ordinary citizens, their country is governed for the benefit of a small political and associated consumer class that supports its privileged lifestyle with resources that should be used for national development while people like themselves continue to live in conditions of distress. Although not equally prominent and intense everywhere, this popular assessment of the prevailing political and economic order is widespread.

These complaints are not new. As discussed in the introduction, this constellation of grievances sparked mass demonstrations and even riots, sometimes on more than one occasion, in Morocco, Algeria, Tunisia, Egypt, Palestine, Jordan, and elsewhere as early as the 1980s and 1990s, as they had done in Egypt and Iran in the late 1970s. In these instances, as well as in some countries where public discontent did not give rise to rioting or even large-scale and sustained demonstrations, large segments of the public have for several decades been alienated from the regimes by which they are governed and sought leaders whose priorities do not center on their own power and privilege. As expressed in the early 1990s by a scholar of Egyptian origin, there is a "severe, multi-dimensional, and protracted crisis faced by many regimes in the Muslim world. This crisis has been evidenced by a decline of state legitimacy and has resulted in 'state exhaustion.'"[13] Similarly, describing the mood in the Arab world during this period, a Jordanian journalist wrote:

> [The problem is] autocratic rulers and non-accountable power elites who pursue whimsical, wasteful and regressive policies.[14]
> [There is] a profound desire for change—for democracy and human rights . . . for accountability of public officials, for morality in public life . . . and for a new regional order characterized by honesty, dignity, justice and stability.[15]

Government officials often contend that these complaints about regime performance are unreasonable and exaggerated. They assert that demands for rapid progress are unrealistic, with many citizens, and especially the young, failing to appreciate that development goals can only be achieved over the long haul. Officials also frequently insist that much has been accomplished, sometimes suggesting that complaints are the result not of government failures but, rather, of aspirations fostered by successful development efforts, most notably in the field of education. Whatever the accuracy of these rebuttals, however, they rarely strike a responsive chord among the disillusioned and alienated segments of the public, presumably because so many find confirmation in their own lives of the charge that something fundamental is amiss in the nation as a whole. These men and women reason, logically, although perhaps somewhat simplistically, that if the government were allocating resources wisely, in accordance with the true interests of the populace, they, their families, and so many of their friends would not be confronted with stagnation or even a decline in their modest standards of living.

The desire for an alternative to the political and economic status quo has led some, and perhaps many, to believe that a more appropriate and responsive political formula might be found in Islam. Both indigenous and foreign analysts writing during the 1980s and 1990s and in the years that followed emphasize that a growing interest in political Islam has been fueled, at least in part, by disaffection with those in power. As reported in studies of Tunisia and Morocco at the end of the 1980s, the growth of the Islamist movement is "a symptom of a deeper malaise within society"[16] and will continue as long as "the problems of social disadvantage and deprivation and of political marginalization" remain unaddressed.[17] Similarly, writing several years later about the Arab world in general, a political scientist from the United Arab Emirates argued that "as long as governments in the Arab world resist political participation and the tolerance of different political opinions, the strength of Islam as a political ideology will continue to be a serious alternative."[18] And more recently still, as noted in a broad overview by a British scholar of Sudanese origin, "the rise of the Islamic movements is a symptom of the dire crises that beset the land of Islam. . . . [They] emerged as a reaction to the crisis they wanted to get out of."[19]

Complaints about the governing regime and its policies have also been reflected in the strength of Islamist parties at the ballot box when competitive elections were permitted, as in Jordan, Tunisia, and Algeria in the late 1980s and early 1990s, and more recently in Turkey, Palestine, Yemen, Morocco, Egypt, Kuwait, and elsewhere. The dynamic fueling the relationship between political and economic discontent and the electoral strength of Islamist parties, reflecting a connection that transcends ideology and doctrine and what voters are against as much as what they are for, is nicely captured in the statement of a young Algerian who explained to an American journalist why he had supported the Islamic Salvation Front (FIS) in the local and regional elections of June 1990:

> In this country, if you are a young man . . . you have only four choices: you can remain unemployed and celibate because there are no jobs and no apartments to live in; you can work in the black market and risk being arrested; you can try to emigrate to France to sweep the streets of Paris or Marseilles; or you can join the FIS and vote for Islam.[20]

As this account suggests, the FIS was the only available and viable opposition movement through which it was possible to cast a meaningful vote against the regime. For the most part this has been and remains the case, since authoritarian governments have usually been more successful, and sometimes more motivated, in working to suppress secular opposition movements. As reported in a recent overview of electoral politics and political participation in the Arab world, "the major opposition movements and parties across the region today are Islamist parties and actors [whereas] secular opposition parties seem to have lost the sway and influence they possessed in the 1960s and 1970s."[21] For this reason, Islamist movements have been able to capture support, or at least votes, from opponents of the political and economic status quo who do not necessarily favor Islamist social and cultural policies. For these individuals, who are not the Islamists' core constituency, support presumably reflects a judgment that an Islamist political movement is the best available alternative, and one that is preferable, whatever its drawbacks, to the regime in power. To the extent that this is the case, at least some voters do not lend their support to Islamist movements because of, but perhaps rather in spite of, these movements' social agenda. Perhaps they also assume, or at least hope, that the party will use whatever influence it possesses or acquires to address problems of political economy and will put social and cultural objectives on the back burner.

There is also some evidence that even in countries where voters have been offered meaningful alternatives, as in Jordan, Yemen, Morocco, and Palestine, for example, Islamist movements have had considerable success in attracting voters who are motivated by political and economic considerations rather than by religious or ideological predispositions. Among the reasons that Islamist parties are frequently preferred in these instances is the fact that secular elites are often seen as closely associated with the governing regime.[22]

Beyond their frequent monopoly on credible opposition to the governing regime, there are other factors unrelated to an Islamist policy agenda that have helped Islamist parties at the polls. One of these is their connection to religious and social service organizations whose resources they can use not only to reward supporters but also to sway swing voters to their side.[23] Another factor concerns the foreign policy of the regime, especially in Egypt, Jordan, Palestine, and a few other countries. In cases where the government is aligned with the United States, particularly on questions regarding Israel, but also on U.S. Middle East policy more generally, Islamist parties have exploited anti-American sentiment and, again, drawn support from men and women who may not favor the conservative social and cultural policies that Islamists advocate, but are influenced to a greater degree by their dislike of ties to the United States.[24] Finally, as noted in the previous section, Islamist parties have also frequently put forward moderate platforms in order to attract a broader spectrum of voters and, in particular, to increase the likelihood of receiving support from men and women who would be deterred by more controversial religion-inspired policies.[25]

All of these considerations were on display in 2011, the last year in which surveys included in the present study's dataset were conducted. During this very important year, massive popular uprisings associated with what became known as the Arab Spring shook the region. The anti-regime sentiments that animated the Arab Spring were already familiar and often came together at this time as a demand for dignity, *karama*, perhaps best understood as a call for governments that care about their citizens and respect them enough to work seriously and honestly on their behalf. Sometimes intertwined with sectarian, tribal, or regional rivalries, interrelated political and economic grievances fueled public anger, even rage, and were at the core of what brought mass protests and led to the overthrow of the regimes in Tunisia, Egypt, Yemen, and Libya; to violent and sustained confrontations in Bahrain and Syria; and to reforms or other preemptive responses by the regimes in several additional countries.

As discussed above, Islamist parties were important beneficiaries of the public's desire for an alternative to the status quo, obtaining more votes in the 2012 elections in Egypt and Tunisia than might have been expected given the size of their core constituencies, at least as these can be estimated from available surveys. And while this was in part due to superior mobilization efforts and a disorganized secular opposition, it also reflected the fact that the parties were, once again, able to attract votes from a considerable number of Muslim citizens who do not favor Islamist social and cultural policies but were rather motivated by their search for an alternative to the governing regime.

But this may not be the whole story among individuals who are both discontent with the political status quo and do not hold conservative cultural values pertaining to such areas as women's rights and gender relations. The logic of the previous assessment notwithstanding, men and women who possess this combination of attitudes and values, regardless of whether they are or are not prepared to support Islamist political movements, may in fact believe that Islam, as opposed to Islamists, *should* play a role in government and political affairs. One reason for this may be Islam's emphasis on equality, protection of the weak and vulnerable, and help for the needy. Relevant, too, may be a belief that Islam, as a religion of laws, will bring a commitment to justice and the rule of law. There will be disagreement about whether these values and commitments have in practice been any more respected by religious officials and advanced by religious institutions than by their secular counterparts. Nevertheless, to the extent that ordinary citizens who have an unfavorable view of the governing regime find these normative orientations in Islam and believe they will bring a positive and needed element to political affairs, they may indeed endorse the proposition that Islam should exercise influence in government and politics and not be motivated in their judgments by entirely temporal and secular considerations.

Whether or not these latter dynamics do indeed shape the judgments of a significant number of ordinary citizens is a question for empirical analysis. It may be the case, as initially discussed, that among men and women who do not possess conservative social and cultural values, a negative evaluation of the governing regime only very rarely leads to support for the proposition that Islam should exercise influence in political affairs. But, as the latter possibility suggests, there is also a plausible case to be made for the proposition that discontent with the regime in power *does* significantly increase the likelihood of supporting political Islam among those with more liberal values pertaining to women and other social and cultural issues.

Finally, while each of these competing possibilities pertains to citizens who do not possess more traditional and conservative views on social and cultural issues, those who do possess more traditional and conservative views may already be disproportionately likely to favor an important role for Islam in political affairs. Hypothesis 1 expressed this proposition, and the reasoning supporting it was discussed when that hypothesis was presented. But regardless of whether an analysis of the data does or does not lend support to Hypothesis 1, it seems likely, or at least it is reasonable to propose, that if individuals with more traditional and conservative normative orientations have a negative view of the regime in power, they will be more likely to favor an important political role for Islam than will be individuals with similar cultural orientations and a positive evaluation of the regime. They will be disproportionately likely to see Islam as a desirable alternative to a regime they do not like, or whose performance they judge to be inadequate, and this will not be in spite of any concern that this will lead to more conservative social and cultural policies. On the contrary, their desire for an alternative to the political status quo will be reinforced by the possibility that such policies, which they favor, will become more likely if Islam exerts greater influence in political affairs.

Hypothesis 2 may be offered to guide the analysis by which the relevance and explanatory power of these various causal stories can be evaluated.

> H2. Individuals who are more dissatisfied with the character and performance of their political institutions and officials are more likely than are individuals with higher levels of political satisfaction to favor a political formula that gives Islam an important role.

All of the causal stories offered above, for which the fit to reality remains to be tested, assume that the regime in power is largely secular, or at least that it does not have a strong Islamic connection. The dynamic assumed to be operating is that those who are unhappy with the regime are significantly more likely than those with a positive evaluation of the regime to want Islam to play a significant political role precisely because the government and leaders of which they disapprove do not draw upon the religion for guidance and insight. In other words, Islam is the alternative, either institutionally, ideologically, or both, to what people believe they have and do not like.

But some Muslim-majority countries in the Middle East and North Africa have, or have had at some point during the period for which survey data are available, governments that do have a meaningful Islamic connection. This is clearly the case in Saudi Arabia and Iran, for example, as well as others where the connection is sometimes less robust or more transient but clear and important nonetheless. In these cases, the logic informing the analysis above would suggest that citizens with a negative evaluation of the regime by which they are governed would be disproportionately likely to *oppose* giving Islam a meaningful role in political affairs. The proposed causal story thus remains the same, but the direction of the relationship changes; the desire for an institutional and/or ideological alternative to a regime that one does not like leads away from, rather than toward, the view that Islam should exercise influence in government and political affairs.

Yet, this too is not the only possible dynamic. It may be the case that a significant number of citizens make a distinction between a regime with an Islamic connection and the proper role that Islam should play in political life and the affairs of state. Some citizens may believe that the government, notwithstanding any connection it may assert or actually have to religious institutions and officials or to

Islamist movements, has manipulated, distorted, or even hijacked the religion for its own self-serving and largely temporal purposes. To the extent that this is the case, discontent with the regime may *not* predispose citizens to favor a political system in which Islam exercises influence, but may rather predispose them to favor a political system in which influence *is* exercised by Islam, the true and proper Islam, as they understand it—an Islam that is practiced by leaders who honestly and accurately follow, rather than self-interestedly manipulate, the religion's teachings.

In light of these additional possibilities, Hypothesis 2 may be reformulated as Hypothesis 2a and Hypothesis 2b, in which the direction of the posited relationship is proposed to vary according to whether or not people are citizens of a country governed by a regime with an Islamic connection. And, as discussed above in relation to men and women who live in countries with more secular regimes, analysis of the available survey data will go a long way toward assessing the relative utility and explanatory power of plausible but competing causal stories about the relationship between an individual's evaluation of the regime and his or her views about the role Islam should play in politics and government.

> H2a. Individuals who are more dissatisfied with the character and performance of their political institutions and officials are more likely than are individuals with higher levels of political satisfaction to *favor* a political formula that gives Islam an important role *if they are citizens of a country governed by a secular regime.*

> H2b. Individuals who are more dissatisfied with the character and performance of their political institutions and officials are more likely than are individuals with higher levels of political satisfaction to *oppose* a political formula that gives Islam an important role *if they are citizens of a country governed by a regime with a strong Islamic connection.*

Economic Circumstances and Economic Satisfaction

The various and alternative causal stories that inform the hypotheses about political judgments and regime evaluation may have an equal or even greater measure of explanatory power when the complaints held by ordinary citizens involve economic rather than political circumstances. The two categories of concern often reinforce one another, of course, coming together under the rubric of political economy. As the discussion in the previous section makes clear, complaints about a country's political rulers and the regime over which they preside may be and usually are fueled by discontent about the economic situation, as well as by discontent about the absence of political freedoms and/or the violation of human rights. On the other hand, even to the extent that this is indeed the case, one category of concern may carry much more explanatory power than the other. In any event, if discontent with the status quo is one of the drivers of citizen attitudes about Islam's political role, as suggested in the previous section, and should discontent with the status quo be based to a substantial extent on a negative evaluation of economic circumstances, even if there are also complaints of a more explicitly political character, the following hypotheses, Hypotheses 3a and 3b, may also be derived from the causal stories offered earlier.

> H3a. Individuals with lower levels of economic satisfaction are more likely than are individuals with higher levels of economic satisfaction to *favor* a political formula that gives Islam an important role *if they are citizens of a country governed by a secular regime.*

> H3b. Individuals with lower levels of economic satisfaction are more likely than are individuals with higher levels of economic satisfaction to *oppose* a political formula that gives Islam an important role *if they are citizens of a country governed by a regime with a strong Islamic connection.*

Findings from the first two waves of Arab Barometer surveys, both of which have provided some of the data included in the larger dataset assembled for the present study, shed light on the place of economic concerns, and on their importance relative to political concerns, in the thinking of ordinary citizens about the environment in which they reside. The interview schedule administered in the nineteen surveys conducted in twelve countries between 2006 and 2011 through the Arab Barometer included several questions that are pertinent in this context. One of these asked respondents to identify the most important problem facing their country. Another asked respondents to select from a short list that included both political and economic factors the one that they judged to be the most important feature of democracy.

In responding to the first of these questions, an overwhelming majority of respondents listed an economic problem, such as poverty, unemployment, or high and rising prices. In the first wave of surveys, carried out in 2006–2007, 55.4 percent of all respondents answered by identifying an economic problem, and another 25.0 percent listed corruption as the most important problem facing their country. Similarly, in the second wave of surveys, carried out in 2010–2011, 62.8 percent of the respondents listed an economic problem and another 14.5 percent stated that corruption was their country's most important problem. These findings strongly suggest that economic considerations occupy a central place, and probably a dominant place, in people's thoughts when they evaluate the regime by which their country is governed.

In response to the second question, asking about the most important feature of democracy, political features, such as changing the government through elections or having the freedom to criticize the government, and economic features, such as a political system that provides for basic economic needs or fosters equality between rich and poor, were each listed with roughly equal frequency. As shown in table 3.4, 49 percent of the respondents in the first wave of surveys listed a political

Table 3.4. Most Important Features of Democracy among Respondents in First and Second Waves of the Arab Barometer

There is a difference in opinion among people regarding the most important features of democracy. If you had to choose one, which of the following features would you say is the most important?

	Wave one	Wave two
The opportunity to change the government through elections	29%	26%
Freedom to criticize the government	20	13
Narrowing the gap between rich and poor	23	14
Providing basic items (such as food and housing,) to every individual	28	19
Equality of political rights between citizens	—	12
Eliminating financial and administrative corruption	—	16
Total	100%	100%

feature, and 51 percent listed an economic feature. Similarly, as the table also shows, in the second wave, political features and economic features were again each selected by about half of all respondents.

These findings suggest both a distinction and a co-mingling of political and economic considerations. On the one hand, economic concerns are clearly prominent; they are not only widespread but also appear to persist over time. Accordingly, to the extent that criticisms of the government are primarily complaints about the regime's economic performance, judgments about the status quo that might appear to be based on political considerations may actually be based on evaluations of the economic situation. If this is indeed the case, the causal stories from which Hypotheses 2, 2a, and 2b were derived may be inadequate if economic assessments are not considered. Findings about these hypotheses may therefore vary as a function of whether or not a measure of economic satisfaction is included in the analysis, and conclusions about the explanatory power of regime evaluation may in fact be spurious if such a measure is not included.

On the other hand, whatever the degree to which economic complaints fuel and drive judgments about the status quo, it does not follow that explanatory power resides in economic evaluations alone—or that the causal stories pertaining to regime evaluation offered above are in the final analysis not very plausible or persuasive. On the contrary, it is entirely reasonable to proceed on the assumption, in advance of any hypothesis testing, that both political judgments and economic judgments have, or at least may have, independent and significant explanatory power. As the findings presented in table 3.4 indicate, what citizens expect from a governing regime, and hence, presumably, the basis on which they determine whether the status quo is or is not satisfactory, includes both political and economic considerations, with one of these perhaps being more central to the thinking of some individuals and the other perhaps being more central to the thinking of other individuals.

A final consideration pertaining to the potential utility of economic evaluations in accounting for variance in attitudes about the role Islam should play in government and political affairs is the immediacy of economic concerns for most individuals. Although there is not necessarily a strict alignment between an individual's assessment of the economic situation in general—of one's country, region, or group—and an individual's assessment of their own economic situation and that of their family, it is highly likely that the two are in fact related for most people, and that the former is most often shaped by the latter. It probably is the case that some well-off men and women in the Middle East and North Africa, recognizing that there is considerable poverty and inequality in their society, assess their own economic situation favorably while evaluating the broader economic environment more negatively. A divergence of this kind does not appear to be very common, however. An analysis of second wave Arab Barometer data, for example, which contain questions about both personal and national economic circumstances, shows a very strong correlation between evaluations pertaining to one's country and those pertaining to oneself and one's family. The coefficient is .391, which is highly statistically significant ($p < .001$, $N = 12,483$).

Additionally, in most countries there are relatively few individuals with a level of affluence that sets them dramatically apart from most of their co-nationals and for whom personal and national economic assessments might reasonably be expected to differ sharply. In the larger dataset assembled for the present study, based on forty-four surveys in fifteen countries, and with a total of 67,680 men and women, only 12.4 percent of the respondents reported being "very satisfied" with the economic situation of their household. Thus, the causal story from which Hypotheses 3a and 3b are derived, involving a pathway leading from economic assessments to evaluations of the status quo to a desire for a change in the way that Islam connects, or doesn't connect, to the governing regime, would seem to begin with and be carried forward in particular by an individual's *immediate* economic situation.

Education: Exposure and Mobility

Political attitude research in many countries and on many topics has documented the explanatory power of education. For example, men and women with higher levels of education tend to differ significantly from those with lower levels of education by being more likely to be engaged in civic and political life and more likely to be open to diverse political and cultural perspectives. Moreover, although the relationship between education on the one hand and political and social attitudes on the other has long been documented by studies in developed democracies, data from research in developing countries have often, albeit not always, found a connection as well. For example, data collected by the World Values Survey (WVS) between 1999 and 2002 found gaps in trust in government between better-educated and less well-educated individuals of sixteen percentage points in Turkey, twenty-five percentage points in South Africa, and nineteen percentage points in Morocco. In each case, trust was higher among less well-educated individuals.[26] With respect to the political role of religion, a subject that is directly relevant for the present study, the WVS reported education-related gaps in these three countries of, respectively, thirty-six, twenty-five, and eighteen points in the percentage of respondents agreeing with the proposition that more people with strong religious beliefs should hold public office.[27] In each case, agreement with this proposition was higher among less well-educated individuals. At the same time, a more recent study using data from the first wave of Arab Barometer surveys, with control variables included in the analysis, found a statistically significant inverse relationship between education and support for political Islam in some Arab countries, but not others.[28]

These and other established relationships between education and political orientations represent tendencies; they are not deterministic but are rather probabilistic, meaning that men and women who differ in level of education are *likely* to differ in their attitudes and behavior, but this is not *always* the case. Nor, as indicated by the Arab Barometer findings mentioned above, is there even a probabilistic relationship in all instances. Nevertheless, public opinion research has very often shown that education has significant explanatory power, and for this reason it deserves to be the focus of additional causal stories that seek to account for variance in the views held by ordinary citizens about the role that Islam should play in government and political affairs.

Two broad categories of explanatory factors are central to the causal stories most frequently advanced to account for the impact of education. One of these concerns learning and exposure, involving the acquisition of information about the world beyond one's own community and exposure to arguments and perspectives with which one previously had no more than limited familiarity. Education involves more than the acquisition of additional or new factual information, however. The learning and exposure associated with education also bring, at least potentially, greater awareness of how things could be and very possibly may be different, a corresponding increase in openness to embracing or at least considering new ideas, and, contributing to these insights, a more sophisticated understanding of cause and effect in societal and political dynamics.

A second category of factors contributing to the impact and explanatory power of education centers on the opportunities that education provides for personal and professional mobility. Men and women who are better educated acquire both skills and credentials that enable them to be more successful than individuals who are less well-educated, other things being equal, in obtaining jobs, wealth, social position, and prestige within their communities. And this in turn increases the likelihood that their lifestyles and experience, and presumably also their interests and priorities, will further set them apart from individuals who have not received as much schooling. Personal and professional advantages do not automatically flow to those who are well educated, of course, just as those who are less well-educated are not necessarily precluded from advancing and achieving their goals in life and work. Nevertheless, a higher level of education does disproportionately give to those who receive it an array of abilities and opportunities that, in the aggregate, are not possessed to the same degree by individuals with a lower level of education.

As noted, the empirical evidence on which these causal stories are based is much more likely to have come from some societies than others, with studies in the Muslim-majority countries of the Middle East and North Africa, while by no means absent, constituting but a small proportion of the relevant body of research. This does not mean, however, that mechanisms and pathways that trace the impact of education on political attitudes through exposure and mobility do not apply to the Middle East and North Africa. On the contrary, both logic and familiarity with the region make plausible an expectation that education does indeed play a role in shaping the political orientations of the region's Muslim publics.

The application of these insights about the explanatory power of education leads to alternative and competing hypotheses when seeking to account for variance in views about the role Islam should play in political affairs. First, following what is perhaps the most plausible proposition to be derived from the preceding discussion, it may be hypothesized that men and women who are *less* well-educated are disproportionately likely, relative to those who are better educated, to favor a significant political role for Islam. Considerations associated with both exposure and mobility make this relationship plausible, and likely. With respect to exposure, less well-educated individuals are likely to be less familiar with the more secular political formulae that prevail outside the Muslim world, or that may even characterize the secular authoritarianism of national politics in their own country. Rather, at least relative to those who are better educated, they are likely to have greater appreciation for and attachment to models of governance and political authority based on sources and institutions that are more immediately familiar, including, and probably especially, those associated with Islam.

Considerations of mobility and status also suggest that level of education helps to account for variance in views and preferences about Islam's political role. In this case, however, as with the previously discussed causal stories linking regime evaluation and economic satisfaction to attitudes about political Islam, the direction of the relationship probably varies as a function of whether or not citizens reside in a country governed by a regime with an Islamic connection. Other things being equal, less well-educated men and women, relative to those who are better educated, are likely to be socially and economically disadvantaged and less secure in their professional lives; and for these reasons they are more likely to be dissatisfied with the status quo and the direction of the country more generally. This, in turn, leads to the proposition that lower education pushes toward support for a political formula that assigns to Islam a role that differs from the one it played in the country at the time the respondent was interviewed.

As the preceding suggests, the pathway emphasizing exposure and the pathway emphasizing mobility and status lead to the same proposition for citizens who reside in a country governed by a regime that is essentially secular—a regime that does not have a strong and institutionalized connection to Islam. In this case, both the condition of a narrower worldview and more limited exposure to a broader array of political models, as well as the condition of relative disadvantage and fewer opportunities for personal and professional advancement, give rise to the same proposition: lower levels of education predispose citizens toward greater support for political Islam.

Alternatively, to the extent that both of the pathways described above are indeed operative, the two sets of conditions lead to *different* expectations about the relationship between education and preferences regarding Islam's political role among men and women who reside in a country governed by a regime that *does* have a significant Islamic connection. More specifically, while it follows from the pathway emphasizing exposure that education is inversely related to support for political Islam regardless of the regime by which people are governed, it follows from the pathway emphasizing mobility that the relationship between education and support for political Islam is inverse for citizens governed by more secular regimes but, by contrast, positive for citizens governed by a regime with an important Islamic connection.

Against all this is one final possibility about the way that considerations of mobility, opportunities, and status shape the relationship between education and attitudes toward political Islam. Despite the appeal of the proposition that a lower level of education brings diminished opportunity and, for this reason, fosters discontent with the status quo and produces support for a political formula that differs from the one that prevails, there is also an argument to be made for the proposition that, at least in some countries, discontent with the status quo may actually be greater among those who are *better* educated. The reason for this is that education sometimes, and increasingly often, does not actually bring higher social status and professional advancement. Although education promises these things and fuels expectations that the promise will be kept, these expectations are often unrealized. With widespread unemployment and underemployment giving rise, especially among younger men and women, to a cohort described in North Africa as *les diplômés chômeurs*,[29] discontent due to unrealized expectations may actually be higher among better educated individuals than among their less well-educated countrymen, and so it may be these individuals who are disproportionately likely to favor a political system that differs from the status quo with respect to the role to be played by Islam.

The following hypotheses capture all of these various possibilities, each of which is derived from and supported by a plausible causal story. Taken together, they set forth the alternative and competing propositions about the explanatory power of education to be tested.

> H4. Individuals with *lower* levels of education are more likely than are individuals with higher levels of education to *favor* a political formula that gives Islam an important role *regardless of whether or not they are citizens of a country governed by a secular regime or a regime with a strong Islamic connection.*

> H4a1. Individuals with *lower* levels of education are more likely than are individuals with higher levels of education to *favor* a political formula that gives Islam an important role *if they are citizens of a country governed by a secular regime.*

> H4a2. Individuals with *lower* levels of education are more likely than are individuals with higher levels of education to *oppose* a political formula that gives Islam an important role *if they are citizens of a country governed by a regime with a strong Islamic connection.*

> H4b1. Individuals with *higher* levels of education are more likely than are individuals with lower levels of education to *favor* a political formula that gives Islam an important role *if they are citizens of a country governed by a secular regime.*

> H4b2. Individuals with *higher* levels of education are more likely than are individuals with lower levels of education to *oppose* a political formula that gives Islam an important role *if they are citizens of a country governed by a regime with a strong Islamic connection.*

Findings

As has been emphasized throughout the discussion, the citizens of Muslim-majority countries in the Middle East and North Africa reside in a context in which there are important, and often intense, debates about whether Islam should play a role and exercise influence in government and political affairs. There are competing models, or at least frameworks, among which men and women must choose. And since people differ in the degree to which they either favor or oppose a political formula that assigns an important place to Islam, there is, in the language of social science, variance to be explained.

A recent study of religion and politics nicely summarizes the context within which this variance exists, makes explicit the choices with which it presents ordinary citizens, and, consistent with the hypotheses offered above, suggests that many determinants of popular judgments and predispositions are to be found not in the religion itself but in the context of state and society.

> In the contemporary Middle Eastern context, the expansion of choice has come in the realm of religion, but the reasons are not so much religious as political, economic and social . . . The religious choices now available emerge from an evolving set of political and social circumstances that probably contribute more to understanding the choices than the study of religious scripture.[30]

Against this background, the explanatory power of each of the hypotheses and associated causal stories set forth above will be assessed. As discussed in chapter 1, the dependent variable is a scale ranging from very positive to very negative views about political Islam, and since this variable is continuous, the analysis will employ ordinary least squares (OLS) regression. The independent variables, set forth in the hypotheses presented above, include attitudes toward gender equality, judgments about the governing regime, economic satisfaction/dissatisfaction, and level of education. The survey items used to measure attitudes toward gender equality and evaluation of the governing regime were presented in chapter 1, as were the procedures used to construct these and other multi-item indices. The measure of economic satisfaction is a two-item index based on quintile of income computed using all respondents in the same survey and a question asking respondents to rate their economic situation on a scale ranging from "very satisfactory" to "very unsatisfactory." As also discussed in chapter 1, the analysis pools the data from the forty-two surveys containing questions about political Islam and includes weights to correct for sample size differences and same-country population overlap. Personal religiosity, which is measured by another multi-item index and is strongly correlated with support for political Islam, will be included as a control variable, as will sex and age.

In addition, given the possibility that the explanatory power of one or more hypotheses may not be the same for different age cohorts or for men and women, a possibility that is consistent with the findings of several studies using data from Arab countries,[31] the data will be disaggregated on the basis of sex and age cohort, taken together, and separate regressions will also be carried out for each demographic category. Age is divided into two cohorts for these analyses: under thirty-five and thirty-five and older, and this, combined with sex, yields four categories of respondents for whom separate OLS regressions will be carried out. Personal religiosity will continue to be included in these regressions as a control variable.

Table 3.5a. OLS Regression Coefficients Showing the Influence on Support for Political Islam of Attitudes toward Gender Equality, Regime Evaluation, Economic Satisfaction, and Education among Respondents from Countries Governed by a Regime without an Islamic Connection

	Model 1	Model 2	Model 3
Higher support for gender equality	−.109***	−.118***	−.114***
	(.008)	(.008)	(.008)
More positive regime evaluation	−.014		−.009
	(.008)		(.008)
Higher level of economic satisfaction		−.016**	−.018**
		(.006)	(.006)
Higher level of education	−.037***	−.033***	−.025**
	(.008)	(.007)	(.008)
Controls			
Greater personal religiosity	.128***	.144***	.141***
	(.008)	(.008)	(.008)
Female sex	.032*	.031*	.030
	(.016)	(.016)	(0.17)
Older age	−.009	−.014*	−.010
	(.006)	(.006)	(006)
Constant	.092	.142***	.113*
	(.041)	(.043)	(.046)
Number of observations	38,974	38,974	38,974

Note: Higher values on dependent variable indicate higher support for political Islam; table presents unstandardized coefficients; standard errors are in parentheses.
*significant at .05 level; **significant at .01 level; ***significant at .001 level.

The remainder of this chapter presents the results of these individual-level analyses. Thereafter, in chapter 4, following the two-level approach described in chapter 1, country-level variables will be introduced in order to determine whether and how findings about individual-level relationships vary as a function of the attributes and experiences of countries at the time they were surveyed.

Tables 3.5a and 3.5b present findings for the pooled analyses using all respondents. Table 3.5a gives the unstandardized regression coefficients and standard errors for respondents from countries that were governed by a regime without a strong Islamic connection at the time of the survey. Table 3.5b presents coefficients and standard errors for respondents from countries that were governed by a regime with a strong Islamic connection at the time of the survey.[32]

Table 3.5b. OLS Regression Coefficients Showing the Influence on Support for Political Islam of Attitudes toward Gender Equality, Regime Evaluation, Economic Satisfaction, and Education among Respondents from Countries Governed by a Regime with an Islamic Connection

	Model 1	Model 2	Model 3
Higher support for gender equality	−.130***	−.133***	−.120***
	(.011)	(.012)	(.012)
More positive regime evaluation	.149***		.142***
	(.011)		(.012)
Higher level of economic satisfaction		.020*	.011
		(.009)	(.009)
Higher level of education	−.090***	−.104***	−.092***
	(.011)	(.011)	(.012)
Controls			
Greater personal religiosity	.270***	.293***	.274***
	(.011)	(.012)	(.012)
Female sex	.032	.027	.015
	(.023)	(.024)	(.024)
Older age	−.018*	−.010	−.013
	(.009)	(.009)	(.009)
Constant	.282***	.238***	.252***
	(.059)	(.065)	(.066)
Number of observations	20,715	20,715	20,715

Note: Higher values on dependent variable indicate higher support for political Islam; surveys in countries governed by a regime with an Islamic connection include Iran 2005; Iraq 2004, 2006, and 2011; Lebanon 2007; Palestine 2006; Saudi Arabia 2003 and 2011; Sudan 2011; and Turkey 2001 and 2007. Table presents unstandardized coefficients; standard errors are in parentheses. *significant at .05 level; **significant at .01 level; ***significant at .001 level.

Gender Equality

Turning first to Hypothesis 1, the tables provide strong and consistent support for the proposition that individuals who hold more conservative views on gender equality, and very possibly on a broader array of social and cultural issues, are more likely than individuals who hold more progressive views to believe that Islam should play an important role in political affairs. Both among men and women from countries governed by a regime without a strong Islamic connection and among men and women from countries governed by a regime with a strong Islamic connection, there is a strong and statistically significant inverse relationship between support for gender equality and support for political Islam. Among both subsets of respondents, $p < .001$, indicating that it is extremely unlikely that a relationship this strong could have been obtained by chance alone and, as a result, that the analysis has led to a false conclusion about the connection between views about gender equality and views about Islam's place in political life.

This finding about Hypothesis 1 is not surprising, but it does make clear that social and cultural orientations play an important role in shaping attitudes toward political Islam. As discussed earlier, there is a considerable divergence of opinion about whether women and men should have equal rights and opportunities in various spheres. Additionally, some people attach much importance to what Islam has to say about women's status and gender relations and favor conservative and literalist interpretations of Islam on this issue. Whatever may be the bases for the belief that women should not have the same rights and opportunities as those available to men, however, including, possibly, motivations that have little or nothing to do with religion, those who take this position are disproportionately likely to want Islam to exercise influence in political affairs. The reasons for this, presumably, are the considerations of perceived value congruence and policy expectations that were discussed earlier.

It is also important to note that perceived value congruence and policy expectations not only push those who are less favorably predisposed toward gender equality toward support for political Islam, they also, for the same reasons, push those who favor gender equality toward the view that Islamic prescriptions, institutions, and officials should *not* play a role in shaping the political direction of their societies. In both cases, and notwithstanding the "moderate" platforms that some Islamist leaders and movements have increasingly put forward, ordinary citizens are disproportionately likely to believe that government officials who are influenced by Islam will advance a particular social and cultural agenda, one of which they either approve or disapprove, and this in turn is an important determinant of their views about the role that Islam should play in government and political affairs.

Regime Evaluation

Hypothesis 2 posits a connection between judgments about the governing regime and support for political Islam. More specifically, Hypothesis 2a proposes that individuals who are more dissatisfied with the character and performance of their political institutions and officials are disproportionately likely to favor a political formula that gives Islam an important role in political affairs if they are citizens of a country governed by an essentially secular regime; and Hypothesis 2b proposes that individuals who are more dissatisfied with their political institutions and officials are disproportionately likely to disapprove of a political formula that gives Islam an important role in political affairs if they are citizens of a country governed by a regime with a strong Islamic connection.

The positive and highly statistically significant coefficient reported in table 3.5b shows that regime evaluation has explanatory power among respondents from countries that were governed by a regime with an Islamic connection at the time they were surveyed, thus providing evidence in support of Hypothesis 2b. Indeed, the strength of the respective regression coefficients indicates that in these countries regime evaluation has even more independent explanatory power than views about gender equality. Alternatively, table 3.5a, in which the coefficient is not statistically significant, does not provide evidence in support of Hypothesis 2a: regime evaluation does not have significant explanatory power among respondents from countries governed by an essentially secular regime.

The causal story associated with these hypotheses is straightforward and plausible, and it is surprising that discontent with an essentially secular regime does not lead more frequently to support for an alternative that is Islamic. As discussed earlier, there are descriptive and country-specific accounts that claim the existence of such a connection. One of the previously quoted studies argued, for example, that "as long as governments in the Arab world resist political participation and the tolerance of different political opinions, the strength of Islam as a political ideology will continue to be a serious alternative."[33] In fact, however, at the individual level of analysis and with respect to region-wide trends during the time period covered by the survey data brought together in the present study, it appears that a higher level of discontent with a secular authoritarian regime does not push men and women toward the view that it would be better for their country if Islam played an important role in political affairs. It has been the case, of course, as various studies have credibly and persuasively shown, that Islamist movements have been able to gain popular support under conditions of secular authoritarianism. But the findings presented in table 3.5a suggest that it is not because these movements offer an *Islamic* alternative, but rather, to the extent they build support beyond a core constituency and among politically alienated citizens more broadly, it is for reasons with no more than a very limited connection to the religious content of their platforms.

Additional insight is offered by the support for Hypothesis 2b provided in table 3.5b. Among countries as diverse as Iran, Turkey, Iraq, Saudi Arabia, Sudan, and others, taken as a whole, discontent with a regime that has an Islamic connection predisposes individuals to want a political alternative and, apparently, to believe that this is not to be found in Islam. A possibility considered when reflecting on the pathways that might connect regime evaluation and views about political Islam was that politically discontent citizens in these societies might disapprove of the particular Islamic regime by which they are governed without believing that Islam and the principles it embodies are best kept apart from political life. In this hypothetical case, these men and women would believe that their government is not really or properly Islamic and that the needed alternative is not a secular government but rather one that truly and honestly respects the Islamic values of equality and justice. In fact, however, while these values and principles are indeed found in Islam, this is not the way that a negative evaluation of the ruling regime predisposes citizens to think about Islam and its political role. Rather, if people do not approve of government officials and policies, they want an alternative that does not look to Islam for guidance but rather separates between religion and political life.

Regime evaluation and economic satisfaction are related, although perhaps not as strongly as might have been expected, and for this reason tables 3.5a and 3.5b include not only a full model, Model 3, but also models in which attitude toward political Islam is regressed against only one of these two independent variables. This makes it possible to determine whether there are spurious relationships. In this case, political discontent and economic discontent might both be related to attitudes toward political Islam, as well as to each other, and a relationship involving one of the variables would be shown to be spurious, meaning it would possess predictive but not explanatory power, if it were statistically significant when the other variable is not included in the model but not statistically significant when the second variable is included. There do not appear to be any spurious relationships involving regime evaluation, however. The findings in Model 1, in which regime evaluation but not economic satisfaction is included, are identical to the findings in Model 3, in which both variables are included.

Economic Satisfaction

Hypotheses 3a and 3b posit relationships involving economic discontent that parallel the ones involving political discontent that are proposed in Hypotheses 2a and 2b. Specifically, Hypothesis 3a proposes that individuals with lower levels of economic satisfaction are disproportionately likely to favor a political formula that gives Islam an important role if they are citizens of a country governed by a secular regime; and Hypothesis 3b proposes that individuals with lower levels of economic satisfaction are disproportionately likely to oppose a political formula that gives Islam an important role if they are citizens of a country governed by a regime with a strong Islamic connection.

Table 3.5a provides evidence in support of Hypothesis 3a. Among citizens of countries with a more secular government, higher levels of economic dissatisfaction do indeed increase the likelihood of having a more positive view of political Islam. As discussed earlier, the pathway linking economic dissatisfaction to support for political Islam may involve one or more of several interrelated elements. On the one hand, perceived differences in character between the ruling regime and a government that would give an important place to Islam may be an underlying dynamic. People who are unhappy with the status quo presumably want a *consequential* alternative, something that is very different, perhaps as different as possible. On the other hand, to at least some extent, they may want a government that is not only very different but that is also specifically Islamic, however they might understand this, presumably because of the values and principles for which they believe Islam will bring respect. In any event, the findings presented in table 3.5a provide support for those previously mentioned studies, and others, that report a connection between discontent with the status quo and a favorable disposition toward political Islam, but the table also shows that under conditions of secular authoritarianism, or perhaps quasi-authoritarianism, it is economic discontent and not political discontent that drives this relationship.

The pattern is different in countries governed by a regime with a strong Islamic connection. In this case, economic dissatisfaction does not push in one direction or another with respect to views about political Islam. Rather, as discussed above, the dimension of discontent with the status quo that makes a significant and independent contribution to support for political Islam is political and concerns the regime. But while it is in the political domain that explanatory power is to be found in countries governed by a regime with an Islamic connection, Model 2 in table 3.5b shows that there is a statistically significant relationship between economic satisfaction and attitudes toward political Islam when evaluation of the regime is not included in the analysis. Further, although not shown in the table, there is a statistically significant relationship, with $p < .01$, between economic satisfaction and regime evaluation among respondents from these countries. Economic satisfaction is therefore a part of the causal story, albeit a secondary part. It plays a role in shaping evaluations of the regime, which, in turn, have a significant impact on what people think about the political role of Islam. More specifically, among respondents from countries governed by a regime with a strong Islamic connection, individuals with lower levels of economic satisfaction are more likely to have an unfavorable view of their government and, as a result, to be less likely to favor a political formula that assigns an important place to Islam.

Education

Turning finally to education, the independent variable in Hypotheses 4, 4a1, 4a2, 4b1, and 4b2, the tables show that in both subsets of countries, respondents with lower levels of education are more likely to have a favorable view of political Islam than are individuals with higher levels of education. As discussed earlier, education carries with it both greater exposure to arguments and perspectives with which one previously had no more than limited familiarity and also greater opportunities for personal and professional mobility and improved socioeconomic status. Either of these pathways associated with education could, conceivably, play a role in shaping attitudes toward political Islam.

The finding of an inverse relationship between lower education and a positive view of political Islam in countries with a government that has an Islamic connection, where this inverse relationship is actually somewhat stronger than in countries with a government that does not have an Islamic connection, suggests that explanatory power lies primarily in the dimension of exposure and not in the dimension of mobility. These less well-educated individuals are disadvantaged by the status quo, at least in relative terms; and they also have more negative evaluations of the regime by which they are governed, which a separate analysis shows to be the case. Thus, if the causal story associated with education were centered on limited or blocked mobility, these individuals would presumably want a different political formula for their country, one that separates religion and politics. But this is not the case. These less well-educated men and women are disproportionately likely to want a political system that does incorporate an Islamic dimension, and so it is reasonable to conclude that this view, so far as education is concerned, is fostered by more limited exposure to alternative patterns of governance and political authority.

An additional set of possibilities related to education was considered in Hypotheses 4b1 and 4b2. These hypotheses proposed that better educated individuals in countries governed by a secular regime would be more likely to favor political Islam, and that better educated individuals in countries governed by a regime with an Islamic connection would be less likely to favor political Islam. The rationale for these propositions emphasized considerations of mobility, or more specifically of unfulfilled expectations, noting that unemployment and underemployment, particularly among the young, fosters discontent with the status quo and might therefore mean that it is the better educated individuals, rather than those who are less well educated, who are disproportionately likely to favor a political formula that differs from the one by which their country is governed. The data do not provide support for this causal story, however, thus contributing further to the conclusion, stated above, that less well-educated individuals are more likely than better educated individuals to favor a system of government that gives an important place to Islam because they have had less exposure to and are less familiar with differing and more distant patterns of governance and political authority.

Although not connected to our hypotheses, personal religiosity was included in the analyses as a control variable because of its strong relationship to attitudes toward political Islam. This relationship is shown in tables 3.5a and 3.5b. In both subsets of countries, higher personal religiosity is strongly and positively related to support for political Islam, and in both cases this is the strongest relationship in any of the models. Interestingly, although the relationship is statistically significant at the .001 level in both instances, it is much stronger among respondents from countries governed by a regime with a strong Islamic connection than among respondents from countries governed by a regime without a strong Islamic connection. Sex and age, which will now be considered as conditionalities, are not significantly related to attitudes toward political Islam in the full model, Model 3, either in table 3.5a or in table 3.5b.

Demographic Differences

The patterns shown in tables 3.5a and 3.5b are based on analyses of all respondents. It is possible, however, that some of the statistically significant relationships found in the tables characterize some segments of the population but not others. To explore this possibility, hypotheses have been tested separately among respondents in each of four demographic groupings based on sex and age cohort taken together: men ages thirty-four and under, men ages thirty-five and over, women ages thirty-four and under, and women ages thirty-five and over. The results are presented in tables 3.6a and 3.6b.

The findings in table 3.6b are very straightforward and offer little additional insight. The table is based on data from surveys carried out in countries governed by a regime with an Islamic connection, and it shows that patterns of statistical relationships in each of the four demographic categories are almost identical, and therefore, of course, almost identical as well to the pattern shown in table 3.5b. As in the analysis based on all respondents in these countries, the findings in table 3.6b show that among men ages thirty-four and under, among men ages thirty-five and over, among women ages thirty-four and under, and among women ages thirty-five and over, support for political Islam is inversely related to support for gender equality, positively related to a positive evaluation of the governing regime, and inversely related to education. The one additional observation is that, among men ages thirty-four and under, economic satisfaction is positively related to support for political Islam. Apart from this latter finding, however, the conclusion to be drawn is that the insights about pathways and causal stories derived from an analysis of all respondents do not apply only to particular subsets of the population but rather have general applicability, and hence explanatory power, across society as a whole.

Table 3.6a, which is based on respondents from countries governed by a regime without an Islamic connection, shows a different pattern. In this case, the pattern is not the same in the four demographic categories. In all four categories, there is a strong and statistically significant inverse relationship between support for gender equality and support for political Islam. It thus appears that the explanatory power of social and cultural predispositions, or at least those pertaining to the status of women, is generalizable to diverse sectors of the population. Beyond this, however, neither of the other two statistically significant relationships shown in table 3.5a is found in all four, or even three, of the demographic categories. The inverse relationship between economic satisfaction and support for political Islam is found only among women, including those in both age categories, and the inverse relationship between education and support for political Islam is found only among older individuals, including both men and women. In addition, regime evaluation, which is not significantly related to attitudes toward political

Table 3.6a. OLS Regression Coefficients Showing the Influence on Support for Political Islam of Attitudes toward Gender Equality, Regime Evaluation, Economic Satisfaction, and Education among Younger Men, Older Men, Younger Women, and Older Women from Countries Governed by a Regime without an Islamic Connection

	Men 34 and under	Men 35 and over	Women 34 and under	Women 35 and over
Higher support for gender equality	−.136*** (.016)	−.117*** (.016)	−.106*** (.017)	−.082*** (.019)
More positive regime evaluation	−.016 (.015)	−.029* (.015)	.016 (.017)	.002 (.019)
Higher level of economic satisfaction	−.001 (.012)	−.008 (.012)	−.035** (.012)	−.028* (.014)
Higher level of education	.010 (.017)	−.029* (.014)	−.024 (.016)	−.056*** (.017)
Control				
Greater personal religiosity	.142*** (.014)	.156*** (.015)	.123*** (.018)	.121*** (.022)
Constant	−.021 (.063)	.066 (.053)	.198** (.062)	.251*** (.059)
Number of observations	9,780	9,610	10,396	8,946

Note: Higher values on dependent variable indicate higher support for political Islam; table presents unstandardized coefficients; standard errors are in parentheses.
*significant at .05 level; **significant at .01 level; ***significant at .001 level.

Islam when all respondents are included in the analysis, is related, inversely, among men ages thirty-five and over.

It is only possible to speculate about the reasons that particular relationships have explanatory power among some segments of the population but not others. With respect to the relationship involving economic satisfaction, the associated causal story proposed earlier emphasized discontent with the status quo as an important driver of judgments about political Islam, and it suggested that discontented citizens in countries governed by an essentially secular regime are disproportionately likely to seek a credible and consequential alternative and to find this alternative in Islam. One reason that this dynamic is more common among women may be that women, as the household members most responsible for the family's welfare, are more concerned than men about their disadvantaged economic circumstances. If so, they may be more motivated than men to endorse an alternative to the status quo and/or more attracted than men by Islam's emphasis on

Table 3.6b. OLS Regression Coefficients Showing the Influence on Support for Political Islam of Attitudes toward Gender Equality, Regime Evaluation, Economic Satisfaction, and Education among Younger Men, Older Men, Younger Women, and Older Women from Countries Governed by a Regime with an Islamic Connection

	Men 34 and under	Men 35 and over	Women 34 and under	Women 35 and over
Higher support for gender equality	−.120***	−.149***	−.110***	−.082**
	(.024)	(.023)	(.025)	(.028)
More positive regime evaluation	.131***	.153***	.117***	.173***
	(.022)	(.021)	(.025)	(.028)
Higher level of economic satisfaction	.036*	.003	.001	.005
	(.018)	(.018)	(.019)	(.021)
Higher level of education	−.068**	−.084***	−.073**	−.130***
	(.024)	(.020)	(.025)	(.025)
Control				
Greater personal religiosity	.227***	.289***	.295***	.299***
	(.021)	(.021)	(.026)	(.029)
Constant	.094	.210**	.229**	.350***
	(.087)	(.073)	(.088)	(.082)
Number of Observations	5,130	5,226	5,344	4,871

Note: Higher values on dependent variable indicate higher support for political Islam; surveys in countries governed by a regime with an Islamic connection include Iran 2005; Iraq 2004, 2006, and 2011; Lebanon 2007; Palestine 2006; Saudi Arabia 2003 and 2011; Sudan 2011; and Turkey 2001 and 2007. Table presents unstandardized coefficients; standard errors are in parentheses. *significant at .05 level; **significant at .01 level; ***significant at .001 level.

equality and help for the needy. Another possibility, particularly among younger women, is that women with limited economic opportunities may take on "fundamentalist and traditionalist" belief systems in order to increase their value as marriage partners. This possibility is suggested by a recent study that analyzed WVS data on Muslim respondents in eighteen countries.[34]

Less well-educated individuals are disproportionately likely to believe that Islam should play a role in government and political affairs, and it appears that the reason for this is not to be found in the reduced life chances associated with lesser education but rather in a lower level of exposure to diverse and more distant patterns of governance and political authority. To the extent that it is indeed the exposure rather than the status mobility dimension of education that carries the explanatory power, the reason that a lower level of education increases the likelihood of support for political Islam among older but not younger individuals in countries governed by a regime without an Islamic connection may be that younger people are more likely, through social media and other Internet phenomena, to be less dependent on education to gain familiarity with the world beyond their traditional communities.

If this is the case, it might be asked why a lower level of education increases the likelihood of support for political Islam among younger as well as older individuals in countries governed by a regime with an Islamic connection. In fact, however, although it is statistically significant, the relationship is not as strong among younger individuals in these countries. And it is strongest of all among older women, the population category that is probably least likely to gain exposure to diverse models of societal and political organization beyond that provided by education. Accordingly, to the assessment that less well-educated individuals are disproportionately likely to support political Islam because they have had less exposure to other political and social systems may be added the observation that this is most likely to be the case among men and women who have had fewer opportunities, beyond those provided by education, to become familiar with the world outside their own communities.

Finally, the pathway linking a negative evaluation of the governing regime to support for political Islam in countries governed by a regime without an Islamic connection almost certainly involves the desire for a consequential alternative to the political status quo. The reason that this attitudinal dynamic characterizes older men but not any other demographic category may flow from the fact that men, as a group, tend to be more politically conscious than women and that older men, compared to younger men, are likely to have a greater sense of their country's history. As a result, older men may have a keener sense than do individuals in other demographic categories of the longevity of the secular authoritarian regime by which their country is governed, and they may also be more aware than others of the role that Islamist movements have historically played in opposing that regime. It may therefore be the case that discontent with the status quo in secular authoritarian political settings is most likely to increase support for political Islam among individuals who are more politically conscious and also, in part through personal experience, more knowledgeable about their country's modern history.

It is important to move beyond a straightforward report of the statistically significant relationships shown in tables 3.5a, 3.5b, 3.6a, and 3.6b and an associated summary of whether and among which demographic categories the survey data brought together for this study provide evidence in support of various hypotheses. It is also important to offer insights about the underlying pathways and causal stories on which the statistically significant relationships shed light. In other words, it is important not only to determine whether and how, to take one example, an individual's level of education affects the likelihood that he or she will believe that Islam should occupy an important place in government and political affairs. It is also necessary to ask *why* this is the case—to inquire about the reasons, in this instance, that less well-educated men and women are disproportionately likely to believe that Islam should indeed play an important role in government and politics. For this reason, both in formulating hypotheses and in discussing the results of analyses by which these hypotheses have been tested, I have offered in this chapter a number of ideas and insights about the pathways linking each independent variable to the dependent variable and have sought to derive plausible and potentially persuasive causal stories about the dynamics shaping attitudes toward political Islam.

At the same time, it must be acknowledged that these ideas and insights inevitably and necessarily go beyond the data. Although informed by past research, they were initially created through reflection and reasoned speculation, employing what is sometimes called the sociological imagination, when formulating the hypotheses; and they have subsequently been clarified and refined based on findings about significant variable relationships. Nonetheless, they are not themselves findings. They are rather informed and reasoned interpretations or, more accurately perhaps, speculations. They may be correct, and they are certainly deserving of serious consideration. But they may also be incomplete, or perhaps of secondary importance in understanding why individuals come to hold certain views about Islam's political role, and it is also possible that they are entirely wide of the mark. Hence, although the present chapter aspires to identify at least some of the causal stories that tell *why* individuals come to hold different views about Islam's place in political life, these insights, being unavoidably subjective and thus in the nature of "best guesses," are also self-consciously offered as an incremental contribution and a stimulus to further reflection and research.

The present chapter has investigated the determinants of support for political Islam at the individual level of analysis. In chapter 4, the conditioning effect of country-level factors will be considered. In accord with the second step of the two-level research design described in chapter 1, the regressions run in the present chapter will be run separately for each of the forty-two surveys that contain questions pertaining to political Islam. The resulting coefficients will then become measures of the dependent variables in analyses in which the unit of analysis is the survey, hence $N = 42$, and attributes of countries at the time they were surveyed will be independent variables. This cross-survey analysis will make it possible to identify country-level and temporal characteristics that define the locus of applicability of significant individual-level relationships and, in this way, to map in conceptual terms whether and how, and by extension why, the explanatory power of individual-level factors varies over space and time.

4 How and Why Explanations Vary across Countries

Individual-Level Analysis

The views of ordinary citizens about the role that Islam should play in government and political affairs are not monolithic. On the contrary, many men and women in the Muslim-majority countries of the Middle East and North Africa believe that Islam should occupy a place of importance in the political life of their society; many others disagree, believing that religion is an essentially private matter and should be separated from politics; and still others hold views that place them at some point in between these two poles of opinion. This division of opinion was illustrated in the preceding chapter in table 3.1.

Against the background of this division of opinion, chapter 3 sought to move from description to explanation and asked *why* individuals hold different views about Islam's political role. The focus was on individual-level dynamics shaping predispositions and preferences, on causal stories and the associated pathways that might, in the language of social science, account for the observed variance in attitudes toward political Islam. Toward this end, the chapter sought explanatory insights by formulating four sets of hypotheses. The first of these proposed that an individual's views about the political role that Islam should play are shaped, in part, by his or her cultural values. A second hypothesis proposed that attitudes toward political Islam are determined, in part, by judgments about the regime by which an individual's country is governed. A third hypothesis proposed that an individual's economic circumstances and level of economic satisfaction are among the determinants of views about political Islam, and a fourth proposed that explanatory power is also to be found in an individual's level of education.

In presenting each hypothesis, the structure and direction of the proposed variable relationship was made explicit. In three instances, the conditioning impact of whether respondents did or did not reside in a country governed by a regime with an Islamic connection was also considered. Equally important, ideas about the logic that made each hypothesis plausible were offered. This logic, or rationale, described one or more causal stories that gave each proposition a degree of persuasiveness sufficient to warrant its empirical assessment. In other words, the rationale identified a nontrivial pathway leading to either positive or negative attitudes toward political Islam that, on its face, was persuasive enough for insight to be gained even if an empirical test subsequently determined that the hypothesized relationship did not possess explanatory power.

To test these hypotheses, and by extension to evaluate the causal stories from which each was derived, data from the forty-two surveys containing questions about political Islam were pooled for the analyses presented in chapter 3. With weights to correct for sample size differences and for overlap between the populations of countries surveyed at different points in time included in the analysis, models were run to compute regression coefficients for all respondents and for respondents in four separate demographic categories: younger men, older men, younger women, and older women. The findings of these individual-level analyses were presented in tables 3.5a, 3.5b, 3.6a, and 3.6b. In discussing the explanatory implications of these findings, I offered assessments about the pathways that do and do not appear to play a role in shaping views about political Islam. The main conclusions resulting from these analyses and discussions are summarized below.

Cultural Values

Value congruence and expectations about public policy play a significant role in shaping views about political Islam. Accordingly, holding more conservative views on social and cultural issues predisposes an individual to believe that Islam should play an important role in political affairs; and correspondingly, holding more progressive views on social and cultural issues predisposes an individual to believe that that Islam should not play an important role in government and politics.

The analyses reported in chapter 3, which used attitudes toward gender equality as a measure of social and cultural values, found support for this dynamic when all respondents were included in the analysis and also in separate analyses of respondents in each of the four demographic categories. Further, this was the case both in analyses based on respondents in countries governed by a more secular regime and in analyses based on respondents in countries governed by a regime with an Islamic connection.

Regime Evaluation

People who are dissatisfied with the performance or policies of the regime by which their country is governed, and who for this reason lack confidence in their country's political leaders and institutions, will favor a political system that constitutes a consequential alternative to the status quo. Accordingly, a negative evaluation of the governing regime predisposes an individual who resides in a country governed by a secular regime to believe that Islam should play an important role in political affairs; and correspondingly, a negative evaluation of the governing regime predisposes an individual who resides in a country governed by a regime with an Islamic connection to believe that Islam should not play an important role in political affairs.

The analyses reported in chapter 3 found support for this causal story among citizens of countries governed by a regime with an Islamic connection. This was found to be the case when all respondents were included in the analysis and also in separate analyses of respondents in each of the four demographic categories. By contrast, among respondents in countries governed by a secular regime, the analysis found evidence of a pathway leading from a negative evaluation of the government to support for political Islam only among older men.

Economic Satisfaction

People who are dissatisfied with their personal economic circumstances, and who for this reason desire a government with different policies and priorities, will favor a political system that constitutes a consequential alternative to the status quo. Accordingly, economic dissatisfaction predisposes an individual who resides in a country governed by a secular regime to believe that Islam should play an important role in political affairs; and correspondingly, economic dissatisfaction predisposes an individual who resides in a country governed by a regime with an Islamic connection to believe that Islam should not play an important role in political affairs.

The analyses reported in chapter 3 found support for this causal story when all respondents in countries governed by a secular regime were included in the analysis. More specifically, however, this was the case only among younger women and older women and not among men in either age category. Among citizens of countries governed by a regime with an Islamic connection, economic dissatisfaction fostered opposition to political Islam only among younger men.

Education

Education brings the acquisition of information about the world beyond one's own community and exposure to arguments and perspectives with which one is likely to have previously had no more than limited familiarity. For this reason, education reduces support for political Islam and increases support for a political system in which Islam does not play an important role.

The analyses reported in chapter 3 found support for this causal story both in countries governed by a secular regime and in countries governed by a regime with an Islamic connection when all respondents were included in the analysis. In the former, however, this was the case for respondents in only two demographic categories: older men and women. In the latter, by contrast, a lower level of education predisposed individuals in all four demographic categories to believe that Islam should play an important role in government and political affairs.

These points summarize the most important takeaways from the individual-level findings reported in chapter 3. The present chapter seeks to identify the conditioning impact on these individual-level relationships of time-adjusted country-level attributes and circumstances.

Survey-Level Analysis

Since the findings presented in chapter 3 are based on the pooled analysis of data from forty-two surveys, the aggregate coefficients and levels of statistical significance reported in tables 3.5a, 3.5b, 3.6a, and 3.6b are not necessarily, and indeed are not, indicative of the relationships to be found in every one of the surveys brought together for the present study. Variable relationships that are strong and significant in many or at least some of the surveys, and thus account in large measure for the patterns observed in pooled analyses, are not strong and significant in a number of other surveys. Further, relationships that are not strong and significant in many surveys, leading to a conclusion based on pooled analyses that the hypothesized pathway does not have much explanatory power, nonetheless *are* strong and significant in a number of other surveys. Thus, given that individual-level factors that account for variance in attitudes toward political Islam among respondents in all of the surveys taken together do not have same measure of explanatory power among respondents in every one of the forty-two separate surveys, the need, pursued in the present chapter, is to identify the time-specific attributes of those societies in which particular causal stories do and do not account for variance in the views held by ordinary citizens about the place that Islam should occupy in the political life of their country.

Toward this end, I use the survey, rather than the individual, as the unit of analysis in this second stage of a series of two-level analyses. The dataset includes forty-two surveys that contain questions with which it has been possible to measure attitudes toward political Islam. These are listed in table 1.1 of chapter 1. In fact, however, since the analyses include weights to correct for population overlap when multiple surveys have been taken in the same country at intervals of less than four years, as also described in chapter 1, the effective N in these analyses is thirty-six when data on the relevant country-level attributes are available for all of the surveys in the dataset. Findings about each hypothesized individual-level relationship for each survey are dependent variables in these cross-survey analyses; and attributes of countries at the time they were surveyed, or with measures of these attributes lagged by five or ten years in some instances, are the independent variables. This two-level research design, and particularly the treating of country-level attributes as independent variables rather than simply listing what was found in each individual country during the year it was surveyed, makes two important and closely interrelated analytical contributions.

First, this research design yields insights that are applicable, or at least potentially applicable, beyond any single country or specific group of countries and any particular period of time. Instead of reporting that a given individual-level characteristic or orientation, such as attitude toward gender equality, for example, predisposes individuals toward one position or another with respect to political Islam in some countries in some years but not in other countries or in other years, this approach identifies the political, economic, and/or social characteristics of the environment within which attitude toward gender equality has been found to have explanatory power. The analysis will thus yield an insight that goes beyond the observation that views about equality between women and men account for variance sometimes, but only sometimes, or perhaps often or rarely, as the case may be; it will rather have specified in conceptual terms when this individual-level orientation does and does not have, or is disproportionately likely to have, explanatory power. The analysis will in this way produce evidence of a potentially generalizable explanatory insight, one that can be tested with survey data, or perhaps even different kinds of data, drawn from other societies possessing the relevant conditioning attributes. This, in turn, will contribute to the production of an increasingly accurate and complete map, specified in terms of variable attributes, of the explanatory power of attitudes toward gender equality.

Second, the analysis will not only identify when, meaning under what conditions, attitude toward gender equality or any other individual-level independent variable has explanatory power, it will also provide a basis for informed theorizing about *why* particular country-level attributes constitute conditions under which that independent variable has a meaningful impact on the dependent variable, in this case attitudes toward political Islam. This theorizing requires going beyond the data and offering reasoned speculation about the dynamics and causal stories to which findings appear to point. But while these analytical insights remain to be refined through further reflection and evaluated through additional empirical research, they are necessary steps in the quest for genuine understanding. Theorizing about pathways and causal stories, or speculating about them, if one prefers, is required in order to make incremental but nonetheless continuing progress toward an understanding of the interplay between individual-level and country-level explanatory factors and, thereby, toward further uncovering some of the mechanisms by which attitudes toward political Islam are shaped. In this way, this analysis will shed light on why and how, rather than merely whether and when, ordinary citizens come to hold particular views about the political role to be played by Islam.

One dimension of the analysis that addresses these objectives involves identifying country-level attributes that constitute conditions under which an individual-level variable relationship is disproportionately likely to be statistically significant. This is illustrated in table 4.1a. Focusing on the inverse relationship

Table 4.1a. Impact of Country's Level of Secondary School Enrollment and Prior Proportion of the Population under the Age of Fifteen on the Inverse Individual-Level Relationship between Support for Gender Equality and Support for Political Islam among Younger Women

		Relationship not statistically significant $(p > .05)$	Relationship statistically significant $(p < .05)$
Level of secondary school enrollment	Lower	19 61.3%	1 12.5%
	Higher	12 38.7%	7 87.5%
		$N=39, p=.015$	
Percentage of population under fifteen ten years prior to survey	Lower	15 46.9%	7 87.5%
	Higher	17 53.1%	1 12.5%
		$N=40, p=.048$	

Note: Probabilities are based on chi-square values that were computed with weighting, whereas actual rather than weighted frequencies are shown. The number of surveys included in the analysis is less than forty-two because the interview schedule in several surveys did not include all relevant questions. Level of secondary school enrollment is cut at 81 percent; proportion of the population under the age of fifteen ten years prior to the survey is cut at 41 percent.

between support for gender equality and support for political Islam reported in chapter 3, the table compares the frequency with which the relationship is statistically significant at or below the .05 confidence interval among younger female respondents in countries that, at the time they were surveyed, had higher levels and lower levels of secondary school enrollment, respectively, and also in countries that ten years prior to the time they were surveyed had, respectively, a higher proportion and a lower proportion of the population under the age of fifteen.

The hypothesized inverse relationship between attitudes toward gender equality and attitudes toward political Islam was confirmed among this subset of respondents, younger women, meaning that it is strong enough to be statistically significant and thus very likely to characterize the population from which it was drawn, in eight of the surveys in the dataset. Table 4.1a shows that seven of these eight surveys were in countries with a higher level of secondary school enrollment and, again, that seven of the eight were in countries in which, ten years earlier, a smaller percentage of the population was under the age of fifteen. The probability values reported in the table show that the relationship is statistically significant

Table 4.1b. Binary Logistic Regression Showing the Impact of Country's Level of Secondary School Enrollment and Prior Proportion of the Population under the Age of Fifteen on the Inverse Individual-Level Relationship between Support for Gender Equality and Support for Political Islam among Younger Women

	Model 1	Model 2	Model 3
Higher level of secondary school	2.395**		2.170*
enrollment	(1.147)		(1.186)
Higher percentage of population under		−.165**	−.137*
fifteen lagged by ten years		(.075)	(.078)
Constant	−2.785***	4.947*	2.551
	(1.030)	(2.782)	(3.110)

Note: The dependent variable is a dichotomous measure indicating whether or not the individual-level relationship is significant at or below the .05 level. The analysis includes weights to adjust for population overlap, as discussed in the text. Given the small *N*, which is thirty-five after weighting, $p < .1$ may be considered statistically significant.
The table presents logit coefficients with standard errors in parentheses.
* $p < .1$; ** $p < .05$; *** $p < .01$.

in both instances, indicating that each of the two country-level attributes—a higher level of secondary school enrollment and a lower prior proportion of the population under fifteen—has a measurable conditioning effect and describes a societal environment in which unfavorable views about gender equality are disproportionately likely to lead to favorable views about political Islam among younger women.

This observation is further confirmed in table 4.1b, which uses binary logistic regression analysis to examine the explanatory power of each country-level attribute with the other included in the analysis and thus held constant. The table shows that the relationships are not as strong, but are still statistically significant, when both country-level attributes are included in the analysis. Given the small *N*, which is thirty-five after weighting, since only forty surveys included questions pertaining to gender equality, $p < .1$ may be considered statistically significant and sufficient to indicate that a higher level of secondary school enrollment and a smaller proportion of the population under the age of fifteen constitute country-level conditions under which attitudes about gender equality are disproportionately likely to play a role in shaping views about political Islam.

In two-level analyses of survey data, interest in hypothesized individual-level variable relationships is not limited to those that are statistically significant. In addition to identifying the country-level attributes that specify conditions under which an individual-level relationship is disproportionately likely to be statistically significant, it is also instructive for coefficients that indicate how much change

Table 4.2. Impact of Country's Degree of Civil Liberties and Level of Female Secondary School Enrollment on the Inverse Individual-Level Relationship between Support for Gender Equality and Support for Political Islam among All Respondents

	Model 1	Model 2	Model 3
Greater degree of civil liberties	.055***		.056***
	(.020)		(.016)
Higher level of female secondary school enrollment		−.056***	−.057***
		(.018)	(.016)
Constant	−.178***	−.128***	−.146***
	(.011)	(.014)	(.012)

Note: Values of the dependent variable ranges from −.232, indicating a strong inverse relationship between support for gender equality and support for political Islam at the individual level of analysis, to −.018, indicating little relationship between the two individual-level variables. The table presents unstandardized coefficients; standard errors are in parentheses.
$^*p < .1; ^{**} p < .05; ^{***} p < .01.$

in the value of an individual-level dependent variable results from a change in the value of an individual-level independent variable, regardless of whether or not the relationship is statistically significant, to be regressed against country-level attributes. Regression coefficients resulting from individual-level analyses thus become dependent variables in cross-survey analyses, and country-level attributes, treated as independent variables, are examined in an attempt to determine how, and by extension why, the coefficients vary.

The kind of findings that result from two-level analyses in which regression coefficients are the dependent variable are illustrated in table 4.2. Focusing again on the hypothesized inverse relationship between attitudes toward gender equality and support for political Islam, as discussed in chapter 3, and basing findings this time on an analysis that includes all respondents, the table shows the influence of variation in two country-level attributes: degree of civil liberties and level of female secondary school enrollment, both at the time the country was surveyed. These country-level attributes are thus the independent variables in models in which coefficients expressing the strength of the inverse relationship between support for gender equality and support for political Islam at the individual level of analysis constitute the dependent variable. Given that only an inverse individual-level relationship has been found to have explanatory power, as reported in chapter 3, the dependent variable includes only negative coefficients, which in fact characterize thirty-one of the forty surveys in which questions about gender quality were asked. With weighting, this reduces the N in table 4.2 to twenty-six. The values of the dependent variable range from −.232 to −.018, with the latter coefficient being the only instance in which $p > .05$.

The findings presented in table 4.2 indicate that as the degree of civil liberties in a country increases and/or as the proportion of girls enrolled in secondary school decreases, the value of the coefficient expressing the individual-level relationship between support for gender equality and support for political Islam increases, moving toward 0 from a low of −.232. The table thus shows that the societal environment defined by these country-level attributes has an influence on the individual-level relationship, with the degree to which opposition to gender equality is associated with support for political Islam decreasing as a function of the degree of civil liberties in a country and increasing as a function of the extent of its female secondary school enrollment. It is notable that each of the two country-level attributes has an independent impact on the individual-level relationship, with $p < .01$ for each when the other is included in the analysis, as shown in Model 3 of the table.

Tables 4.1a, 4.1b, and 4.2 have been presented in order to illustrate and clarify the nature of the analyses by which the findings to be presented and discussed in this chapter have been generated. The tables point to the influence of country-level attributes and suggest that the significance and strength of individual-level relationships in which support for political Islam is the dependent variable are not distributed randomly across countries with different political, economic, or demographic profiles. This is not to say that it will be possible to identify the influence of country-level attributes on all of the individual-level relationships reported in chapter 3. On the contrary, some of the relationships reported in chapter 3 may not be disproportionately likely to have explanatory power in particular kinds of national settings. Nevertheless, to the extent that individual-level factors do have more of an impact on attitudes toward political Islam in some environments than others, as is at least sometimes the case, any serious effort to understand why ordinary citizens come to different views about Islam's place in government and political affairs requires that programs of research include an effort to discover and map the influence of country-level attributes.

The country-level attributes in the dataset constructed for the present study, which were discussed in chapter 1 and listed in table 1.6, have been used to investigate whether and in what way individual-level relationships in which attitude toward political Islam is the dependent variable have disproportionate explanatory power in particular kinds of societal environments. Many and in fact most of these country-level attributes do not have a conditioning effect on individual-level relationships. But some *are* associated with variation in the degree to which an individual-level independent variable accounts for variance in views about the political role to be played by Islam, and in these instances it is both possible and important to offer insights about causal stories that involve country-level as well as individual-level factors. As discussed, even when the data do point to country-level influences, as in tables 4.1a, 4.1b and 4.2, data limitations permit no more than informed speculation about whether the relationship involves a causal connection and, if so, about the nature of the pathways to which it appears to point. This would be the case if the investigation were limited to the individual level of analysis, however; and so, acknowledged limitations notwithstanding, attributes of the country in which individuals reside must be included in the analysis in order to achieve a fuller understanding of the pathways that lead Muslim men and women either toward or away from support for political Islam.

Cultural Values and Support for Political Islam

Of all the hypotheses presented and tested in chapter 3, the one involving cultural values, operationalized in terms of attitudes toward gender equality, has been the most frequently confirmed. As shown in table 4.3, which indicates the number of surveys in which it is confirmed at each level of statistical confidence among all respondents and among subsets of respondents grouped by sex and age, the hypothesized inverse relationship is confirmed among all respondents at the .05 level or below in thirty of the forty surveys that provide the necessary data. The hypothesis was not tested in two of the forty-two surveys used to test other individual-level hypotheses because these surveys did not include questions about gender equality. The hypothesis positing a relationship between lower support for gender equality and higher support for political Islam is also more straightforward than some of the other propositions introduced in chapter 3 because the direction of the relationship is the same in countries governed by a regime with an Islamic connection and in countries governed by an essentially secular regime.

Even though there is very often a statistically significant relationship between attitudes toward gender equality and attitudes toward the role that Islam should play in government and political affairs, this is not always the case. Accordingly, it is likely, or at least possible, that the extent to which opposition to gender equality increases support for political Islam is influenced by the character and circumstances of the country in which people live. This is also likely to be the case among different subsets of the population, among whom, as shown in table 4.3, the frequency with which there exists a statistically significant relationship varies considerably. Among both younger and older women in particular, attitudes toward gender equality are less likely to have a significant impact on attitudes toward political Islam than is the case among men in either age category. Opposition to gender equality pushes toward support for political Islam to a statistically significant degree in only nine surveys among younger female respondents, and in only eight for which $p < .05$. This is the case among older female respon-

Table 4.3. Number of Surveys in which an Inverse Relationship between Support for Gender Equality and Support for Political Islam Is Statistically Significant and Range of the Negative Coefficients that Express this Inverse Relationship

	All respondents	Younger men	Older men	Younger women	Older women
$p < .001$	27	1	2	3	—
	67.5%	2.5%	5.0%	7.5%	
$p < .01$	2	7	7	3	1
	5.0%	17.5%	17.5%	7.5%	2.5%
$p < .05$	1	11	10	2	8
	2.5%	27.5%	25.0%	5.0%	20.0%
$p < .1$	—	2	1	1	7
		5.0%	2.5%	2.5%	17.5%
Not sig.	10	19	20	31	24
	25.0%	47.5%	50.0%	77.5%	60.0%
Total N (weighted)	40	40	40	40	40
	(35)	(35)	(35)	(35)	(35)
Coefficient from/to	−.232/	−.311/	−.339/	−.491/	−.405/
	−.018	−.022	−.002	−.034	−.015

dents in sixteen surveys, but this is still less often than among either younger or older male respondents and, further, in seven of these surveys the relationship is significant only at the .1 level of confidence—a level at which, given the very large *N,* individual-level relationships are not considered to be significant.

All of this suggests, as discussed above and illustrated by tables 4.1a and 4.1b, that the explanatory power of attitudes toward gender equality in accounting for variance in the views held by ordinary citizens about Islam's place in political life itself varies across countries and/or over time and, therefore, that the extent to which these attitudes are a driver of views about political Islam may at least sometimes depend on the influence and conditioning effect of identifiable country-level attributes.

Unemployment level is the only country-level attribute that specifies conditions under which the individual-level relationship between attitudes toward gender equality and views about political Islam is disproportionately likely to be statistically significant at or below the .05 level when the analysis is based on all respondents. More specifically, opposition to gender equality is disproportionately likely to push toward support for political Islam to a statistically significant degree in countries with lower levels of employment. Whereas half of the thirty

Table 4.4. Impact of Country's Level of Unemployment on the Inverse Individual-Level Relationship between Support for Gender Equality and Support for Political Islam among All Respondents

		Relationship not statistically significant ($p > .05$)	Relationship statistically significant ($p < .05$)
Level of unemployment	Lower	1 10.0%	15 50.0%
	Higher	9 90.0%	15 50.0%
		$N=40, p=.061$	

Note: Probabilities are based on chi-square values that were computed with weighting, whereas actual rather than weighted frequencies are shown. Level of unemployment is cut at 14 percent.

statistically significant individual-level relationships noted in table 4.3 are in countries with a lower level of unemployment, this is the case among only 10 percent, or one, of the ten individual-level relationships that are not statistically significant at the .05 level. Cutting the unemployment level at 14 percent and computing chi-square to assess the connection between lower national unemployment on the one hand and the presence of a statistically significant inverse individual-level relationship between support for gender equality and support for political Islam on the other, $p=.061$. This is shown in table 4.4.

As discussed above and illustrated in table 4.2, coefficients expressing the strength of individual-level relationships are also being treated as dependent variables in survey-level analyses in which national attributes are the independent variables. The range and variance associated with these coefficients, as well as the number of relationships that are statistically significant at each level, are shown in table 4.3. When findings about all respondents are included in the survey-level analysis, negative coefficients expressing the inverse relationship between support for gender equality and support for political Islam vary from −.232 to −.018. As previously shown in table 4.2, the values of these coefficients decrease, meaning that negative values move away from 0 and the inverse individual-level relationship becomes stronger, as degree of civil liberties decreases and as level of female secondary school enrollment increases.

Analyses based on all respondents may be less instructive than those based on subsets of respondents grouped according to sex and age. The former is an aggregate of the latter, and to the extent that country-level attributes conditioning the inverse individual-level relationship between support for gender equality and support for political Islam are not the same among all subsets of respondents, explanatory insights derived from a survey-level analysis that includes all respondents may be somewhat less instructive. This analysis will specify conditions under which attitude toward gender equality is disproportionately likely to have explanatory power in general, even though this does not apply to some, or perhaps any, identifiable subsets of the population. Nevertheless, the findings reported above do suggest some of the country-level dynamics that may be at work.

That opposition to gender equality is disproportionately likely to push toward support for political Islam in countries with lower unemployment levels suggests that cultural values have greater explanatory power in the absence, real or perceived, of competition for jobs. This may be because high unemployment fosters uncertainty and concerns that, when present, tend to override the influence of cultural factors. Findings about the conditioning effect of fewer civil liberties and higher female secondary school enrollment suggest additional possibilities about the pathways linking country-level and individual-level factors. On the one hand, fewer civil liberties reduces the space for political discourse and this, in turn, as in the case of unemployment and economic concerns, makes it less likely that other preoccupations, political in this instance, will override or at least significantly reduce the influence of cultural factors. On the other hand, cultural values, especially those pertaining to the rights and status of women, are likely to be more important shapers of attitudes toward political Islam in societies with higher levels of female secondary school enrollment precisely because education raises awareness and expectations and, as a result, increases the salience, and hence the explanatory power, of gender-linked considerations.

These suggestions about the conditioning pathways linking country-level attributes to individual-level variable relationships are only informed speculation, of course. They go beyond the data and should thus be viewed with caution, or even skepticism. They are offered in order to make a start in thinking about why, rather than simply how, the character of the political, economic, or social environment in which an individual resides influences the degree to which his or her views about political Islam are shaped by cultural values. More generally, as is the case throughout this chapter, the primary objective in offering interpretations and informed speculation that go beyond the data is to stimulate further reflection and encourage additional research that will, incrementally, lead to a fuller understanding of underlying multilevel causal stories.

Younger Men

Turning to younger men, an inverse relationship between support for gender equality and support for political Islam that is statistically significant at the .05 level has been found, as shown in table 4.3, in nineteen of the forty surveys that

Table 4.5a. Binary Logistic Regression Showing the Impact of Country's Level of Adult Literacy and Economic Inequality on the Inverse Individual-Level Relationship between Support for Gender Equality and Support for Political Islam among Younger Men

	Model 1	Model 2	Model 3
Higher adult literacy	−1.856**		−1.903*
	(.964)		(1.016)
Higher economic inequality		−1.230*	−1.334*
		(.725)	(.783)
Constant	1.316	.550	2.093**
	(.877)	(.521)	(1.051)

Note: The dependent variable is a dichotomous measure indicating whether or not the individual-level relationship is significant at or below the .05 level. Level of adult literacy is cut at 63.3 percent; the 1–100 point GINI coefficient indicating greater economic inequality is cut at 36.5 percent. The table presents logit coefficients; standard errors are in parentheses.
* $p < .1$; ** $p < .05$; *** $p < .01$.

contained questions pertaining to gender equality. Table 4.5a presents the results of a binary logistic regression analysis in which the presence or absence of a statistically significant individual-level relationship is the dependent variable. It shows that a statistically significant relationship is disproportionately likely to be found in countries with low levels of adult literacy and high levels of economic equality, the latter measured by the UN's GINI index in which higher scores indicate greater inequality. Taken together, these attributes would appear to describe a more traditional society, one that is not socially developed enough to have a high rate of literacy, at least in relative terms, and with an economy that is not sufficiently developed to have given rise to a greater disparity of wealth.

In addition, treating coefficients expressing the inverse relationship between support for gender equality and support for political Islam as the dependent variable, table 4.5b presents the results of an OLS regression analysis and shows that the value of these coefficients increases, going from a low of −.311 to a high of −.002 and indicating a reduction in the strength of the individual-level relationship as the level of adult literacy in the country increases and as the county's GDP increases. These findings, too, suggest that it is in societies that are more traditional and less affluent that attitudes toward gender equality are most likely to play a role in shaping attitudes toward political Islam. Accordingly, if these assessments are correct, the proposition to be taken away from tables 4.5a and 4.5b is that the greater the degree to which a Muslim-majority country is more traditional and less economically developed, the greater the likelihood that an unfavorable attitude toward gender equality will lead to a favorable attitude toward political Islam among its younger male citizens.

Table 4.5b. Impact of Country's Level of Adult Literacy and Gross Domestic Product on the Inverse Individual-Level Relationship between Support for Gender Equality and Support for Political Islam among Younger Men

	Model 1	Model 2	Model 3
Higher adult literacy	.073**		.064*
	(.033)		(.035)
Higher gross domestic product		.000**	.000*
		(.000)	(.000)
Constant	−.219***	−.190***	−.238***
	(.030)	(.018)	(.032)

Note: Values of the dependent variable range from −.311, indicating a strong inverse relationship between support for gender equality and support for political Islam at the individual level of analysis, to −.022, indicating little relationship between the two individual-level variables. GDP is measured in U.S. dollars.
The table presents unstandardized coefficients; standard errors are in parentheses.
* $p < .1$; ** $p < .05$; *** $p < .01$.

Older Men

Among older men, there is again a statistically significant relationship at or below the .05 level between lower support for gender equality and higher support for political Islam in nineteen surveys. These relationships are disproportionately likely to be found in countries that, at the time they were surveyed, had higher ratings on the UN Human Development Index and, in particular, were unlikely to have very low ratings. This is shown in table 4.6. Statistical confidence falls very slightly above the .1 level, however, with $p = .101$, and so this finding, although potentially instructive, should be viewed with caution.

Coefficients expressing the strength of the inverse relationship between support for gender equality and support for political Islam vary between −.339 and −.002. There is a statistically significant relationship between these coefficients, treated as the dependent variable, and a five-year lag of the Transparency International 0–10 Corruption Perception Index. Higher scores on the index indicate less corruption. With weighting, $N = 35$ and the OLS regression coefficient expressing the survey-level relationship between the lagged measure of corruption on the one hand and the inverse individual-level relationship between support for gender equality and support for political Islam on the other is .032, with a standard error of .016 and $p < .1$. This indicates that the lower the level of corruption, the smaller the negative value that expresses the inverse relationship between attitudes toward gender equality and political Islam and, hence, the weaker the relationship. Alternatively, the higher the level of corruption, the greater the negative value of the coefficient and the stronger the relationship.

Table 4.6. Impact of Country's Level of Human Development on the Inverse Individual-Level Relationship between Support for Gender Equality and Support for Political Islam among Older Men

		Relationship not statistically significant ($p > .05$)	Relationship statistically significant ($p < .05$)
Human Development Index rating	Lower	8 38.1%	2 10.5%
	Higher	13 61.9%	17 89.5%
		$N=40, p=.101$	

Note: Probabilities are based on chi-square values that were computed with weighting, whereas actual rather than weighted frequencies are shown. The 0–1 Human Development Index, with higher values indicating greater human development, is cut at .625.

While the analytical insight to be drawn from these findings is not entirely clear, it is worth noting that this pattern is in some ways the exact opposite of the pattern observed among younger men. Whereas attitude toward gender equality was found to have more explanatory power among younger men in societies that are more traditional and/or less developed and that also have fewer disparities of wealth, among older men attitude toward gender equality has more explanatory power in societies that are more developed—or at least that do not have a very low level of development—and in which a history of greater corruption suggests a measure of economic disparity. This suggests, offering a potentially generalizable insight that may be tested in future research, that value congruence and associated policy expectations play a greater role in shaping the views of older men about Islam's political role to the extent that they reside in an environment that is less traditional and in which corruption is more widespread. It is possible that many older men consider themselves disadvantaged in this environment, or at least believe they would be more comfortable and have greater status in a more traditional social and economic environment. If so, these perceptions of the environment in which they do in fact reside may help to explain how and why country-level attributes condition the linkage between cultural values and judgments about political Islam among this category of individuals.

Younger Women

Among younger women, as shown in table 4.3, there are only eight surveys in which there was an inverse relationship between support for gender equality and

Table 4.7. Impact of Country's Level of Female Secondary School Enrollment, Prior Proportion of the Population under the Age of Fifteen, and Life Expectancy on the Inverse Individual-Level Relationship between Support for Gender Equality and Support for Political Islam among Younger Women

	Model 1
Higher proportion of female secondary school enrollment	−.162***
	(.033)
Higher percentage of population under fifteen, ten years prior to survey	.102***
	(.030)
Higher life expectancy	.009***
	(.004)
Constant	−.768***
	(.252)

Note: Values of the dependent variable range from −.491, indicating a strong inverse relationship between support for gender equality and support for political Islam at the individual level of analysis, to −.034, indicating little relationship between the two individual-level variables. The table presents unstandardized coefficients; standard errors are in parentheses.
* $p < .1$; ** $p < .05$; *** $p < .01$.

support for political Islam that is statistically significant at or below the .05 level of confidence. Attributes of the countries in which these significant relationships are disproportionately likely to be found were identified earlier in tables 4.1a and 4.1b. As the tables show, the relevant country-level attributes are a higher level of secondary school enrollment and a lower percentage of the population under the age of fifteen, ten years prior to the year of the survey.

The coefficients that express the inverse relationship between support for gender equality and support of political Islam vary from a low of −.491, indicating a very strong inverse relationship, to a high of −.034, indicating a relationship that is not strong enough to be statistically significant. The three country-level attributes that are significantly related to these coefficients are shown in table 4.7. These include secondary school enrollment for women, proportion of the population under the age of fifteen, ten years prior to the survey, and life expectancy. More specifically, the table shows that a stronger inverse relationship between support for gender equality and support for political Islam, reflected in a lower (or higher negative) value of the dependent variable, is associated with more women in secondary school, a small youth bulge, and lower life expectancy.

These findings suggest that value congruence and policy expectations are disproportionately likely to play a role in shaping the views about political Islam held by younger women in societies that are less developed and have a larger traditional sector, as suggested by lower life expectancy. These are societies in which, in addition, there is probably at least somewhat less competition for jobs and perhaps status mobility in general, which a smaller youth bulge would seem to indicate. Finally, these are societies in which a higher proportion of secondary-school-aged children, and girls in particular, are attending school, which suggests that younger individuals have comparatively bright prospects for personal and professional advancement. A causal story that may be deduced from these findings, at least as a stimulus to further reflection, is that the three attributes in combination define an environment in which some younger women, especially if they are better educated, have greater confidence in their future prospects. If so, those with a greater commitment to gender equality may be disproportionately likely to oppose a political role for Islam for fear that this would restrict the opportunities that societal conditions appear to be making available to them. At the same time, to the extent that a country, being less developed, also has many younger women who are not well educated and/or who reside in the more traditional and conservative sectors of society, these women may tend to favor continuity over change and thus to believe that the rights and status of women and men should not be equal. If this is the case, following the logic discussed in chapter 3 in connection with Hypothesis 1, this may predispose these individuals to look to Islam to provide the formula by which society is organized and governed. Each of these patterns, to the extent it is present, will be reflected in a strong inverse relationship between support for gender equality and support for political Islam.

Older Women

Among older women, there are nine surveys in which the individual-level relationship between attitudes toward gender equality and attitudes toward political Islam is significant at or below the .05 level of confidence. As shown in table 4.3, there are seven additional surveys in which the relationship is significant at the .1 level of confidence. These are not included in the present assessment of country-attribute conditioning effects. Among older women, the only country-level attribute that specifies when a statistically significant inverse relationship between support for gender equality and support for political Islam is disproportionately likely to be found is a ten-year lag of the percentage of the population under the age of fifteen. As shown in table 4.8, eight of the nine significant relationships are in countries in which, ten years prior to the year in which it was surveyed, less than 41 percent of the population was under fifteen. The relationship is significant at the .05 level.

The coefficients that express the inverse relationship between support for gender equality and support for political Islam range from a high of −.015 to a low of −.405; and a ten-year lag of the percentage of the population under fifteen is, again, the only country-level attribute significantly related to these coefficients to a statistically significant degree. OLS regression analysis shows that this survey-level

Table 4.8. Impact of Country's Prior Proportion of the Population under the Age of Fifteen on the Inverse Individual-Level Relationship between Support for Gender Equality and Support for Political Islam among Older Women

		Relationship not statistically significant ($p > .05$)	Relationship statistically significant ($p < .05$)
Percentage of population under fifteen, ten years prior to survey	Lower	13 41.9%	8 88.9%
	Higher	18 58.1%	1 11.1%
		$N=40, p=.051$	

Note: Probabilities are based on chi-square values that were computed with weighting, whereas actual rather than weighted frequencies are shown. The number of surveys included in the analysis is less than forty-two because the interview schedule in several surveys did not include all relevant questions. Proportion of the population under the age of fifteen years, ten years prior to the survey, is cut at 41 percent.

relationship is significant at the .05 level, with $N=35$, B=.089, and S.E.=.038. The positive value of the OLS coefficient (B) indicates that a smaller population under fifteen predicts to a higher negative coefficient and hence a stronger inverse relationship between support for gender equality and support for political Islam.

Once again, it is only possible to speculate about the causal story and pathways to which these findings may point. Other things being equal and considered in the aggregate, older women are the least well-educated and most traditional category of the population, at least relative to other demographic categories based on sex and age. Thus, it might have been expected that the impact on older women would come from a *greater*, not a smaller, increase in the youthful population. The dynamic in this case would presumably be that a greater proportion of young people in the population would tend to make older women feel more marginal and this in turn would push them to embrace, or hold on to, traditional cultural values, and favor, as a result, a political formula they consider to be congruent with these values. In fact, however, the data do not support this plausible albeit speculative interpretation. Rather, they show that a *smaller* youth bulge increases the likelihood that conservative cultural values will push toward support for political Islam among older women. Given this finding, the pathway proposed above might be modified in the following way. Rather than older women becoming more marginalized and hence more tied to tradition as a result of more young people reaching adulthood and entering the societal mainstream, the absence of this youthful push may reduce the extent to which there is pressure for change among those individuals, including and perhaps particularly older women, who make up the most traditional segments of the population. And this then, potentially, or in part, may help to explain why and how a smaller youth bulge conditions the inverse relationship between support for gender equality and support for political Islam among older women.

Conclusion

The present chapter's survey-level analyses add an important dimension to the individual-level findings presented in chapter 3. As shown in table 4.3 with respect to gender equality, and as will be shown shortly with respect to other individual-level independent variables, hypotheses confirmed by the pooled analyses reported in chapter 3 do not describe dynamics that apply to all of the surveys included in the dataset constructed for the present study. On the contrary, the hypothesized inverse relationship between support for gender equality and support for political Islam is confirmed in analyses based on all respondents in only thirty of the forty surveys that contained the items needed to test the hypothesis. Further, and perhaps more important, in none of the analyses based on one of the four subsets of respondents is the hypothesis confirmed in even half of the surveys. Accordingly, since the hypothesis sometimes is and sometimes is not confirmed, it is has been important to investigate the country-level attributes that account for this variance in the strength and significance of the individual-level relationships for which chapter 3 presents evidence.

It is also worth calling attention in this connection to the distribution of this variance across the four categories of respondents based on sex and age. It is not surprising that there are a larger number of significant relationships in analyses based on all respondents, since this may reflect the influence of strong relationships among one or more of the respondent subsets, as well as the much larger N when all respondents are included. What is less expected, and thus more intriguing, is the finding that gender equality has significant explanatory power much more frequently among men than among women. While it might have been assumed that preferences pertaining to the status of women are more important to women than men and thus are more likely to have an impact on women's predispositions about other issues, such as political Islam, among both younger women and older women attitudes toward gender equality in fact account for variance in views about political Islam to a degree that is statistically significant less than half as frequently as they do among men. To the extent that value congruence and associated policy expectations play a role in determining whether people do or do not want Islam to exert political influence, it seems, somewhat counterintuitively, that men more often than women base their judgments about Islam's place in political affairs, in part, on what they believe should be the rights and status of women. One part of the operating dynamic to which this finding points, presumably, is that men who are concerned about competition from women, and for this reason more opposed to gender equality, are disproportionately likely, correctly or incorrectly, to look to Islamist policies to protect the privileged status that men often enjoy.

Finally, with respect to causal stories about the conditioning effect of country-level attributes, it should be repeated that the pathways and societal dynamics discussed above are only informed speculations offered as a stimulus to further reflection and research. It is for readers to assess the degree to which these propositions are persuasive, or at least plausible. At the very least, however, the proposed causal stories recognize and make a start at addressing the puzzles that have been identified by empirical analyses and that flow from findings about country-level attributes that have an impact on the relationship between attitudes toward gender equality and attitudes toward political Islam.

Regime Evaluation and Support for Political Islam

Chapter 3 considered and tested the proposition that a negative evaluation of the governing regime will push either toward or away from support for political Islam depending on whether or not individuals are citizens of a country governed by a regime that has a significant Islamic connection. Expressed in two complementary hypotheses, Hypothesis 2a and Hypothesis 2b, the discussion also made explicit the broader and imagined causal story from which these arguments were derived. For the analyses presented in chapter 3, countries classified as having a regime with an Islamic connection included Iran, Saudi Arabia, Iraq, Sudan, Turkey, and, at some times but not others, Palestine and Lebanon. Governing regimes in other countries, and at certain times in Palestine and Lebanon, were classified as not having an Islamic connection.

The argument that disapproval of the ruling regime is an important driver of support for political Islam in countries governed by a regime that is secular, or at least largely secular, and that has strong authoritarian tendencies as well, has been advanced in a number of studies, including my own. Further, both qualitative and quantitative research has provided some empirical support for this assessment. In fact, however, the findings presented in chapter 3, taken as a whole, suggest that there are notable limits to the explanatory power of regime evaluation under conditions of secular authoritarianism. As shown in tables 3.5a and 3.6a, the hypothesized relationship between a negative assessment of the regime in power and a positive attitude toward political Islam found support only in the pooled, individual-level analysis based on younger men. Beyond this, Hypothesis 2a was not confirmed when the analysis was based on all respondents or on any one of the three other subsets of respondents. Some of the implications of this finding, as well as the reasons it is not contradicted by the frequently strong electoral performance of Islamist opposition parties, were discussed in chapter 3.

Table 4.9. Number of Surveys in which an Inverse Relationship between Evaluation of the Governing Regime and Support for Political Islam Is Statistically Significant and Range of the Negative Coefficients that Express this Inverse Relationship

	All respondents	Younger men	Older men	Younger women	Older women
$p < .001$	8	—	—	—	—
	36.4%				
$p < .01$	2	3	3	1	1
	9.1%	15.0%	13.0%	5.3%	4.3%
$p < .05$	1	1	3	3	—
	4.5%	5.0%	13.0%	15.8%	
$p < .1$	2	3	1	1	1
	9.1%	15.0%	4.3%	5.3%	4.3%
Not sig.	9	13	16	14	21
	40.9%	65.0%	69.6%	73.7%	91.3%
Total N (weighted)	22	20	23	19	23
	(18)	(18)	(19)	(17)	(19)
Coefficient from/to	−.208/	−.242/	−.257/	−.594/	−.588/
	−.002	−.014	−.023	−.001	−.001

The limited degree to which a negative evaluation of the governing regime predisposes ordinary citizens to favor a political formula guided by Islam is also shown in table 4.9. The table is based on the surveys in which the coefficient expressing this individual-level, within-system relationship is a negative value, with the coefficients themselves indicating the extent to which greater disapproval of the government is associated with greater support for political Islam. It shows that the number of surveys in which Hypothesis 2a is confirmed at or below the .05 level of confidence is quite low.

The total number of surveys with which Hypothesis 2a and Hypothesis 2b were tested is forty-two, that being the number of surveys in the present study's dataset that include the necessary questions. Of these, as shown in table 4.9, nineteen to twenty-three have a negative coefficient value expressing the inverse relationship between a positive evaluation of the regime and favorable attitude toward political Islam. The hypothesized inverse relationship, Hypothesis 2a, is confirmed at or below the .05 level in only eleven of the surveys when the analysis is based on all respondents. Among the four demographic subsets, there are never more than six surveys, and in one case only a single survey, in which there is a statistically significant inverse relationship. All but one of the surveys that yielded a statistically significant inverse relationship were conducted in countries governed by a secular regime.

Table 4.9 also shows the range of the negative coefficients that result from analyses based on all respondents and each subset of respondents. Relatively few of these coefficients express relationships that are statistically significant. Nevertheless, as in the investigation of conditionalities associated with the inverse relationship between support for gender equality and support for political Islam, the variance encompassed by these coefficients provides another opportunity to explore whether and how country-level attributes influence the strength of the association between a negative evaluation of the regime and a belief that Islam should play a significant role in the way the country is governed. Insights, again, apply to countries governed by a secular regime, and indeed, with very few exceptions, these negative coefficients all result from analyses of survey data collected in countries whose government does not have an Islamic connection. Among one of twenty-three cases among older men and in two of nineteen cases among younger women, analyses that yielded a negative coefficient are from surveys in countries whose government does have an Islamic connection.

Turning first to country-level attributes that condition the individual-level relationship among all respondents, the only attribute that specifies conditions under which a negative view of the government is disproportionately likely, to a statistically significant degree, to push toward a positive view of political Islam is a lagged measure of low secondary school enrollment. Of the eleven relationships shown in table 4.9 that are statistically significant at or below the .05 level, seven, or 63.6 percent, are in countries in which, at the time they were surveyed, the percentage of secondary-school-aged children enrolled in school was 69 percent or below. Of the eleven relationships shown in table 4.9 that are *not* significant at or below the .05 level, only two, or 18.2 percent, had enrollment levels below 69 percent at the time the survey was conducted. These findings, as well as the probability value indicating that the difference is statistically significant, are shown in table 4.10.

As is often the case, the pathways and dynamics underlying this conditional relationship are not self-evident. Nevertheless, it is important to encourage reflection on the mechanisms that may be at work and to offer some ideas about explanatory insights to which the findings may point. One consideration is that having fewer students attending and graduating from secondary school a decade earlier will have contributed to an environment in which fewer individuals, especially young adults, have had an opportunity to acquire the skills and credentials necessary for personal and professional advancement. Further, this situation may also foster a more general view that the government is not doing enough to create the conditions for social mobility and, as a consequence, is failing to meet the needs of its population, or at least its less fortunate members.

Table 4.10. Impact of Country's Prior Level of Secondary School Enrollment on the Inverse Individual-Level Relationship between a Positive Evaluation of the Governing Regime and Support for Political Islam among All Respondents

		Relationship not statistically significant ($p > .05$)	Relationship statistically significant ($p < .05$)
Ten-year lag of level of secondary school enrollment	Lower	2 18.2%	7 63.6%
	Higher	9 81.8%	4 36.4%
		$N = 22, p = .016$	

Note: Probabilities are based on chi-square values that were computed with weighting, whereas actual rather than weighted frequencies are shown. Level of secondary school enrollment is cut at 69 percent.

In this environment, men and women with an unfavorable view of the regime, regardless of the substance of their complaints, may be disproportionately likely to favor what they judge to be a consequential alternative to the regime in power, in this case a political system guided by Islam. The appeal of political Islam to those who are unhappy with the existing regime may also be reinforced by the religion's proclaimed emphasis on equality and help for those in less favorable social and economic circumstances. This proposed dynamic for the most part restates the rationale that was offered when Hypothesis 2a was introduced in chapter 3. In addition, however, the findings presented in table 4.10 suggest, when the analysis is based on all respondents, that this pathway is most likely to be operative when a secular authoritarian regime governs a country in which opportunities for social mobility are, or at least are perceived to be, relatively limited. Apparently, if this interpretation is correct, concerns about limited opportunities for advancement intensify the more general antiregime sentiments held by some men and women and increase the likelihood that these individuals will favor an Islamic alternative to the secular regime by which they are currently governed.

Country-attribute correlates of the twenty-two negative coefficients expressing the relationship between unfavorable attitudes toward the regime and favorable attitudes toward political Islam suggest insights that are consistent with this assessment. These coefficients range in the analysis based on all respondents from a low of −.208 to a high of −.002, as shown in table 4.9, and the most important country-level attribute related to them to a statistically significant degree is the World Bank's economic inequality (GINI) index. More specifically, the value of the coefficient expressing the relationship between judgments about the regime and judgments about political Islam increases as the GINI index decreases. Since

Table 4.11. Impact of Country's Degree of Economic Inequality and Level of Political Rights on the Inverse Individual-Level Relationship between a Positive Evaluation of the Governing Regime and Support for Political Islam among All Respondents

	Model 1	Model 2	Model 3
Higher economic inequality	−.008**		−.009**
	(.004)		(.004)
Fewer political rights		.028	.032*
		(.021)	(.018)
Constant	.215	−.243**	.077
	(.138)	(.112)	(.150)

Note: Values of the dependent variable range from −.208, indicating a strong inverse relationship between a positive evaluation of the governing regime and support for political Islam at the individual level of analysis, to −.002, indicating little relationship between the two individual-level variables.
The table presents unstandardized coefficients; standard errors are in parentheses.
$* p < .1; ** p < .05; *** p < .01.$

higher (lower negative) coefficients indicate a weaker relationship between anti-government sentiment and support for political Islam, and since higher GINI scores indicate greater economic inequality, the analysis, reported in table 4.11, shows that the greater the level of economic inequality, the greater the degree to which antigovernment views push toward a desire for Islam to play a role in government and political affairs.

A second country-level attribute also appears to play a role, although second-arily, in conditioning the relationship between attitudes toward the government and attitudes toward political Islam when all respondents are included in the analysis. This is level of political rights as measured by the Freedom House seven-point scale in which lower scores indicate fewer rights. When considered alone, this attribute is not related to a statistically significant degree to coefficients expressing the association between views about the government and views about Islam's place in political life. However, as also reported in table 4.11, level of political rights becomes significant when included in the analysis along with economic inequality, with the relationship between antiregime sentiments and support for political Islam growing stronger as the degree of political rights increases. Further, the conditioning effect of the GINI index becomes stronger when level of political rights is included in the analysis, moving from a relationship in which $p = .045$ to one in which $p = .022$.

Given the small number of cases, with $N = 22$, these findings should be treated with some caution. Indeed, if the associations are assessed using a nonparametric statistic, Spearman's rho, which does not consider any possible interaction between the two country-level attributes, the probabilities involving both economic inequality and level of political rights are just barely significant at the .1 level. Nevertheless, the findings do point to an interesting and potentially very instructive causal story, and one that is generally consistent with the inferences drawn from table 4.10. Just as limited opportunities for social mobility, real or at least perceived, increase the degree to which a negative evaluation of the regime pushes toward support for political Islam, this relationship, expressed in Hypothesis 2a, grows stronger as economic inequality increases. In addition, however, somewhat but not entirely counterintuitively, this dynamic appears to be reinforced by political openness. While the existence of greater political rights might reduce overall political discontent, it apparently contributes to an environment in which economic inequality has a particularly strong conditioning effect and thus increases the likelihood that those men and women who *do* have an unfavorable view of the regime will favor a political formula guided by Islam.

Younger Men

Among younger men, as table 4.9 shows, negative attitudes toward the regime increased the likelihood of supporting political Islam to a statistically significant degree in only four surveys. This might be surprising since, as reported in chapter 3 and shown in table 3.6a, it is only among younger men that the hypothesized inverse relationship between negative attitudes toward the government and positive attitudes toward political Islam was confirmed in the pooled analysis. Nevertheless, given the small number of surveys in which the hypothesis was confirmed at or below the .05 level, the likelihood of a significant relationship is not associated with any of the country-level attributes included in the dataset.

The findings are different, however, when coefficients expressing the relationship between the two sets of individual-level attitudes are treated as the dependent variable and regressed against selected country-level attributes. In this case, the results are consistent with and offer additional insight into the causal story that was advanced when Hypothesis 2a was proposed in chapter 3. The country-level attributes that predict to a stronger relationship between negative attitudes toward the regime and support for political Islam, independently and to a statistically significant degree, are greater corruption, lagged by five years, and higher adult literacy. These findings are shown in table 4.12, with the range of the negative coefficients shown in table 4.9 constituting the dependent variable.

The rationale advanced when Hypothesis 2a was introduced in chapter 3 emphasized a desire for fairness and opportunity that the existing regime was judged to be failing to provide and which, presumably, would be present in greater measure if the governing regime were influenced by Islam. And indeed, consis-

Table 4.12. Impact of Country's Level of Corruption (lagged) and Level of Adult Literacy on the Inverse Individual-Level Relationship between a Positive Evaluation of the Governing Regime and Support for Political Islam among Younger Men

	Model 1	Model 2	Model 3
Five-year lag of lower level of corruption	.044**		.059***
	(.015)		(.012)
Greater adult literacy		−.002*	−.002**
		(.001)	(.001)
Constant	−.291***	.015	−.162**
	(.058)	(.071)	(.066)

Note: Values of the dependent variable range from −.242, indicating a strong inverse relationship between support for a positive evaluation of the governing regime and support for political Islam at the individual level of analysis, to −.014, indicating little relationship between the two individual-level variables.

The table presents unstandardized coefficients; standard errors are in parentheses.

* $p < .1$; ** $p < .05$; *** $p < .01$.

tent with this causal story, the findings presented in table 4.12 indicate that not only is this the case to some degree in general among younger men, as reflected in the pooled analysis, it is particularly likely to be the case to the extent that the population is better educated and the regime itself has a history of corruption. In this environment, the population, and apparently younger men in particular, are likely to have higher expectations and thus to be more discontent if they do not find opportunities for advancement. To then have this discontent intensified by a significant level of corruption, for which there is independent evidence and of which the population is presumably well aware, reflects the lack of fairness in the allocation of opportunities and resources that is driving this population's political judgments. Thus, in sum, not surprisingly but nonetheless significantly, greater political discontent among younger men living in countries governed by a secular authoritarian regime is particularly likely to push toward a desire for Islam to play a political role to the extent that these countries are also characterized by a better educated population and a higher level of corruption.

Older Men

Table 4.9 shows that there are six surveys in which the inverse relationship between a positive assessment of the government and a positive view of political Islam is significant at or below the .05 level, which is a larger number of significant relationships pertaining to Hypothesis 2a than among any of the other subsets of respondents. Nevertheless, there is no country-level attribute in the dataset that specifies conditions under which a statistically significant relationship is disproportionately likely to be found.

By contrast, there is an important country-level attribute that is related to a statistically significant degree to the negative coefficients that express the inverse relationship proposed in Hypothesis 2a. As shown in table 4.9, these twenty-three coefficients range from a high of −.023 to a low of −.257, with the latter, lower, number indicating the strongest association between a negative evaluation of the regime and a desire for Islam to exert political influence. The country-attribute correlate of these coefficients, which in all but one instance are based on surveys in countries governed by an essentially secular regime, is a five-year lag of political status. More specifically, the degree to which a negative evaluation of the government pushes toward the view that Islam should play an important political role is significantly more likely in countries that, five years prior to the conduct of the survey, were less free as measured by Freedom House. This is shown in an OLS regression analysis. With lower Freedom House scores indicating less freedom, $B = .055$ and $p = .065$. However, given that $N = 23$, a nonparametric statistic may be a better measure, and findings remain robust when Spearman rho is computed for this purpose: $rho = .450$ and $p = .031$.

The conditioning dynamic to which this finding about a low level of political freedom appears to point is consistent with the causal story proposed when Hypothesis 2a was introduced in chapter 3, as well as the interpretations derived from the survey-level analyses of all respondents and younger men offered above. In these latter instances, support for political Islam increased as a function of opposition to the regime to the extent that a country was characterized by greater economic inequality and fewer political rights. Similarly, among older male respondents, this is the case as well to the extent that the country has been less free during its recent history. Although the Freedom House measure has been lagged by only five years, it is interesting that it is among older men, who are obviously at least somewhat more familiar with the country's history than are younger individuals, that it is the past rather than present level of freedom that has explanatory power. In any event, despite some variations in the specific country-level attributes whose explanatory power has been found in analyses based on different subsets of respondents, it seems clear that the relationship between negative attitudes toward a secular government and the desire for an alternative guided by Islam is conditioned, and intensified, by a national environment characterized by greater political and economic inequality.

Younger Women

As with younger men, table 4.9 shows that among younger women negative attitudes toward the governing regime increased the likelihood of supporting political Islam to a statistically significant degree in only four of the surveys in the dataset.

Nevertheless, despite the small number of significant relationships, there are two country-level attributes that specify conditions under which these relationships are disproportionately likely to be found. One is level of political rights as measured by Freedom House, and the other is level of adult literacy. With respect to political rights, all four significant relationships are in countries with a rating of 5 or below on the Freedom House scale, with lower scores indicating greater political rights. And while all four, or 100 percent, of the significant individual-level relationships among younger women are in countries with more political rights, at least in relative terms, fewer than half of the fifteen surveys in which a negative evaluation of the regime is *not* related to support for political Islam to a significant degree are in countries with greater political rights. Probabilities based on both chi-square and Spearman's rho, nonparametric statistics that are most appropriate given the small N, show that the relationship is statistically significant at or very slightly above the .05 level.

The pattern is similar for adult literacy. All four significant relationships are in countries with higher levels of adult literacy—over 80 percent, whereas only one-third of the individual-level relationships that are *not* significant are in countries with similarly high levels of adult literacy. Probabilities based on chi-square and Spearman's rho again show these relationships to be statistically significant, with $p=.029$ and $p=.016$, respectively.

The data do not permit the kind of multivariate analysis that would test the impact of each country-level attribute with the other held constant, and so the most that can be said with full confidence is that each predicts to a greater likelihood that negative evaluations of the governing regime will push toward support for political Islam among younger women without necessarily having independent explanatory power. In fact, however, the two attributes probably reinforce one another, as suggested by the finding that all of the statistically significant individual-level relationships are in countries that are higher in *both* political rights and adult literacy, whereas only 20 percent of the individual-level relationships that are not significant are in countries with higher ratings on both country-level attributes. And since higher levels of political rights and adult literacy both indicate greater political and social development, it is reasonable to conclude, despite the small N, that this defines an environment in which, among younger women, negative evaluations of the regime are disproportionately likely to give rise to a favorable view of political Islam.

A consistent but slightly different picture emerges when the dependent variable is not the presence or absence of a statistically significant inverse individual-level relationship between positive attitudes toward the government and positive attitudes toward political Islam but rather coefficients that express the strength of this individual-level relationship. In this case, only level of political rights is associated to a statistically significant degree with Hypothesis 2a among younger women. More specifically, the value of the negative coefficient indicating the degree to which an unfavorable judgment of the governing regime is associated with a favorable judgment of political Islam decreases, thus indicating a stronger inverse relationship, as a function of decreasing scores on the Freedom House's political rights index. Based on the nonparametric statistic, Spearman's rho, $p < .05$.

The reasons that discontent with the political status quo might lead ordinary citizens to seek a consequential alternative in the form of political Islam were discussed when Hypothesis 2a was introduced in chapter 3. The pooled analysis presented in chapter 3 showed that this hypothesis does not have substantial and widespread explanatory power among younger women; yet it turns out that this is not the whole story. There are in fact societal conditions under which the relationship between a negative view of the regime and a positive view of Islam *is* more likely to be strong and significant among younger women. These conditions are defined by a higher level of social and especially political development, at least in relative terms; and while it is only possible, again, to speculate about the attitude-shaping dynamics to which this points, some preliminary ideas may be offered as a stimulus to further reflection and theorizing. On the one hand, Islamist groups may have greater opportunities to organize and disseminate their message in a political environment that is at least somewhat more open. On the other, these groups may provide the most available and acceptable avenues for civic participation among younger women—in contrast to older women, who are less engaged in civic life, and to men, who have a broader array of opportunities. For this reason, younger women who are discontent with the prevailing political order may be particularly likely to be guided by an Islamist perspective when thinking about alternative political formulae.

Older Women

As reported in table 4.9, there is only one survey in which negative evaluations of the governing regime are disproportionately likely, to a statistically significant degree, to lead to support for political Islam among older women. There are, however, three country-level attributes that are related to a statistically significant degree to the negative coefficients expressing the inverse relationship between a positive view of the regime and a positive attitude toward political Islam among this subset of respondents. These coefficients range from a low of −.588 to a high of −.001, as reported in table 4.9, and the country-level attributes associated with a stronger inverse individual-level relationship, indicated by a lower (higher negative) coefficient, are a low level of adult literacy, a low level of female secondary school enrollment, and a low level of human development based on the UN index. These associations are shown in table 4.13, which presents Spearman's rho coefficients and the associated probabilities.

It is important to note that the three country-level attributes are themselves very highly correlated, with $p < .001$ in two of the three bivariate combinations.

Table 4.13. Correlation between Level of Female Secondary School Enrollment, Level of Adult Literacy, and Level of Human Development and the Inverse Individual-Level Relationship between a Positive Evaluation of the Regime and Support for Political Islam among Older Women

	Stronger relationship between a negative evaluation of the governing regime and support for political Islam	
	Spearman's rho	*p*
Female secondary school enrollment	.499	.015
Adult literacy	.463	.026
UN Human Development Index rating	.403	.056

Note: Values of coefficients expressing the relationship between a negative evaluation of the governing regime and support for political Islam range from −.588, indicating a strong inverse relationship, to −.018, indicating little relationship between the two individual-level variables. Weights were included in the analysis when computing rho values and probabilities.

It may thus be reasonably inferred that they are all indicators of an underlying attribute: level of socioeconomic, or perhaps just social, development. Data limitations, and specifically the low *N*, again do not permit the kind of multivariate analysis that would be necessary to determine whether any one of the three attributes has more explanatory power than the others. In fact, however, all three point to the same conclusion: that the lower a country's level of social development, the greater the likelihood that support for political Islam will increase among older women as a function of discontent with, and distrust of, the governing regime.

It is notable that some of these country-level attributes associated with social development, particularly adult literacy, also had a conditioning effect on Hypothesis 2a among younger men and younger women; but in these cases the direction of the relationship is different, with higher adult literacy and higher social development increasing the likelihood that a negative evaluation for the regime would lead to a favorable attitude toward political Islam. Among older women, by contrast, it is *lower* levels of development that increase the connection between discontent with the government and support for political Islam. The causal story to which this would appear to point is that since older women are already the demographic category least likely to be engaged in civic life and exposed to diverse political arrangements, at least in relative terms and other things being equal, and since this comparatively restricted worldview is likely to be sheltered and perhaps even reinforced by the less developed and less socially mobilized character of the society in which they live, it is probably a more limited awareness of nontraditional political systems that makes older women particularly likely to look to Islam if they desire an alternative to the political status quo.

In this case, as in the discussion of findings based on other subsets of respondents, it is only possible to speculate about the multilevel attitude-shaping dynamics that may be at work. But there do appear to be country-level attributes that condition the individual-level relationship between judgments about the regime and judgments about political Islam, attributes that characterize social, political, and/or economic environments in which negative evaluations of the government are most likely to foster the view that Islam should play a role in political life. It is thus important to offer ideas, even tentative ideas, about the causal connections that are behind these conditioning relationships; and plausible and potentially instructive pathways have been proposed for this purpose and as a stimulus to further reflection and research.

Regime Evaluation and Opposition to Political Islam

Chapter 3 argued and offered evidence that in countries governed by a regime with an Islamic connection, individuals who are more dissatisfied with the character and performance of their political institutions and officials are more likely than are individuals with higher levels of political satisfaction to *oppose* a political formula that gives Islam an important role. Hypothesis 2b reverses the direction of the relationship discussed above, Hypothesis 2a, and Hypothesis 2b turns out, as reported in chapter 3, to have explanatory power more frequently and more broadly than Hypothesis 2a. As shown in tables 3.5b and 3.6b, the hypothesis was confirmed with $p < .001$ in pooled analyses based on all respondents and also on each of the four respondent subsets based on sex and age. While a negative evaluation of the regime sometimes pushes toward support for political Islam in countries ruled by a government that is essentially secular, and does so to a greater degree among some categories of citizens in some political, economic, or social environments, as shown and discussed above, the impact of regime evaluation on judgments about political Islam is much stronger and much more consistent when Islamist elements are not part of the opposition but are rather part of the political establishment. In this case, logically, dislike of the regime pushes away from the view that Islam should play a role in government and political affairs.

The frequency with which Hypothesis 2b is confirmed at each level of statistical significance is shown in table 4.14. Of the twenty surveys in which there is a positive relationship between a favorable attitude toward the government and a favorable attitude toward political Islam among all respondents, and hence also a positive relationship between an *un*favorable attitude toward both, the relationship is significant at or below the .05 level in fourteen instances, with $p < .001$ in

Table 4.14. Number of Surveys in which a Positive Relationship between Evaluation of the Governing Regime and Support for Political Islam Is Statistically Significant and Range of the Positive Coefficients that Express this Relationship

	All respondents	Younger men	Older men	Younger women	Older women
$p < .001$	10	2	4	1	2
	50.0%	9.1%	21.1%	4.3%	10.5%
$p < .01$	1	2	1	2	3
	5.0%	9.1%	5.3%	8.7%	15.8%
$p < .05$	3	5	1	3	2
	15.0%	22.7%	5.3%	13.0%	10.5%
$p < .1$	2	—	—	1	2
	10.0%			4.3%	10.5%
Not sig.	4	13	13	16	10
	20.0%	59.1%	68.4%	69.6%	52.6%
Total N (weighted)	20	22	19	23	19
	(18)	(18)	(17)	(19)	(17)
Coefficient from/to	.002/	.002/	.019/	.002/	.008/
	.327	.309	.365	.442	.364

ten of these. Ten of these fourteen surveys, or 71.4 percent, are in countries governed by a regime with an Islamic connection, which is consistent with Hypothesis 2b and highly significant, since only eleven of the forty-two surveys in the dataset that contain the necessary items, or 26.2 percent, were conducted in countries in which the regime has such a connection. Among the four subsets of respondents, the relationship is significant at or below the .05 level in no fewer than six and as many nine instances. A large majority of these significant relationships are in countries governed by a regime with an Islamic connection, with proportions ranging from 66.7 percent to 83.3 percent.

Although most of the fourteen statistically significant relationships resulting from analyses based on all respondents are from surveys in countries governed by a regime with an Islamic connection, this is not the case in every instance and, in any event, there are several other country-level attributes that also specify conditions under which Hypothesis 2b is disproportionately likely to be confirmed. These country-level attributes are level of economic inequality, measured by the World Bank GINI index, and level of unemployment. More specially, as shown in table 4.15, both greater economic inequality and higher unemployment define

Table 4.15. Impact of Country's Level of Economic Inequality and Level of Unemployment on the Positive Individual-Level Relationship between a Positive Evaluation of the Governing Regime and Support for Political Islam among All Respondents

		Relationship not statistically significant ($p > .05$)	Relationship statistically significant ($p < .05$)
Level of economic inequality	Lower	5 83.3%	4 28.6%
	Higher	1 16.6%	10 71.4%
		$N=20, p=.060$	
Level of unemployment	Lower	4 66.7%	4 28.6%
	Higher	2 33.3%	10 71.4%
		$N=20, p=.067$	

Note: Probabilities are based on chi-square values that were computed with weighting, whereas actual rather than weighted frequencies are shown. Level of economic inequality coefficient is cut at 36.5 percent; level of unemployment is cut at 14 percent.

societal conditions under which a negative evaluation of the government is disproportionately likely, to a statistically significant degree, to push toward opposition to political Islam. It is not possible to determine from table 4.15 whether the impact of each country-level attribute is significant with the other held constant, but the two would seem to reinforce one another, creating a mass–elite economic gap that defines the conditions under which the dynamic that informs Hypothesis 2a is most likely to be operating. Indeed, of the twenty surveys yielding positive coefficients in analyses based on all respondents, eight were conducted in countries that are higher in *both* economic inequality and unemployment, and in seven of these eight a negative evaluation of the government pushes toward a negative view of political Islam to a statistically significant degree.

Several other country-level attributes turn out to have explanatory power when the dependent variable is the positive coefficient expressing the individual-level relationship between an unfavorable attitude toward the government and an unfavorable attitude toward political Islam. The twenty positive coefficients range from .002 to .327. Level of civil liberties, as measured by Freedom House, and life expectancy are the two attributes that correlate with these coefficients to a statistically significant degree, with the positive value of the individual-level coefficient,

Table 4.16. Impact of Country's Level of Life Expectancy and Level of Political Rights on the Positive Individual-Level Relationship between a Negative Evaluation of the Governing Regime and Opposition to Political Islam among All Respondents

	Model 1	Model 2	Model 3
Higher life expectancy	−.013***		−.010**
	(.004)		(.004)
Fewer civil liberties		.104**	.072*
		(.038)	(.036)
Constant	1.005***	.070**	.770**
	(.288)	(.025)	(.289)

Note: Values of the dependent variable range from .002, indicating little relationship between the two individual-level variables, to .327, indicating a strong relationship between a negative evaluation of the governing regime and opposition to political Islam at the individual level of analysis.

The table presents unstandardized coefficients; standard errors are in parentheses.

* $p < .1$; ** $p < .05$; *** $p < .01$.

and hence the strength of the relationship posited by Hypothesis 2b, increasing as levels of both civil liberties and adult life expectancy decrease. Using Spearman's rho, a nonparametric statistic, $p = .015$ for civil liberties and $p = .007$ for life expectancy. Both country-level attributes are also significant in an OLS regression analysis, with $p = .062$ for civil liberties and $p = .028$ for life expectancy, as shown in table 4.16. As noted previously, multivariate analyses should be interpreted with caution when the N is low, as in the present instance. Still, while caution is in order, the regression analysis does suggest that both of the country attributes, which in fact are not related to one another to a statistically significant degree, have independent explanatory power.

Consistent with findings about the societal environment in which Hypothesis 2a is most likely to have explanatory power in countries governed by a secular authoritarian regime, these findings pertaining to Hypothesis 2b suggest that an unfavorable political economy again increases the likelihood that political discontent will have an impact on attitudes toward political Islam. With respect to Hypothesis 2b, which posits a direct relationship between unfavorable attitudes toward the government and toward political Islam and has explanatory power primarily although not exclusively in countries where the regime has an Islamic connection, the dynamic would again seem to be that these unfavorable conditions increase the appeal of an available and consequential alternative to the status quo and then in turn, by virtue of this appeal, make that alternative more likely to be embraced as political disaffection and discontent with the government increase.

To the extent that there are a few instances in which Hypothesis 2b has significant explanatory power in societies that are not governed by a regime with an Islamic connection, the pathway flowing from a negative evaluation of the government would not in this case involve the appeal of a readily available and consequential political alternative but rather, possibly, in some instances under conditions of secular authoritarianism, be animated by a desire for liberal and inclusive democracy to which both the ruling regime and the Islamist alternative are judged to be hostile.

Younger Men

There are twenty-two surveys in which the coefficient expressing the relationship between a favorable attitude toward the government and a favorable attitude toward political Islam among younger men is a positive value. Of these, there are nine in which the relationship is statistically significant at or below the .05 level. These nine are found disproportionately, to a degree that is statistically significant, in countries that have fewer civil liberties, as measured by Freedom House, and a higher level of corruption, as measured by Transparency International. Both nonparametric chi-square and binary logistic regression confirm the significance of these relationships. When considered separately, $p < .01$ for civil liberties and $p < .05$ for corruption. When both county-level attributes are considered in the binary logistic regression analysis, $p < .05$ for civil liberties and $p < .1$ for corruption.

The same two country-level attributes also have significant explanatory power in accounting for variance in the value of the positive coefficients expressing the individual-level relationship between a favorable attitude toward the government and a favorable attitude toward political Islam, and hence an unfavorable attitude toward both as well. These coefficients range from a low of .002 to a high of .309, as reported in table 4.14. Both nonparametric Spearman's rho and OLS regressions have been computed to assess the relationship between the two country-level attributes and these coefficients resulting from the individual-level analysis among younger men. Both statistical tests confirm that coefficient values increase to a statistically significant degree as a function of fewer civil liberties and a higher level of corruption. The results of the regression analysis are presented in table 4.17.

The country-level attributes with a conditioning effect on the relationship between a negative attitude toward the governing regime and an unfavorable attitude toward political Islam among younger men are among those found to have significant explanatory power in analyses based on all respondents. It thus appears that the same attitude-shaping dynamic is at work among this subset of individuals. Unfavorable political and economic conditions, especially those pertaining to governance, increase the likelihood that a negative evaluation of the regime will

Table 4.17. Impact of Country's Level of Corruption and Level of Civil Liberties on the Positive Individual-Level Relationship between a Negative Evaluation of the Governing Regime and Opposition to Political Islam among Younger Men

	Model 1	Model 2	Model 3
Lower level of corruption	−.111**		−.072*
	(.038)		(.039)
Fewer civil liberties		.118***	.082**
		(.035)	(.038)
Constant	.197***	.073***	.139***
	(.032)	(.021)	(.039)

Note: Values of the dependent variable range from .002, indicating little relationship between the two individual-level variables, to .309, indicating a strong relationship between a negative evaluation of the governing regime and opposition to political Islam at the individual level of analysis.

The table presents unstandardized coefficients; standard errors are in parentheses.

* $p < .1$; ** $p < .05$; *** $p < .01$.

lead ordinary citizens to embrace the view that Islam should not occupy an important place in government and political affairs. This is most often the case in countries governed by a regime with an Islamic connection, but in a few instances it is the case under conditions of secular authoritarianism as well.

Older Men

There are only six instances in which Hypothesis 2b is confirmed among older men, and the only country-level attribute that specifies conditions under which this is disproportionately likely to be the case is life expectancy, specifically, and perhaps surprisingly, higher life expectancy. Four of the six significant individual-level relationships, 66.7 percent, are found in countries with a life expectancy of 71.4 year or greater, whereas among the thirteen other instances in which a positive coefficient expresses the relationship between attitudes toward the governing regime and attitudes toward political Islam there are only three, 23.1 percent, in countries with a life expectancy of this many or more years. Chi-square, computed with weights, yields $p = .087$.

Degree of civil liberties is the only country-level attribute that is correlated to a statistically significant degree with the nineteen positive coefficients, which range from .019 to .365, that express the individual-level relationship posited in Hypothesis 2b. More specifically, the value of the coefficient is disproportionately likely to be higher, expressing a stronger direct relationship between similar attitudes, either positive or negative, toward both the governing regime and political

Islam, in countries with fewer civil liberties. An analysis based on Spearman's rho, again weighted to correct for population overlap when surveys in the same country are less than four years apart, yields $p = .038$.

The finding about fewer civil liberties suggests that the conditioning dynamics proposed above are operative among older as well as younger men. By contrast, the finding about greater life expectancy suggests an additional element in the way that societal environment affects the individual-level relationship posited in Hypothesis 2b. Since life expectancy is often an indicator of human development—indeed, it is one of three variables in the UN Human Development Index—one possibility is that societies characterized by greater life expectancy and greater human development possess more citizens who hold or are at least very familiar with nontraditional values, and this may then incline older men who are politically discontent away from, rather than toward, support for a political formula based to a significant extent on the country's normative traditions. This is speculative, of course, and in fact the finding about greater life expectancy is not especially robust. Nevertheless, an attitude-shaping dynamic associated with greater life expectancy does significantly increase the likelihood among older men that a more negative evaluation of the governing regime will push toward greater opposition to political Islam, most often but not exclusively in countries governed by a regime with an Islamic connection. The pathway offered above is proposed, as elsewhere, as a stimulus to further reflection about the way that country-level and individual-level factors interact to account for variance in the way that ordinary citizens think about political Islam.

Younger Women

There are twenty-three surveys in which regression analyses examining the individual-level relationship between regime evaluation and support for political Islam among younger women yields a positive coefficient. As shown in table 4.14, these vary from .002 to .442; and six involve a relationship that is statistically significant at or below the .05 level. Four of the six, or 66.7 percent, are in countries governed by a regime with an Islamic connection, whereas this is the case among only five, or 29.4 percent, of the remaining seventeen.

The six statistically significant relationships among younger women are disproportionately likely to be found in countries that are characterized by four very strongly intercorrelated country-level attributes related to social and human development. These are life expectancy, level of secondary school enrollment, level of female secondary school enrollment, and degree of urbanization. Specifically, Hypothesis 2b is significantly more likely to be confirmed among countries with a lower rating on each of these attributes. Probabilities based on Spearman's rho are .016 for female secondary school enrollment, .018 for general secondary school enrollment, .032 for life expectancy, and .051 for level of urbanization. Probabilities based on chi-squares computed with dichotomous measures yield similar results. As noted, the four country-level attributes are themselves significantly interrelated, with a correlation coefficient (r) of .662 in one instance and r > .7 in all others. The four thus are all indicators of the same general characteristic: level of social or human development. While it is possible that some of these indicators have more independent explanatory power than others, the main conclusion is that a lower level of development in a country increases the likelihood that its younger women who hold negative views of the regime will also hold negative views of political Islam.

A somewhat similar pattern emerges when the dependent variable is the twenty-three coefficients expressing the individual-level connection between a positive attitude toward the government and toward political Islam, or a negative attitude toward both. None of the four country-level attributes identified above is correlated with these coefficients to a statistically significant degree, nor is the UN Human Development Index, with which all *are* very strongly correlated, with the lowest rho value being .609 and $p < .001$ in every instance. But a dichotomous measure of the Human Development Index *is* correlated to a significant degree with the positive individual-level coefficients based on the analysis of younger women, with rho yielding $p < .05$ and with weights included in the analysis. Specifically, the coefficients are higher, indicating a greater tendency for a negative evaluation of the regime to push toward a negative judgment of political Islam when the country has a low level of development, specifically at or below .625 on the UN scale. The scale ranges from 0, the lowest level of development, to 1, the highest level of development.

Although country-level attributes relating to political economy had a conditioning effect on Hypothesis 2b among younger men, and to some extent among older men as well, it is interesting to note that among younger women it is social and human development that plays a conditioning role. A dynamic suggested by this conditioning is that since traditional cultural norms are likely to be stronger in less developed societies, and since these norms tend to disadvantage women in the Muslim Middle East, the complaints fueling antiregime sentiments among women may be based in large part on the government's failure to promote gender equality, real or perceived, rather than on more explicitly economic and political considerations.

These sentiments may be particularly pronounced among younger women, since they are likely to have higher aspirations and expectations. Therefore, to the extent these younger women also view political Islam as indifferent, if not actually hostile, to improving the status of women, the strength of traditional norms in the broader society they inhabit may for this reason increase the likelihood that those among them with stronger antiregime sentiments will also have more negative views of political Islam. To the extent that this dynamic is operative among younger women, a low level of development probably does not directly reinforce a causal connection between negative views of the government and negative views of political Islam but rather contributes to the emergence or strengthening of underlying sentiments that simultaneously influence the two judgments and thus increase the extent to which they covary.

Older Women

There are seven surveys in which Hypothesis 2b is confirmed at or below the .05 level of confidence in analyses based on older women. There are, however, no country-level attributes that define a societal environment in which these significant relationships are disproportionately likely to be found. With respect to the nineteen coefficients expressing a positive relationship between attitudes that are either favorable or unfavorable toward both the governing regime and political Islam, coefficients that range from .008 to .364, there is one country-level attribute that appears to have a conditioning effect. This is level of adult literacy, or more accurately a dichotomized measure of adult literacy. Surprisingly, however, given the pattern of conditionalities noted among younger women, among older women the individual-level coefficients are higher, and the relationship between similarly positive or similarly negative attitudes both toward the regime and political Islam is stronger, when adult literacy, cut at 63.4 percent, is *higher*. Both Spearman's rho and a comparison of means test show this relationship to be statistically significant, with $p < .05$.

Although the logic is not entirely persuasive, or at least not fully fleshed out, one possibility concerning the attitude-shaping dynamic associated with this finding may be that whereas younger women are more concerned about their circumstances in societies with a lower level of social development, older women feel more insecure in societies with a higher level of development. To the extent this is the case among a reasonable number of older women, either one of two alternative pathways may incline them toward similar attitudes toward the governing regime and political Islam. Further, it is possible that each is operative among some individuals and thus, taken together, they increase the likelihood that older women in more developed societies will have either a more unfavorable attitude toward both the regime in power and an alternative represented by political Islam or, conversely, a more favorable attitude toward both.

On the one hand, mirroring the dynamic operative among younger women, some older women may feel that development is bringing opportunities to younger but not to older individuals, and especially not to older women. For this reason they may be discontent with the regime but also reject political Islam because of a belief that it would similarly do little or nothing to improve their status. This would probably be the case most frequently among those who are better-educated and live in urban areas. On the other hand, older women who are less well-educated and/or reside in less urbanized environments constitute the most traditional and sheltered segment of society, other things being equal, and for this reason they may, perhaps somewhat reflexively, express support for the government out of deference to authority and for political Islam because of the religion's central and familiar place in the history and culture of their country, as well as in the conduct of their own daily affairs.

Economic Dissatisfaction and Support for Political Islam

As with attitudes toward gender equality and regime evaluation, chapter 3 also introduced individual-level hypotheses in which economic satisfaction is the independent variable. Hypothesis 3a proposed that individuals with lower levels of economic satisfaction are more likely than are individuals with higher levels of economic satisfaction to favor a political formula that gives Islam an important role if they are citizens of a country governed by a secular regime. Hypothesis 3b proposed that individuals with lower levels of economic satisfaction are more likely than are individuals with higher levels of economic satisfaction to oppose a political formula that gives Islam an important role if they are citizens of a country governed by a regime with a strong Islamic connection. The chapter also discussed the logic that made these hypotheses plausible and the imagined causal story from which they were derived.

The pooled individual-level analysis reported in chapter 3 provided some support for Hypotheses 3a and 3b, although it was limited in both cases, and especially in the case of Hypothesis 3b. It showed that a lower level of economic satisfaction pushes toward support for political Islam in countries governed by a regime without an Islamic connection—an essentially secular authoritarian regime—when all respondents are included in the analysis and also in analyses based on older women and on younger women. In countries governed by a regime with an Islamic connection, it showed that a lower level of economic satisfaction pushes away from support for political Islam among younger men.

The number of surveys in which Hypothesis 3a is confirmed at or below the .05 level of statistical confidence is shown in table 4.18. The table also reports the number and range of the OLS coefficients in surveys where, as proposed in Hypothesis 3a, there is an inverse relationship between economic satisfaction and the view that Islam should exercise influence in political affairs. The number of surveys that yielded negative coefficients ranges from a low of twenty-two in analyses based on older men to a high of thirty in analyses based on younger women. The table also shows that there are relatively few surveys in which these coefficients indicate a relationship that is strong enough to be statistically significant. Indeed,

Table 4.18. Number of Surveys in which an Inverse Relationship between Economic Satisfaction and Support for Political Islam Is Statistically Significant and Range of the Negative Coefficients that Express this Inverse Relationship

	All respondents	Younger men	Older men	Younger women	Older women
$p < .001$	5	—	1	—	—
	20.0%		4.6%		
$p < .01$	1	1	—	—	1
	4.0%	4.3%			4.2%
$p < .05$	3	1	—	1	—
	12.0%	4.3%		3.3%	
$p < .1$	—	1	3	3	2
		4.3%	13.6%	10.0%	8.4%
Not sig.	16	20	18	26	21
	64.0%	87.0%	81.8%	86.7%	87.4%
Total N (weighted)	25	23	22	30	24
	(20)	(19)	(19)	(25)	(20)
Coefficient from/to	−.137/	−.201/	−.325/	−.178/	−.286/
	−.001	−.001	−.002	−.001	−.004

with the exception of analyses based on all respondents, there is no subset of respondents for which there are more than two surveys that yield relationships that are significant at or below the .05 level.

Consistent with the hypotheses and findings presented in chapter 3, the vast majority of the surveys on which table 4.18 is based, the surveys in which a negative coefficient expresses the relationship between economic satisfaction and support for political Islam, were conducted in countries governed by a regime without an Islamic connection. More specifically, the proportions vary from 76.7 percent, which is twenty-three of the thirty surveys in the case of younger women, to 87.5 percent, which is twenty-one of twenty-four surveys in the case of older women. Similarly, of the nine statistically significant inverse relationships observed in the analysis of all respondents, seven, or 77.8 percent, were conducted in countries governed by an essentially secular regime.

The presence or absence of a regime with an Islamic connection is not the only country-level variable attribute that conditions the connection between economic satisfaction and views about political Islam. The strength of the inverse relationship posited by Hypothesis 3a, and in some cases its statistical significance as well, is also influenced by the character of the broader political, economic, and/or social environment in which people reside. Among all respondents, a statistically significant relationship is disproportionately likely to be found in countries

Table 4.19. Impact of Country's Level of Female Secondary School Enrollment on the Inverse Individual-Level Relationship between Economic Satisfaction and Support for Political Islam among All Respondents

		Relationship not statistically significant ($p > .05$)	Relationship statistically significant ($p < .05$)
Level of female secondary school enrollment	Lower	3 18.8%	6 66.7%
	Higher	13 81.2%	3 33.3%
		$N = 20, p = .012$	

Note: Probabilities are based on chi-square values that were computed with weighting, whereas actual rather than weighted frequencies are shown. Level of secondary school enrollment is cut at 84 percent.

* $p < .1$; ** $p < .05$; *** $p < .01$.

that have lower levels of overall secondary school enrollment, lower levels of female secondary school enrollment, and lower scores on the UN Human Development Index.

The strongest of these relationships, which is shown in table 4.19, involves female secondary school enrollment. With enrollment cut at 84 percent, 66.7 percent of the nine individual-level relationships that are significant at or below the .05 level are found in countries with lower enrollment levels, whereas only 18.8 percent of the relationships that are not statistically significant, based on all respondents, are found in countries that have fewer than 84 percent of their school-aged female population in school. Based on chi-square, a nonparametric statistic, $p = .012$. Relationships involving lower overall secondary school enrollment and lower ratings on the Human Development Index are less robust but nonetheless significant at the .1 level. This is confirmed using chi-square with the attributes dichotomized, as in table 4.19, and also using Spearman's rho to assess continuous measures. Like chi-square, rho is a nonparametric statistic

Two of these three country-level attributes are also related to the negative coefficients expressing an inverse individual-level relationship between economic satisfaction and support for political Islam, the relationship proposed in Hypothesis 3a. As shown in table 4.18, these twenty-five coefficients range from a low of −.137 to a high of −.001. Among all respondents, coefficient values decrease, expressing a stronger inverse relationship, as a function of decreasing scores on the Human Development Index and decreasing levels of female secondary school enrollment. Based on Spearman's rho with continuous measures of the two country-level attributes, and also on a difference of means test with dichotomous measures, $p < .05$ in all instances. Lower overall second school enrollment based on a dichotomous measure is also statistically significant at the .1 level, and a ten-year lag of overall enrollment is significant at the .05 level. These findings are similar to those about environments in which the relationship posited by Hypothesis 3a is disproportionately likely to be statistically significant. In this case, too, the inverse relationship between economic satisfaction and support for political Islam is likely to be stronger among individuals who live in a country with a lower level of human and social development and, in particular, that offers fewer opportunities for advancement to women.

As has been the case in some other instances, the pathway linking a lower level of human and social development at the national level to the explanatory power of economic dissatisfaction at the individual level is not immediately apparent. Since the circumstances of daily life and the opportunities for advancement are to some extent unsatisfactory for most ordinary citizens in this environment, at least in relative terms, it might have been assumed that economic discontent would be at least somewhat pronounced and influence political judgments not only among many who support political Islam but also among many who do not want Islam to play a role in political life, thereby giving it little explanatory power. The data suggest that this is not the case, however.

A possible dynamic linking country-level and individual-level factors may be that higher levels of economic dissatisfaction in this environment indicate a particularly strong disapproval of the existing political system, the system deemed responsible for the lower level of development, and so this dissatisfaction pushes toward support for a clear alternative. In addition, although economic dissatisfaction pushes toward support for political Islam most often in countries governed by a secular authoritarian regime, there are a few instances in which this occurs in countries that have a lower level of development but do not have a government with an essentially secular orientation. In these instances, and perhaps some others, Islam's appeal among those with higher levels of economic discontent may not be based as much, or at least not only, on the view that things would be better under a less secular government, but also, perhaps, that the existing government, despite its Islamic connection, is not truly guided by the religion's principles of equality and justice. In any event, while further reflection and research will be needed to identify and explicate the underlying causal connections, it does appear that the degree to which economic dissatisfaction accounts for variance in support for political Islam increases to the extent that people reside in a country with a lower level of human and social development, especially one that gives fewer opportunities to women.

Younger Men

As reported in table 4.18, there are only two surveys in which the relationship posited in Hypothesis 3a is significant at or below the .05 level among younger men.

Table 4.20. Impact of Country's Degree of Political Rights and Proportion of Women in Labor Force on the Inverse Individual-Level Relationship between Economic Satisfaction and Support for Political Islam among Younger Men

	Model 1	Model 2	Model 3
Fewer political rights	.017		.029*
	(.016)		(.016)
Higher proportion of women in labor force		.051*	.052*
		(.028)	(.026)
Constant	−.155*	−.100***	−.259**
	(.090)	(.025)	(.089)

Note: The dependent variable ranges from −.201, indicating a strong inverse relationship between economic satisfaction and support for political Islam at the individual level of analysis, to −.001, indicating little relationship between the two individual-level variables. Higher scores on the Freedom House measure of political rights indicate fewer rights. Proportion of women in the labor force is a dichotomized measure cut at 20 percent.
The table presents unstandardized coefficients; standard errors are in parentheses.
$* p < .1; ** p < .05; *** p < .01.$

Accordingly, there are no generalizable insights about country-level attribute conditionalities to be derived. The conclusion to be drawn is rather that economic dissatisfaction only very rarely helps to explain, to a degree that is statistically significant, why some younger men do and other younger men do not have a favorable attitude toward political Islam, and this is the case regardless of the political, economic, and social environment in which people reside.

Although the inverse individual-level relationship is strong enough to be statistically significant in only two surveys, the negative coefficients that express this relationship are associated to a statistically significant degree with two country-level attributes. The twenty-three coefficients range from a low of −.201 to a high of −.001, and they are much lower, indicating a stronger inverse relationship between economic satisfaction and support for political Islam, in countries that have more political rights, as measured by Freedom House, and in countries that have a lower proportion of women in the labor force. Based on Spearman's rho, $p < .1$ for the relationship involving each country-level attribute. An OLS regression has also been carried out, although the results should be interpreted with caution given the relatively small N. In this case, as shown in table 4.20, level of political rights does not have significant explanatory power when considered alone, but does in the model that includes both country-level attributes. This is instructive, in part, because there is a strong positive correlation between greater political rights and a higher percentage of women in the labor force, yet the former increases and the latter decreases the strength of the individual-level relationship between economic dissatisfaction and support for political Islam.

The reason that the relationship between economic dissatisfaction and support for political Islam is stronger in societies that possess these attributes would seem to involve a number of interrelated elements. On the one hand, Islamist opposition movements are likely to have more opportunities to organize and disseminate their message in countries where there are greater political rights. On the other, fewer women in the labor force suggests that the societies may be more conservative and traditional and, as a result, nontraditional ideological currents are probably less in evidence and, thus, less widely known and potentially appealing. Accordingly, to the extent that discontent with the economic status quo is sufficient to produce an interest in alternative political arrangements, such interest is disproportionately likely in this political and normative environment to increase the view that government and politics should, at least in part, be guided by Islam.

Older Men

Like younger men and all of the other subsets of respondents, there are few surveys in which the relationship posited in Hypothesis 3a is statistically significant among older men. Accordingly, again, there are no country-level attributes that define conditions under which a significant relationship is disproportionately likely to be found.

Again, however, there are country-level attributes that predict to higher and lower values of the coefficients that express the inverse relationship between economic satisfaction and support for political Islam. The coefficients range from −.325 to −.002, with the lower (higher negative) values indicating a stronger relationship. There are, in fact, five attributes that are significantly correlated with these coefficients, with Spearman's rho yielding $p < .05$ in four instances and $p < .01$ in one instance. These attributes, all of which are aspects of social and human development, and which therefore mirror the attributes found to condition the individual-level relationship in analyses based on all respondents, are overall adult literacy, adult female literacy, overall secondary school enrollment, female secondary school enrollment, and the UN Human Development Index. Specifically, in each case, again as in the analysis based on all respondents, scores indicating a lower level of development on each attribute are associated with higher negative coefficient values, indicating thereby that residence in a less developed country increases the degree to which economic dissatisfaction pushes toward support for political Islam.

Speculation about the causal story of which this might be a manifestation was offered above in the discussion of findings based on all respondents. To the extent this story is persuasive, or at least plausible, it will also shed light on the reasons that a lower level of social and human development increases the degree to which economic dissatisfaction pushes toward support for political Islam among older men. As suggested above and offered to encourage further reflection, it is possible that in countries with lower levels of social and human development, which are likely to offer fewer opportunities for personal and professional advancement, perhaps especially to older individuals, economic dissatisfaction is particularly likely to lead to strong disapproval of existing political arrangements, arrangements deemed responsible for the lower level of development, and so this dissatisfaction will tend to increase support for the clear and consequential alternative that political Islam purports to offer.

Younger Women

Once again, as shown in table 4.18, there are very few surveys in which the relationship posited in Hypothesis 3a is statistically significant among younger women, and so there are again no political, economic, or social environments within which a significant relationship is disproportionately likely to be found. There is, however, one country-level attribute that is related to a statistically significant degree to the inverse individual-level relationship between economic satisfaction and support for political Islam among this subset of respondents. This is level of political freedom as measured by Freedom House, an attribute that, interestingly, overlaps to a substantial degree with the Freedom House measure of political rights that was found to have a conditioning effect in analyses based on younger men. Testing Hypothesis 3a among younger women resulted in a negative coefficient in thirty surveys, and these range from a low of −.178 to a high of −.001. Analyses based on Spearman's rho and also on a difference of means test that compared "party free" and "not free" countries showed in both cases, with $p < .1$, that coefficient values were likely to be lower, indicating a stronger inverse individual-level relationship, in countries with higher levels of political freedom.

As suggested in the case of younger men, one reason that a higher level of political freedom increases the likelihood that economic dissatisfaction will push toward support for political Islam may be that Islamist opposition movements have more opportunities to organize, recruit, and disseminate their message in this environment. It is possible that fewer individuals will desire an alternative to existing political arrangements if there exists a measure of political freedom. But to the extent that some individuals are nonetheless discontent with the status quo, and particularly with their own and the country's economic situation, they will be inclined to think about alternatives and may thus be disproportionately receptive to Islamist claims that there will be more justice and help for the needy if the government is guided by the religion.

There are additional country-level elements in the case of younger men, and so the pathways connecting country-level and individual-level shapers of attitudes toward political Islam are not entirely the same. Further, in any event, the proposed causal connection is only speculative. Nevertheless, it is interesting and potentially instructive that under conditions of greater political openness, where Islamist movements are likely to have greater freedom to organize, younger individuals of both sexes who are more economically dissatisfied, and who presumably are therefore unhappy with the political status quo as well, are disproportionately likely to want Islam to play an important role in government and political affairs.

Older Women

With only one survey in which the relationship between economic dissatisfaction and support for political Islam is significant at or below the .05 level among older women, there are again no country-level conditionalities associated with this individual-level relationship. So far as the negative coefficients that express this relationship are concerned, the one and only country-level attribute that accounts for some of the variance in these coefficients is a ten-year lag of level of urbanization. The coefficients themselves, of which there are twenty-four, vary from −.286 to −.004. Both Spearman's rho and OLS regression analysis show, with $p < .1$, that coefficient values are likely to be lower, indicating a stronger inverse relationship between economic satisfaction and support for political Islam, to the extent that older women live in a country that, ten years prior to the time it was surveyed, had a greater proportion of its population living in urban areas.

It is not clear why there should be a stronger connection between economic dissatisfaction and support for political Islam among older women to the extent that they live in countries that were more urban a few years earlier. Nor is it evident that speculating about the pathway behind this conditioning connection will be particularly productive. One possibility that might be considered, however, primarily as a stimulus to further reflection, is that older women, being the most traditional and least socially mobilized segment of the population, at least in relative terms and other things being equal, are disproportionately likely to feel themselves isolated and left behind in societies that, by virtue of being more urban, are also more complex and dynamic. If this is the case, economic dissatisfaction among older women may bring support for alternative political arrangements. Being more traditional and presumably less familiar with and able to evaluate alternative political models, at least in the aggregate and relative to other segments of the population, older women may find that the interaction between a more complex societal environment and their own economic dissatisfaction increases the degree to which they have a positive attitude toward political Islam.

Economic Dissatisfaction and Opposition to Political Islam

Hypothesis 3b, which was tested in the pooled individual-level analysis reported in chapter 3, proposed that individuals with lower levels of economic satisfaction are more likely than are individuals with higher levels of economic satisfaction to oppose a political formula that gives Islam an important role if they are citizens of a country governed by a regime with a strong Islamic connection. As shown in table 3.5b, the hypothesis was not confirmed in a regression analysis based on all respondents when the model also included evaluation of the governing regime. When tested among subsets of respondents, as shown in table 3.6b, it was confirmed in an analysis based on younger men, but not in analyses based on any other subset of respondents.

Although Hypothesis 3b was found to have little explanatory power in the pooled analyses presented in chapter 3, it is possible that this hypothesis, like others tested in pooled analyses, does have a significant impact on attitudes toward political Islam in a number of individual surveys and also, perhaps, that these surveys are disproportionately likely to have been conducted in countries with particular characteristics. In fact, however, this is the case to only a very limited degree. As shown in table 4.21, Hypothesis 3b is confirmed at or below the .05 level of statistical confidence in only four surveys in analyses based on all respondents, in only six surveys in analyses based on younger men—the one respondent subset for which the hypothesis was confirmed in the pooled analysis—and in no surveys in analyses based on the three remaining categories of respondents.

Table 4.21 also lists for all respondents and for each subset of respondents the range of the positive coefficients that indicate the strength of the positive individual-level relationship between economic satisfaction and support for political Islam—or, as stated in Hypothesis 3b, between economic dissatisfaction and opposition to political Islam. Of the forty-two surveys in the dataset that include the items necessary to test Hypothesis 3b, the number in which the test yields a coefficient with a positive value varies from twenty in the case of older men to only twelve in the case of younger women, with the magnitude of the value indicating the strength of the relationship. As in the investigation of country-level conditionalities associated with other individual-level hypotheses, an investigation of whether the relationship posited by Hypothesis 3b is likely to be stronger in particular political, economic, and/or social environments may, again, yield instructive insights about the interaction between individual-level and country-level factors in accounting for variance in support for political Islam.

Among all respondents, the four surveys in which the relationship between economic dissatisfaction and opposition to political Islam is significant at or below the .05 level are all in countries with a lower level of secondary school enrollment, below 69 percent, ten years prior to the conduct of the survey. This is the

Table 4.21. Number of Surveys in which a Positive Relationship between Economic Satisfaction and Support for Political Islam Is Statistically Significant and Range of the Positive Coefficients that Express this Relationship

	All respondents	Younger men	Older men	Younger women	Older women
$p < .001$	—	1	—	—	—
		5.2%			
$p < .01$	2	1	—	—	—
	11.8%	5.2%			
$p < .05$	2	4	—	—	—
	11.8%	21.1%			
$p < .1$	1	1	1	1	—
	5.8%	5.3%	5.0%	8.3%	
Not sig.	12	12	19	11	18
	70.6%	63.2%	95.0%	91.7%	100.0%
Total N (weighted)	17	19	20	12	18
	(16)	(17)	(18)	(11)	(17)
Coefficient from/to	.003/	.012/	.000/	.001/	.000/
	.138	.289	.138	.128	.165

case among 63.6 percent of the surveys in which the relationship is not statistically significant, however, and so, based on chi-square, the relationship is not statistically significant. Based on a comparison of means test in which a continuous measure of lagged secondary school enrollment is used, $p > .1$ as well. Nor does any other country-level attribute specify conditions under which Hypothesis 3b is disproportionately likely to be confirmed.

The seventeen positive coefficients that express the individual-level relationship between economic dissatisfaction and opposition to political Islam among all respondents range from a low of .003 to a high of .138, as shown in table 4.21. Only seven of the surveys that yielded these coefficients were conducted in countries governed by a regime with a religious connection, which is not unexpected given that the pooled analysis based on all respondents presented in chapter 3 did not find support for Hypothesis 3b. There are, however, two other country-level attributes, themselves very strongly intercorrelated, that are related to the positive individual-level coefficients to a statistically significant degree. These are level of political freedom and level of political rights, both based on Freedom House measures. In each case, with $p < .1$, which is an acceptable level of statistical significance given the small N, the value of the coefficient expressing the relationship between economic dissatisfaction and opposition to political Islam is higher, and the individual-level relationship is thus stronger, to the extent that it is based on a survey conducted in a country with greater political openness.

In two instances, among younger men and among younger women, Freedom House measures of political freedom and openness also had a conditioning effect on the inverse relationship proposed in Hypothesis 3a—the proposition that economic dissatisfaction pushes toward *support* for political Islam. It was suggested in these cases that this might be because a more open political environment makes it easier for Islamist opposition movements to organize and disseminate their message and thus gain support for their platform among those who are dissatisfied with their economic situation. But it now appears, interestingly and for reasons about which it is only possible to speculate, that there are also instances in which economic dissatisfaction is disproportionately likely in countries that are more politically open to push toward *opposition* to political Islam.

A possible explanation is that political openness increases the opportunities to seek support for their platform not only for Islamists but also for more secular critics of the status quo and for those who argue that the path advocated by political Islam would not make things better and might actually make them worse. Political openness thus, almost by definition, gives space to a variety of ideological perspectives, not all of which call for political influence to be exercised by Islam. Accordingly, while in some countries where these conditions prevail individuals who are dissatisfied and presumably desire change are disproportionately likely to look to Islam for an alternative to the status quo, in other, more open, political environments these individuals are disproportionately likely to conclude in response to the various political messages being articulated, including, perhaps, the Islamists' own message, that Islam should *not* play a role in government and political affairs.

The takeaway from this analysis, if correct, is that political openness at the country-level conditions the individual-level relationship between economic satisfaction and attitudes toward political Islam in different and essentially opposite ways, strengthening the inverse relationship proposed by Hypothesis 3a in some instances and strengthening the positive relationship proposed by Hypothesis 3b in others. The possibility that this difference in the direction of the individual-level relationship depends on the way that other country-level attributes interact with political openness is a promising avenue for future research.

Younger Men

As shown in table 3.6b, younger men are the one subset of respondents for whom the pooled analysis reported in chapter 3 found support for Hypothesis 3b. As shown in table 4.21, there are nineteen surveys in which the analysis of younger men yielded a positive coefficient, and in six of these the relationship between economic

Table 4.22. Impact of Country's Level of Unemployment (Lagged), Per Capita GDP, and Adult Literacy (Lagged) on the Positive Individual-Level Relationship between Economic Satisfaction and Support for Political Islam among Younger Men

	Model 1	Model 2	Model 3
Higher unemployment (ten-year lag)	.005*	.007***	.007***
	(.003)	(.001)	(.001)
Higher per capita Gross Domestic Product		.102***	.118***
		(.024)	(.023)
Higher adult literacy (ten-year lag)			−.003*
			(.001)
Constant	.007	−.064**	.125
	(.038)	(.027)	(.085)

Note: The dependent variable ranges from .012, indicating little relationship between the two individual-level variables, to .289, indicating a strong positive relationship between economic satisfaction and support for political Islam.
The table presents unstandardized coefficients; standard errors are in parentheses.
* $p < .1$; ** $p < .05$; *** $p < .01$.

dissatisfaction and an unfavorable attitude toward political Islam is statistically significant at or below the .05 level. There is, however, no country-level attribute that defines conditions under which these significant individual-level relationships are disproportionately likely to be found.

The nineteen positive coefficients that express this relationship vary from a low of .012 to a high of .289. Three country-level attributes are related to these coefficients to a statistically significant degree: a lower level of adult literacy lagged by ten years, a higher level of unemployment also lagged by ten years, and higher per capita gross national income. These relationships are shown in table 4.22, which also shows that each country-level attribute conditions the individual-level relationship when the others are held constant. Taken together, these attributes point to an environment in which there is more aggregate wealth but fewer opportunities for individual personal and professional mobility. Under these conditions, apparently defined by a substantial level of real, or at least perceived, economic disparity, increased economic dissatisfaction is disproportionately likely to increase disapproval of political Islam.

It is not surprising that economic dissatisfaction would be intense enough in this environment to have an impact on people's views about the way their country should be governed. It is less clear, however, why this dissatisfaction should push toward opposition to political Islam not only in some countries that are, but even more frequently in countries that are not, governed by a regime with an Islamic connection. Adding further to the puzzle is the finding, presented and discussed above, that for some subsets of respondents, although not for younger men, economic dissatisfaction is disproportionately likely to increase *support* for political Islam in countries where the economic situation is less favorable. The finding that less favorable economic circumstances at the country level in some instances strengthen the relationship proposed by Hypothesis 3a and in other instances strengthen the relationship proposed by Hypothesis 3b may be due to the fact that different indicators define the specific character of an unfavorable economic environment, with the disadvantageous circumstances of ordinary citizens being in the context of greater aggregate wealth in one instance but not the other. Or the direction of the conditioning effect may simply vary from one category of the population to another, which the findings presented here do suggest.

Notwithstanding these ambiguities about the way that unfavorable economic circumstances at the country level and the individual level interact to exert an influence on attitudes toward political Islam, and also notwithstanding uncertainty about the pathways that lie behind the conditioning effect that results from this interaction, among younger men, arguably the category of the population most likely to be concerned about any limitations on opportunities for advancement, the relationship between economic dissatisfaction and opposition to political Islam is disproportionately likely to be stronger to the extent they reside in a country that is more affluent but also is, or at least has been in the recent past, characterized by lower levels of literacy and higher levels of unemployment.

Older Men

For older men, there are twenty surveys in which the test of Hypothesis 3a and Hypothesis 3b yielded a coefficient with a positive value, but in none of these is the individual-level relationship statistically significant at or below the .05 level. The positive coefficients that express the connection between economic dissatisfaction and opposition to political Islam vary from a low of .000 to a high of .138, and there are two country-level attributes that are related to these coefficients to a significant degree. Specially, the coefficient values are higher, and the relationship posited by Hypothesis 3b is thus stronger, in countries that, at the time they were surveyed, were more politically free and had a lower level of economic inequality. Based on Spearman's rho, $p=.016$ for political freedom and $p=.079$ for economic equality. Also, as shown in table 4.23, the relationship between each country-level attribute and the individual-level coefficients remains significant in a regression analysis that includes both attributes, and in fact the interaction between them makes the impact of each even stronger. As in all other cross-survey analyses, weights to adjust for population overlap in countries surveyed only a few years apart have been included.

Table 4.23. Impact of Country's Level of Political Freedom and Economic Inequality on the Positive Individual-Level Relationship between Economic Satisfaction and Support for Political Islam among Older Men

	Model 1	Model 2	Model 3
Greater political freedom	.037**		.042***
	(.016)		(.014)
Greater economic		−.004	−.005**
inequality		(.002)	(.002)
Constant	−.017	.188*	.156*
	(.024)	(.092)	(.076)

Note: The dependent variable ranges from .000, indicating no relationship between the two individual-level variables, to .138, indicating a relatively strong positive relationship. Higher scores on the UNDP Economic Inequality (GINI) Index indicate greater inequality. The table presents unstandardized coefficients; standard errors are in parentheses.
$* p < .1; ** p < .05; *** p < .01.$

Once again, it is only possible to speculate about the attitude-shaping dynamics that lie behind these findings about country-level conditionalities. Several elements suggest themselves, some of which are counterintuitive but which nevertheless offer a causal story that is consistent with the findings reported in table 4.23. Older men are the population category most likely to be familiar with their country's political history and aware of a time when there was less political freedom and greater economic inequality than was the case when they were surveyed. At the same time, being economically dissatisfied, they are probably particularly attuned to their country's present circumstances, including the way it is governed. This pattern of experience, knowledge, and perceptions, if accurate, suggests the possibility that older men who are economically discontent worry that their situation, however unsatisfactory, could and presumably would be substantially worse in a less favorable political and economic environment—indeed, they may fear they would be among those most disadvantaged should the country's overall situation deteriorate.

Although it may seem counterintuitive, this scenario raises the possibility that in a political and economic environment that is relatively favorable in the aggregate, those who are economically dissatisfied, and particularly those who, like older men, have a sense of their country's history, are actually less, not more, predisposed to support ideologies and platforms that represent an alternative to the status quo. Accordingly, Islamism's call for justice and the rule of law is likely to be less salient in this environment and may, in fact, be seen as advocating changes that older men who are economically dissatisfied fear would actually worsen their situation.

Younger Women

As shown in table 4.21, there are no surveys in which the relationship posited in Hypothesis b3 is significant at or below the .05 level among younger women, and so there are no country-level attributes that define an environment in which a significant relationship is disproportionately likely to be found. The twelve coefficients that express the individual-level relationship between economic dissatisfaction and opposition to political Islam, or between economic satisfaction and support for Islam to exert influence in political affairs, vary from a low of .001 to a high of .128. There is one country-level attribute that is related to these coefficients to a statistically significant degree. This is human and social development, as measured by the UN's three-item Human Development Index. Specifically, coefficients are higher, indicating a stronger relationship between economic dissatisfaction and opposition to political Islam, to the extent that the HDI is lower, particularly below .625 on the index's 0–1 scale. Based on both Spearman's rho and a difference of means test, $p < .1$.

To ordinary citizens in countries with a low level of social and human development, political Islam might represent a desirable alternative to the status quo, one that promises new policies that would create more opportunities than presently exist. Or, it might be seen as a force for conservatism that gives priority to religion and culture, is less concerned with the need for development, and to that extent actually reinforces the existing economic and political situation. It is likely that both views are present to some degree among those who live in less developed countries and are unhappy with the status quo, with the relative weight of the two perspectives depending on other country-level attributes, including the character of the government, and on the circumstances of different segments of the population. Younger women who reside in countries that are less developed and who are dissatisfied with their economic situation are disproportionately likely to take the view that an Islamic regime is undesirable, and a major reason for this may be concern that policies guided by Islam, despite the religion's call for equality, would in fact restrict the opportunities available to women. Whether this applies not only to younger women but also to older women, whose life circumstances are more likely to be set and stable, is considered below. Men, for their part, at least as a group, would be less likely to have such concerns.

Other factors are probably part of the causal story as well. Nevertheless, it does seem likely that judgments about political Islam are particularly salient but also not homogeneous among individuals who live in societies with lower levels of social and human development and are dissatisfied with their personal circumstances in this environment. This in turn inclines these individuals toward a negative view of political Islam to the extent that they conclude, as many younger women apparently do, that Islamist policies would hinder rather than improve their life chances.

Older Women

Turning finally to older women, there are eighteen surveys in which the relationship between economic dissatisfaction and opposition to political Islam is expressed by a positive coefficient, and in none of these, again, is the relationship
strong enough to be statistically significant. The coefficients themselves, which
range from .000 to .165, are nevertheless strongly correlated with three country-
level attributes that together characterize a political and economic environment
that is not advantageous from the perspective of ordinary citizens, especially older
citizens. These are: a higher level of corruption, as measured by Transparency International, for which Spearman's rho yields $p < .05$; higher unemployment, for
which the relationship is significant at the .1 level; and a higher percentage of the
population under the age of fifteen, for which the relationship is also significant
at the .1 level. Among older women, therefore, the degree to which economic dissatisfaction is associated with opposition to political Islam increases to the extent
that they live in a country that is more corrupt, has a higher level of unemployment, and has a significant youth bulge.

Although the specifics are different, the conditioning dynamics proposed
with respect to younger women appear to be operative among older women as well.
The individual-level relationship proposed by Hypothesis 3b is stronger among
both respondent subsets to the extent that they reside in a country where the circumstances of ordinary citizens are, in the aggregate, disadvantageous. Among
younger women, it is a low level of social and human development that characterizes the environment, whereas among older women the relevant attributes—
corruption and unemployment—concern political economy. The presence of a
youth budge, which may increase the degree to which older women feel marginalized, may also help to explain why the national context makes a difference.

It is not clear from the data whether any kind of aggregate contextual
disadvantage strengthens the degree to which economic dissatisfaction inclines
women toward an unfavorable view of political Islam, or whether the conditioning pathways that link economic and political disadvantage to the judgments of
older women differ in important ways from those that link social and human
underdevelopment to the judgments of younger women. In either case, however,
among older as well as younger women, it appears that women who reside in countries where the aggregate circumstances of ordinary citizens are less favorable
and who are dissatisfied with their own economic situation are disproportionately likely to have a negative view of political Islam, and a major reason for this,
again, is most likely a belief that policies guided by Islam would further limit their
opportunities.

Education and Support for Political Islam

Education is the fourth and final individual-level independent variable considered in chapter 3. Four hypotheses involving education were presented, and the logic that made each plausible enough to be considered was discussed as well. These hypotheses, variations on Hypothesis 4, proposed that an increase in support for political Islam is associated with, respectively, lower levels of education among citizens of countries governed by a secular regime; higher levels of education among citizens of countries governed by a secular regime; lower levels of education among citizens of countries governed by regime with a strong Islamic connection; and higher levels of education among citizens of countries governed by a regime with a strong Islamic connection.

The results of the pooled individual-level analysis reported in chapter 3 only provide support for the hypotheses positing an inverse relationship between education and support for political Islam, hereafter referred to as Hypothesis 4a. In analyses based on all respondents, as shown in tables 3.5a and 3.5b, there is a strong and statistically significant inverse relationship between education and the view that Islam should exert influence in government and political affairs both among citizens of countries with a secular government and among citizens of countries governed by a regime with an Islamic connection. Among subsets of respondents, as shown in tables 3.6a and 3.6b, the relationship is statistically significant among all subsets in countries whose government has an Islamic connection, but only among older individuals, both men and women, in countries governed by a secular regime.

The finding that a lower level of education pushes toward support for political Islam in countries governed by a regime with an Islamic connection, and not only as well as in countries with a secular government but also more consistently among different segments of the population, strongly suggests that education's explanatory power does not reside in considerations of socioeconomic status but rather in considerations of exposure and knowledge. A lower level of education usually involves lower socioeconomic status and limited personal mobility, and this might foster discontent with the status quo and lead to support for a political regime that differs from the one in power. But since a lower level of education pushes toward support for political Islam when the regime in power has an Islamic connection, it is apparently a different dimension of education that provides the explanatory power. Specifically, as discussed more thoroughly in chapter 3, it is almost certainly the more limited exposure to diverse perspectives and sources of knowledge that education provides that animates the pathway linking lower levels of education to greater support for political Islam.

As in the case of other individual-level independent variables, the existence of a statistically significant relationship in the pooled analysis does not mean that

Table 4.24. Number of Surveys in which an Inverse Relationship between Education and Support for Political Islam Is Statistically Significant and Range of the Negative Coefficients that Express this Inverse Relationship

	All respondents	Younger men	Older men	Younger women	Older women
$p < .001$	10	2	3	2	1
	34.4%	8.7%	10.0%	9.0%	3.1%
$p < .01$	3	1	2	1	3
	10.3%	4.3%	6.7%%	4.5%	9.4%
$p < .05$	4	1	4	1	3
	13.8%	4.3%	13.3%	4.5%	9.4%
$p < .1$	1	—	2	1	2
	3.4%		6.7%	4.5%	6.2%
Not sig.	11	19	19	17	23
	37.9%	82.6%	63.3%	77.4%	71.9%
Total N (weighted)	29	23	30	22	32
	(25)	(20)	(25)	(18)	(27)
Coefficient from/to	−.348/	−.365/	−.469/	−.407/	−.363/
	−.005	−.014	−.002	−.003	−.007

the relationship is significant in every one of the surveys included in the pool. Rather, as shown in table 4.24, the number of surveys in which Hypothesis 4a is confirmed at or below the .05 level of statistical confidence ranges from seventeen, when the analysis is based on all respondents, to four, when the analysis is based on younger men or on younger women. Table 4.24 also reports the negative coefficients, indicating an inverse relationship between education and support for political Islam, that result from testing Hypothesis 4a in each of the forty-two surveys in the dataset that contains the necessary items.

The seventeen surveys in which Hypothesis 4a is confirmed at or below the .05 level when all respondents are included in the analysis are disproportionately likely to have been conducted in countries with greater political rights and, as measured ten years prior to the time of the survey, lower levels of unemployment. Based on Spearman's rho, the association between each of these country-level attributes and the inverse individual-level relationship between education and support for political Islam is significant at the .1 level. When both variables are included in a binary logistic regression analysis, the relationship associated with political rights becomes more robust, falling just short of $p < .05$, whereas for unemployment, $p > .1$ and is not significant.

The importance of political openness in accounting for variance in the strength of the inverse relationship between education and support for political

Table 4.25. Impact of Country's Level of Political Freedom and Female Secondary School Enrollment on the Inverse Individual-Level Relationship between Education and Support for Political Islam among All Respondents

	Model 1	Model 2	Model 3
Greater political freedom	−.059*		−.057*
	(.030)		(.029)
Higher female secondary school enrollment		.063*	.060*
		(.038)	(.036)
Constant	−.024	−.154***	−.068
	(.048)	(.032)	(.053)

Note: Values of the dependent variable ranges from −.348, indicating a strong inverse relationship between the two individual-level variables, to −.005, indicating little relationship between these variables. Female secondary school enrollment is a dichotomous variable cut at 76.9 percent.

The table presents unstandardized coefficients; standard errors are in parentheses.

* $p < .1$; ** $p < .05$; *** $p < .01$

Islam is also reflected in cross-survey analyses that treat the negative coefficients expressing this relationship as the dependent variable. As reported in table 4.24, the twenty-nine coefficients range from −.348 to −.005, and two of the relevant Freedom House measures in the dataset—degree of political freedom and degree of political rights—are related to these coefficients to a statistically significant degree. In both cases, the values of the negative coefficients decrease, indicating a stronger individual-level relationship, as a function of greater political openness. In addition, the coefficients also decrease as a function of lower levels of female secondary school enrollment. Based on Spearman's rho, $p < .1$ for each of these three country-level attributes. None of the attributes has statistical significance when all three are included in an OLS regression analysis. The only regression analysis in which two attributes yield probabilities that are significant, indicating independent explanatory power, is shown in table 4.25. These attributes, for which $p < .1$ in each case, are greater political freedom and lower female secondary school enrollment. The stronger relationship is with political freedom, for which $p = .061$.

The main finding suggested by these analyses is that the explanatory power of education, and a lower level of education in particular, increases in more open political environments. A lower level of unemployment and a lower level of female secondary school enrollment also seem to have some impact, although one indicates a higher level of development and the other a lower level of development, which may not be entirely inconsistent since they refer to different dimensions of development. The relationships associated with these latter attributes are less robust, however, and in at least one case the relationship loses its statistical significance in a multivariate analysis. Focusing then on political openness, the causal connection to which the analysis points may be, perhaps, that discussion and debate about governance and public policy are encouraged, or at least tolerated, to a greater degree in countries that are more free and have more political rights. Less well-educated individuals in this environment, given their more limited exposure to the diverse perspectives and sources of knowledge that education provides, will tend to respond to the greater salience of questions about governance by looking to something familiar, in this case Islam, when thinking about how their country should be governed.

Younger Men

There are twenty-three surveys in which the pooled analysis testing hypotheses about education with the responses of younger men yields a negative coefficient. As shown in table 4.24, these coefficients vary from −.365 to −.014, and in four instances the relationship they express is significant at or below the .05 level. These four statistically significant relationships, although few in number, are disproportionately likely to be found, again, in countries that have more political rights. All four are in countries with more political rights, whereas this is the case in only half of the surveys in which the inverse relationship between education and support of political Islam is not significant. Based on both Spearman's rho and chi-square, both of which are nonparametric statistics, the probability of finding this pattern by chance is below .1. The only country-level attribute that is associated with the negative coefficients that express the relationship posited in Hypothesis 4a is a lagged measure of female secondary school enrollment. With $p < .05$ based on Spearman's rho, coefficient values decrease, indicating a stronger inverse relationship between education and support for political Islam, as a function of decreases in the proportion of girls enrolled in secondary school at a time ten years prior to the conduct of the survey.

As in other cases, it is only possible to speculate about the dynamics that animate these connections between country-level attributes and the explanatory power of education at the individual level of analysis. The pathway associated with more political rights probably involves the greater salience of political discourse suggested above in the discussion of findings based on the analysis of all respondents. The reason this is important among younger men may be that they represent a segment of the population that is particularly attuned to their country's political situation, men tending to be more interested in politics than women and younger individuals being more concerned about the future than older persons. If so, the character and relative openness of the political environment may increase the degree to which younger men reflect on questions of governance; and if they are less well educated, their more parochial perspective, in relative terms and other things being equal, will predispose them to think about political formulae in terms of Islam.

A lagged measure of female secondary school enrollment also specifies conditions under which the inverse relationship between education and support for political Islam is stronger among younger men. As noted above, although the measure was not lagged, this had an impact on the explanatory power of education among all respondents as well. No particularly persuasive pathway associated with this conditioning effect suggests itself, but one possibility is that low female secondary school enrollment indicates a lower level of social development. This in turn may mean that information about diverse political and cultural norms are less broadly diffused and thus even less likely to become familiar to individuals who are not introduced to them through education.

Older Men

There are thirty surveys in which tests of the explanatory power of education yield a negative coefficient in analyses based on older men, and in nine of these surveys the inverse relationship between education and support for political Islam is significant at or below the .05 level. These significant relationships are disproportionately likely to be found in countries with lower levels of social and human development in two interrelated respects: lower life expectancy and, again, lower female secondary school enrollment. Both Spearman's rho and chi-square show these relationships to be statistically significant, with $p < .05$ in the case of life expectancy, as illustrated in table 4.26. Consistent with this pattern, lower scores on the UN Human Development Index, indicating a lower level of development, are associated with lower (higher negative) values of the coefficients that express the inverse relationship between education and support for political Islam. Finally, in contrast to the findings about younger men, the coefficient values again decrease, indicating a stronger inverse individual-level relationship, as a function of decreases in the degree to which a country has greater civil liberties. Each of these latter findings about the connection between a country-level attribute and the inverse individual-level relationship between education and support for political Islam is significant at the .1 level.

To the extent that the pathway pertaining to lower development suggested above is plausible, it appears that it also applies to older men. Offered to encourage further reflection and additional research, the argument, or speculation, is that lower levels of social and human development bring greater persistence of traditional or parochial ideas pertaining to governance and fewer opportunities unrelated to education to become familiar with alternative or newer political forms and perspectives. As a result, less well-educated individuals, including older men, will be more likely in this environment than in countries with higher levels

Table 4.26. Impact of Country's Level of Life Expectancy on the Inverse Individual-Level Relationship between Education and Support for Political Islam among Older Men

		Relationship not statistically significant ($p > .05$)	Relationship statistically significant ($p < .05$)
Life expectancy	Lower	7 33.3%	7 77.8%
	Higher	14 66.7%	2 22.2%
		$N = 30, p = .032$	

Note: Probabilities are based on chi-square values that were computed with weighting, whereas actual rather than weighted frequencies are shown. Life expectancy is cut at 71.4 years.

of development to look to Islam when reflecting on how their country should be governed.

Findings pertaining to civil liberties reveal a potentially instructive difference in the way that political climate conditions the explanatory power of education among older men and younger men. Among younger men, as reported, and in the analysis based on all respondents as well, the inverse relationship between education and support for political Islam is more likely to be strong and/or statistically significant in countries that are more politically open. By contrast, among older men, this relationship is more likely to be stronger in countries that are less politically open. The indicators of political openness used in the two analyses are not the same; among younger men, degree of political rights has a conditioning effect, whereas it is degree of civil liberties that has this effect among older men.

While the difference in indicators might account for dissimilar findings among younger men and older men, it is more likely that degree of political rights and degree of civil liberties are both adequate measures of general political openness and, therefore, that different conditioning dynamics are in fact operating among the two subsets of male respondents. If this is the case, the pathway linking country-level and individual-level explanatory factors among older men does not involve the greater salience of political discourse that is present in more open political systems, as proposed in the discussion of younger men. Rather, perhaps, it may be that the presence of more political restrictions reduces opportunities to articulate and disseminate information about diverse political formulae, and this, especially in societies that have lower levels of social and human development, increases the likelihood that less well-educated individuals, perhaps especially if they are older and less likely to use newer technologies to acquire information, will be disproportionately likely to look to Islam when thinking about matters of governance.

Younger Women

Analyses testing Hypothesis 4a among younger women yield twenty-two negative coefficients, four of which are strong enough to indicate an inverse relationship between education and support for political Islam that is statistically significant. As in the case of younger men, and in contrast to findings based on the
analysis of older men, these significant relationships are disproportionately likely
to be found in countries that are more politically open. Both a higher level of political freedom and a higher degree of civil liberties are strongly correlated with
the presence of a statistically significant individual-level relationship, with Spearman's rho yielding $p < .01$ in the case of political freedom. All four of the surveys
in which Hypothesis 4a is confirmed at or below the .05 level are in countries that
are partly free as opposed to not free, whereas only 38.9 percent of the surveys in
which Hypothesis 4a is not confirmed were conducted in partly free countries.
Using chi-square to assess this comparison, $p = .034$, with, as always, weights for
population overlap included.

Three country-level attributes related to social and human development also
specify an environment in which the relationship posited by Hypothesis 4a is disproportionately likely to be significant among younger women. These are overall
secondary school enrollment, female secondary school enrollment, and adult literacy, and in each case it is a lower level of development that is associated with
the presence of a statistically significant individual-level relationship. The strongest conditioning impact is associated with low female secondary school enrollment, with $p < .05$ based on Spearman's rho. In the case of the other two indicators of a low level of development, $p < .1$.

Country-level attributes indicating greater political openness and lower
social and human development are also related to a statistically significant degree
to the negative coefficients that express the connection between a lower level of
education and a more favorable attitude toward political Islam. The twenty-two
coefficients themselves vary from a low of −.407 to a high of −.003, with lower
(higher negative) coefficient values indicating a stronger inverse relationship. With
respect to development, in addition to lower overall secondary school enrollment,
lower female secondary school enrollment, and lower adult literacy, the negative
coefficients are also related to a statistically significant degree to a level of unemployment that is above 14 percent. Given that subsets of these country-level attributes pertain to the same broader concept, and specifically to political openness
and to low social and human development, respectively, their associations with coefficients expressing the strength of the relationship between education and support
for political Islam, while statistically significant in each case, are not entirely independent of one another.

The country-level attributes that condition the inverse individual-level relationship between education and support for political Islam among younger women

are the same, at least with respect to the more abstract concepts of which they are indicators, as those found to have an impact on this relationship among younger men. Specifically, presumably involving the pathways and conditioning dynamics proposed above, the degree to which a lower level of education pushes toward support for political Islam is disproportionately likely to be significant, or at least strong, among individuals who reside in countries that are more politically open and have a lower level of social and human development. This pattern is more consistent and involves more country-level attributes in the case of younger women, however; and this suggests that the greater salience of political discourse that comes with political openness and the reduced exposure to and diffusion of diverse perspectives that tend to characterize less developed societies condition the explanatory power of education more strongly among some subset of individuals than others. One reason that these conditioning effects have a greater impact among less well-educated younger women may be that, as a group and relative to less well-educated younger men, they are less engaged in the public sphere through work outside the home or participation in civil society organizations and thus even less likely than their male counterparts to have acquired through other means the knowledge, insights, and understandings that education usually transmits.

Older Women

There are thirty-two surveys in which a test of the explanatory power of education among older women yields a negative coefficient, and seven of these express a relationship that is strong enough to be statistically significant at or below the .05 level. The coefficients, as reported in table 4.24, range from a low of −.363 to a high of −.007, with lower (higher negative) values indicating that less education pushes more strongly toward a positive attitude toward political Islam. The country-level attributes that have a conditioning effect on this relationship among older women are for the most part those that have this effect in the case of other subsets of respondents.

Country-level attributes that specify conditions under which Hypothesis 4a is disproportionately likely to be statistically significant among older women are low life expectancy, low overall secondary school enrollment, and low female secondary school enrollment, all three of which are indicators of a low level of social and human development. For each attribute, as illustrated by the findings about female secondary school enrollment shown in table 4.27, six of the seven statistically significant individual-level relationships are in countries with a lower level of development. Based on both Spearman's rho and chi-square, $p < .01$ for female secondary school enrollment and $p < .05$ for the other two attributes. All three of these country-level attributes that are indicators of social and human development are also related to a statistically significant degree to the negative coefficients that

Table 4.27. Impact of Country's Level of Female Secondary School Enrollment on the Inverse Individual-Level Relationship between Education and Support for Political Islam among Older Women

		Relationship not statistically significant ($p > .05$)	Relationship statistically significant ($p < .05$)
Female secondary school enrollment	Lower	6 24.0%	6 85.7%
	Higher	19 76.0%	1 14.3%
		$N=32, p=.003$	

Note: Probabilities are based on chi-square values that were computed with weighting, whereas actual rather than weighted frequencies are shown. Female secondary school enrollment is cut at 76.9 percent.

Table 4.28. Impact of Country's Level of Political Rights and Level of Female Secondary School Enrollment on the Inverse Individual-Level Relationship between Education and Support for Political Islam among Older Women

	Model 1	Model 2	Model 3
Greater political rights	−.040** (.018)		−.032** (.017)
Higher female secondary school enrollment		.090** (.036)	.076* (.035)
Constant	−.346*** (.101)	−.183*** (.029)	−.352*** (.094)

Note: The dependent variable ranges from −.363, indicating a strong inverse relationship between the two individual-level variables, to −.007, indicating little relationship between these variables. The table presents unstandardized coefficients; standard errors are in parentheses.
* $p < .1$; ** $p < .05$; *** $p < .01$.

express the individual-level connection between a lower level of education and support for political Islam.

In addition, again as in the case of other respondent subsets, with the exception of older men, an indicator of political openness, in this case degree of political rights, also has a conditioning effect. Specifically, coefficient values decrease, indicating a stronger individual-level relationship, as the rating provided by Freedom House moves from a lesser to a greater degree of political rights. Thus, greater political openness as well as lower levels of social and human development specify an environment in which less education is disproportionately likely to push ordinary citizens toward the view that Islam should play a role in government and political affairs. Further, although this is not the case in multivariate analyses involving all combinations of country-level attributes, table 4.28 indicates that these relationships have independent conditioning effects. Using the Freedom House measure of political rights and female secondary school enrollment as a measure of development, the table presents the results of an OLS regression analysis and shows that each country-level attribute is significantly related to coefficients that express the explanatory power of education when the other country-level attribute is included in the analysis and held constant.

With the partial exception of older men, the same country-level attributes condition the individual-level relationship between a lower level of education and a higher level of support for political Islam. In all cases, the inverse relationship between education and the view that Islam should play a role in government and political affairs is stronger and more likely to be statistically significant in countries that are more politically open and in countries that have a lower level of social and human development. The partial exception to this general finding is that among older men political openness decreases, rather than increases, the likelihood of a stronger and significant individual-level relationship.

Several suggestions have been offered about the attitude-influencing mechanisms that animate the connection between country-level and individual-level factors, education in this case, that have been found to have explanatory power. Although these are only speculations and go beyond the data, they provide a point of departure for thinking about *why* it should be the case that in certain political and social environments, less well-educated men and women are much more likely than their better-educated conationals to support political Islam.

Conclusion

What We Know and What Comes Next

Among the various traditions in scholarship about Islam is the view that the religion imposes a common ideological imprint on Muslim societies, or at least on those where Muslims are the majority, and that, as a result, it is possible to talk in broad terms about an "Islamic personality" and a collective predisposition that "Islam" produces among Muslim publics. This approach assumes that there is a widely shared understanding of Islamic doctrine, that this in turn fosters uniformity through the institutions and symbols that it embeds in Muslim society, and that for this reason religion is the principal determinant of the way that Muslims think and act. Scholarship in this essentialist tradition has become somewhat less common, and more frequently challenged, in recent years, but is reflected in studies by prominent analysts who have been and frequently continue to be influential. Thus, for example, in seeking to explain historical trends and differences between the Muslim world and the West, various scholars have looked to Islam and argued that the religion is hostile to capitalism and to democracy.

The present study departs from this perspective. While recognizing the value in some of the studies in this scholarly tradition, and while not suggesting that Islam, as Islam, has no explanatory power whatsoever, the findings presented here demonstrate that powerful and probably better explanations are to be found by focusing on variations in the way Islam and its political salience are understood and valued, both within and across societies in the Muslim world. This study thus has proceeded on the assumption, which is supported by its findings, that neither is there a uniform "Muslim" character, at the level of either individuals or societies, nor are explanations of normative and behavioral orientations to be found only, or even primarily, in the character of Islam. Rather than seeking to identify and employ for explanatory purposes the common predispositions to which Islam is presumed to give rise, this analysis has emphasized variance and sought to account for it. A range of explanatory mechanisms have been considered, with the aim of identifying both the particular segments of the population to whom and the particular societal environments in which each mechanism is disproportionately likely to be operative.

Principal Findings and Future Research

This emphasis on variance and a rejection of essentialist and one-size-fits-all explanations does not mean that Islam is unimportant. On the contrary, Islam is present and significant in most Muslim-majority societies in the Middle East and North Africa. A sizeable majority of ordinary citizens—about two-thirds of the population, according to the survey findings reported here—are religious, with the proportion who report praying daily approaching 90 percent; only 10–15 percent are not religious. When asked how they identify themselves, about 70 percent select "above all a Muslim" when responding to a question that asks "Which of the following best describes you?" Only about 20 percent select the nationality of their country, saying "above all I am an Egyptian," or "Iraqi," for example, with only about 10 percent responding "Arab" or another category.

These distributions for the most part are consistent across the many political, economic, and social environments from which the survey data are drawn. Within them, however, and also over time, the picture is one of variation with respect to attitudes toward the role that Islam should play in government and political affairs. Given the degree to which individuals tend to be religious, and also given that Islam is a religion of laws that believers consider to have been divinely revealed for the purpose of governing their community, it is understandable that some would insist, or at least prefer, that their country be governed by a political formula that assigns an important place to Islamic codes, institutions, and authorities. But the extent to which this view is widely held has varied over time in the post–World War II period. And a preference for political Islam is accompanied at the present time by the views of an equal proportion, and sometimes a greater proportion, of ordinary citizens who favor a separation of religion and politics. Thus, there are divergent and often highly contested views about whether there should be a strong connection or, alternatively, a clear separation between Islam and political life.

Taking together the predispositions of the more than 60,000 Muslim respondents in the Carnegie dataset, 43 percent disagree or disagree strongly with the proposition that men of religion should have no influence over the decisions of government, with 6 percent neither disagreeing nor agreeing, and the rest, 51 percent, agreeing strongly or agreeing that men of religion should have no influence over the decisions of government. An approximately similar division of opinion is reflected in responses to several other survey items pertaining to political Islam. Fifty-two percent strongly agree or agree with the proposition that it would be better for their country if more people with strong religious beliefs held public office, while 42 percent disagree strongly or disagree, and the remainder, 6 percent, neither agree nor disagree. Also divided, although slightly skewed in the opposite direction, are responses to an item that states that religious practice is a private matter and should be separated from sociopolitical life. Thirty-nine percent disagree strongly or disagree, while the remainder, except for 5 percent who neither agree nor disagree, reject the proposition and express support for a separation of religion and politics.

The central objective of this study has been to identify and map the determinants of this variation in attitudes about the place that Islam should occupy in government and politics. Four hypotheses were examined, each of which purports to identify individual-level attributes and orientations that play a role in shaping attitudes and predispose ordinary citizens toward or away from support for political Islam. The causal stories from which each is derived were considered as well. The independent variables in these hypotheses are: (1) cultural values, operationalized in terms of views about gender equality; (2) judgments about the governing regime; (3) personal economic circumstances; and (4) education.

This individual-level analysis also considered whether the strength and direction of a proposed variable relationship differ as a function of whether the individual resides in a country governed by an essentially secular regime or a regime with a strong Islamic connection. It also considered the possibility that the explanatory power of each independent variable is not the same among all segments of the population but rather differs across demographic categories based on sex and age. Hypotheses have been tested with all of the independent variables and also control variables, most notably personal religiosity, included in the analysis in order that statistically significant relationships may be presumed to be independent and to strengthen the basis for inferring that these relationships reflect a causal connection.

The explanatory power of all but one of the four hypotheses varies as a function of both regime character and demographic attributes. As a result, the findings reported in chapter 3 are not easily summarized. The exception is the hypothesis that posits that more conservative cultural values push individuals toward greater support for political Islam. Attitudes toward gender equality were employed as an indicator of cultural values more broadly. Regression analyses found that less favorable attitudes toward gender equality are strongly and significantly related to greater support for political Islam and, correspondingly, of course, that more favorable attitudes toward gender equality are strongly and significantly related to greater opposition to political Islam. This relationship holds for younger men, older men, younger women, and older women, and in all cases it holds as well for citizens of countries governed by a secular regime and citizens of countries whose governing regime includes Islamists or otherwise has a strong Islamic connection. The causal story behind this relationship probably involves the motivating expectation that government policies and resource allocations will be less supportive of gender equality to the extent that Islam occupies an important place in political life.

The picture is less consistent with respect to regime evaluation, personal economic circumstance, and education. The hypothesis involving regime evaluation posits that a negative evaluation of the governing regime will lead to a desire for a different kind of government, one that represents a consequential alternative to the one in power, and that an unfavorable assessment of the government will thus push toward support for political Islam in countries governed by secular regimes and away from support for political Islam in countries governed by regimes with an Islamic connection. Interestingly, and perhaps surprisingly, the second half of this two-part causal story has more explanatory power than the first. Among citizens of countries governed by regimes with a strong Islamic connection, such as Saudi Arabia, Iran, and Sudan, but also others where the connection exists but may not be as robust, the relationship between a negative evaluation of the regime and opposition to political Islam is very strong, being statistically significant at the .001 level among respondents in all four of the demographic categories considered.

By contrast, in countries with secular governments, including Egypt, Tunisia, Yemen, and many others, the relationship is statistically significant, and only at the .05 level, among older men but not among individuals in any of the other three demographic categories. It is perhaps not surprising that regime evaluation has the greatest impact on the views of older men, who are probably more politically mature than other population categories and more likely to have a sense of Islam's place in the country's and region's political history. Nevertheless, it is notable, and a subject for further reflection, that an unfavorable judgment of a regime that is secular and in most cases authoritarian does not influence the ideological preferences of younger men, who presumably are the most concerned about the inequality and blocked mobility that contribute to dissatisfaction with the political status quo, and that a negative evaluation of the regime also does not make either younger women or older women disproportionately likely to favor the most consequential, and usually the most readily available, political alternative.

The hypothesis involving economic circumstance mirrors the one involving regime evaluation. It posits that more unfavorable economic circumstances will lead to support for a political formula that constitutes a consequential alternative to the one by which the country is currently ruled, such that economic dissatisfaction will push toward support for political Islam in countries governed by a secular regime and toward opposition to political Islam in countries governed by a regime with an Islamic connection. This hypothesis, too, sometimes does and sometimes does not have explanatory power. For reasons about which it is only possible to speculate, economic dissatisfaction pushes toward support for political Islam among younger women and older women but not among men in either age category in countries with a government that does not have a strong and significant Islamic connection. Since women are more likely than men to be concerned about and responsible for managing the household, including buying food, perhaps this makes them more sensitive to the need to pay bills and put food on the table and hence more likely, to the extent they are more economically dissatisfied, to favor a political formula that differs significantly from the one by which their country is governed.

But this reasoning, if correct, should also apply in countries governed by a regime with an Islamic connection, and that is not the case. In these countries, it is only among younger men that economic dissatisfaction was found to push toward support for an alternative political formula and hence, in this instance, toward an unfavorable opinion of political Islam. While it might be expected that economic dissatisfaction would have the strongest impact on the political assessments of younger men since they are, presumably, those whose lives are most affected by inequality and blocked mobility, this should not be the case only in countries governed by a regime with an Islamic connection. Thus, as with findings about the impact of economic dissatisfaction on the political judgments of women in some environments but not others, it is a matter both for further reflection and to be investigated in future research.

Finally, in addressing the influence of level of education on attitudes toward political Islam, this analysis considered the reasons that both higher education and lower education might predispose individuals to support political Islam. In both political environments, those where a secular government was in power and those where the governing regime had an Islamic connection at the time the survey was conducted, the statistically significant relationship involves an inverse association, meaning that support for political Islam increases as level of education declines. Further, although less well-educated individuals differ from those who are better educated, other things being equal, both in their knowledge and exposure to nontraditional ideas and also in their socioeconomic status and prospects for personal and professional advancement, the fact that less education pushes toward the view that Islam should play a role in government and politics under Islamist regimes as well as under more secular governments strongly suggests that is it the knowledge and exposure aspect of education that drives the relationship.

Educational level has significant explanatory power among all subsets of the population in the pooled analysis of survey data from the countries in the dataset that are governed by a regime with an Islamic connection. But this is not the case among respondents in countries governed by an essentially secular regime. In this case, it is only among older individuals, both men and women, although the relationship is much stronger among women, that persons who are less well educated are disproportionately likely to want Islam to play an important role in the governing of their country. To the extent that the knowledge and exposure consequences of education are the reason for this connection—a connection that may reasonably be presumed to be causal, it is probably because older individuals and especially older women are themselves, other things being equal, more traditional and less likely to use newer social media technologies that might reduce the knowledge and exposure gap between better and less well-educated individuals. The reason why this should be the case only in the pooled analysis of data from countries with a secular government is not immediately self-evident. This is one of a number of intriguing findings from the individual-level analyses about which additional reflection and research would be fruitful.

These findings individually and collectively help to account for the variance in attitudes toward political Islam that exists within and across countries. They do not come together to form a unified theory, however. Indeed, it is not clear that a fully unified theory is possible, since the findings presented in chapter 3 strongly suggest that there is no one-size-fits-all causal story that tells why some men and women would like their country to be governed by a political system that assigns an important place to Islam while others believe that Islam is only relevant to personal practice and should be kept apart from government and politics. These findings may nonetheless be considered building blocks to be used in future efforts to provide more integrated explanations and to investigate the connections between the various individual-level determinants that have been found to have explanatory power. And in the meantime, they provide strong predictive power and a reasonably complete map of the individual-level attributes and orientations, each accompanied by suggestions about the underlying attitude-shaping dynamics, that predispose an individual toward one position or the other about Islam's political role.

Since the findings presented in chapter 3 are based on pooled analyses of data from multiple surveys, it should not be assumed that the findings resulting from these analyses apply in every country at the time it was surveyed. And indeed this is not the case, as shown in the survey-level analyses reported in chapter 4. The purpose of chapter 4 is thus to enlarge the map of factors that play a role in shaping attitudes toward political Islam by identifying country-level attributes that condition the degree to which individual-level determinants have explanatory power. In other words, since the individual-level relationships reported in chapter 3 sometimes are and sometimes are not strong and significant, as already shown by the differences between explanations that apply in countries with, respectively, a secular government and a government with an Islamic connection, it is important to identify and specify in terms of country-level attributes the character of the political, economic, and/or social environments in which attitudes toward gender equality, regime evaluation, personal economic satisfaction, and education are disproportionately likely to push toward a particular judgment about the role Islam should play in political affairs.

Chapter 4 presents a great deal of information about the country-level conditionalities associated with individual-level relationships, and it thus lays a foundation for explanations of variance in judgments about political Islam that are much richer and more complete. For example, opposition to political Islam increases in general among younger women as a function of support for gender equality, which of course means that support for political Islam increases as support for gender equality decreases. But this inverse relationship is disproportionately likely to be strong and significant in countries that have: (1) a lower level of life expectancy, and thus tend to have a lower level of what the UN Development Programme calls "human" development; (2) a greater proportion of school-aged girls enrolled in secondary school; and (3) a smaller proportion of the population under the age of fifteen, and thus have a smaller youth bulge.

Another example of country-attribute conditionalities concerns the finding that support for political Islam increases in general among older men as level of education decreases, and thus decreases as level of education increases. This relationship is disproportionately likely to be strong and significant in countries that have a government that grants its citizens fewer civil liberties and that also have a lower level of female secondary school enrollment and lower life expectancy. Both of the latter two measures are indicators of a lower level of human development.

Deriving coherent causal stories from findings like these is a challenge that can be met to only a limited degree without additional research. It is possible, however, to offer analytical insights, or speculations, that go beyond the data but are nonetheless instructive. Chapter 4 has undertaken to do this wherever propositions that are persuasive, or at least plausible, suggest themselves. With respect to conditionalities associated with the impact of attitudes toward gender equality on judgments about political Islam among younger women, one possibility is that the interaction of a lower level of human development, a smaller youth bulge, and higher female secondary school enrollment creates an environment in which younger women have greater confidence in their future prospects and this, in turn, intensifies opposition to political Islam among those committed to gender equality for fear that Islamist policies will limit their opportunities. With respect to conditionalities associated with the impact of education on judgments about political Islam among older men, it is possible that the presence of more political restrictions reduces opportunities to articulate and disseminate information about diverse political formulae. And, in societies where a lower level of human development brings greater persistence of traditional ideas pertaining to governance, this decreases the likelihood that less well-educated men, if they are older and less likely to use social media technologies that might expose them to new ideas and broaden their political outlook, will look beyond Islam when thinking about the way their country should be governed.

These suggestions about attitude-shaping dynamics that underlie the connection between individual-level determinants and country-level conditionalities build on empirical findings. Nevertheless, they go beyond the data. The findings themselves are sometimes, but only sometimes, based on multivariate analyses. But even in these cases, a small *N* and inadequate controls limit the degree to which the survey-level findings provide a statistical basis for inferring causation. Further, and more important, even if the connections can be assumed to be causal, which in fact they probably are in most or at least many cases, the findings do not by themselves reveal the *reason*s that particular country-level attributes increase the likelihood that a given individual-level determinant will have explanatory power. In other words, only speculations have been offered, and the underlying mechanisms remain to be determined.

But the speculations offered in chapter 4 do provide a basis for moving forward. Each has been provided for the explicit purpose of encouraging further reflection and laying a foundation for future research. Reflections about these and other possible mechanisms and dynamics can be shaped into hypotheses that specify components of the pathway linking country-level conditionalities and individual-level determinants. Thereafter, these propositions can be tested in data-based studies that will, if successful, reduce uncertainty and contribute to a fuller understanding of not only how, but also why, individual-level determinants of attitudes toward political Islam have the greatest explanatory power in particular political, economic, or social environments.

Chapter 4 presents findings and offers interpretations about country-level conditionalities associated with all of the individual-level relationships that analyses presented in chapter 3 show to have a measure of explanatory power across particular subsets of the population. Like the study overall, it thus provides a map that shows where to look for deeper explanations and blocks on which to build in research that seeks to construct integrated multidimensional models.

A New Era?

Among countries as among individuals, there are no one-size-fits-all answers to questions about the position and influence of Islamist political formulae. Not all countries in the Middle East and North Africa experienced to the same degree the trajectory of political Islam described in the introduction. At the same time, taking the region as a whole and focusing on broad ideological currents, the decades since World War II can be divided into different and identifiable periods. The first decades, roughly from the end of the war to the death of Gamal Abdul Nasser in 1970, were characterized by declining interest in Islam both in personal life and as a source of guidance in political affairs. During the 1970s and 1980s, by contrast, Islamist movements gained strength and became increasingly successful in their efforts to build an institutional infrastructure and attract adherents. During the 1990s, following the collapse of the Soviet Union and influenced by what became known as the "third wave" of democratization and growing discontent with the authoritarian regimes governing most of the region, calls for democracy became an important, probably the most important, way that both intellectuals and large numbers of ordinary citizens thought about the political system by which they wished to be governed. There are subplots within the story of each of these periods, and in no case did dominant regional trends characterize to the same degree the political tendencies prevailing in every country. Nevertheless, this periodization offers a useful general description of the region's thinking about political ideologies and political formulae during the years between, say, 1950 and 2010.

During the second decade of the twenty-first century, the region experienced events of sufficient magnitude to raise the question of whether the Middle East and North Africa are now in the early stages of a new era with respect to politics and ideology. With respect to both democracy and political Islam, and also with respect to the connection between them, events triggered by what became known as the Arab Spring have placed this question about periodization on the agenda. For one thing, a number of longstanding secular authoritarian regimes collapsed. For another, in competitive elections in two of these countries—Tunisia and Egypt, which had led and served as exemplars of the Arab Spring—Islamist parties handily won free and fair elections in 2011 but then were forced from office in 2013 amid widespread and often intense public disapproval of their policies and performance. It remains to be seen whether the developments in these countries and the significant political and ideological contests, some of which are violent, taking place elsewhere in the Middle East and North Africa will lead men and women who in the past have supported political Islam to conclude that the religion, or at least those who would govern in its name, should not occupy an important place in government and political affairs after all.

Greater concern for security and stability has been another significant feature of the immediate post–Arab Spring years. The protests of the Arab Spring showed that masses of ordinary citizens were very strongly opposed to the authoritarian regimes ruling their countries and wanted the kind of accountable government that democracy promises. Subsequently, however, uncertainty and even chaos in transitioning countries, as well as sustained violence in some of these same countries and others, most notably Syria but also including Iraq, Libya, and Yemen, appear to have led some individuals to wonder whether democratization requires sacrificing stability and security and to conclude that, if this is indeed the case, democracy may not be so desirable after all. Opinion polls conducted in 2013 and 2014 show some lessening of public support for democracy—although support does remain high overall—and an increase in the proportion of men and women who attach priority to strong leadership.

It is too early to say how events will play out in the countries most affected by these developments, let alone whether they will shape region-wide tendencies in a manner reminiscent of the 1952 coup that brought Nasser to power in Egypt. But it is at least possible that the turbulence and change that have marked much of the region since 2011 are introducing new elements into the search for a compelling political formula in some and perhaps even many countries in the Middle East and North Africa. The growing amount of public opinion data that are now being collected in the region will permit the investigation of whether and in what ways attitudes toward political Islam are changing and whether not only more fully developed but also entirely new causal stories will be needed to understand how individual-level determinants and country-level conditionalities come together to shape the way that ordinary Muslim citizens think about the role their religion should play in government and political affairs.

Notes

Preface

1. David D. Kirkpatrick, "Egyptian Campaign Focuses on Islam's Role in Public Life," *New York Times,* May 11, 2012.
2. Edward Cody, "Tunisia Faces Political Struggle over Islam," *Washington Post,* June 16, 2013.

Introduction

1. Ali Gomaa, "In Egypt's Democracy, Room for Islam," *New York Times,* April 2, 2011.
2. Lecture at the Henry L. Stimson Center, May 9, 2011.
3. Tim Arango, "In Iraq: Bottoms Up for Democracy," *New York Times,* April 16, 2011.
4. Mark Tessler, Amaney Jamal, and Michael Robbins, "Arab Attitudes toward Democracy and Governance: Findings from the 2010–2011 Arab Barometer," *Journal of Democracy* 23 (October 2012): 89–103.
5. John Esposito, *Islam: The Straight Path* (New York: Oxford University Press, 1988), pp. 32–33.
6. Judith Tucker, *Women, Family and Gender in Islamic Law* (New York: Cambridge University Press, 2008), p. 15.
7. For additional discussion of secular education in Egypt during this period, see Albert Hourani, *Arabic Thought in the Liberal Age: 1798–1939* (London: Oxford University Press, 1962), and J. M. Ahmed, *The Intellectual Origins of Egyptian Nationalism* (London: Oxford University Press, 1960).
8. Chedley Khairallah, *Le Mouvement Jeune Tunisien* (Tunis: Bonici, n.d.), pp. 12–14.
9. Leon Carl Brown, "Stages in the Process of Change," in Charles A. Micaud, with Leon Carl Brown and Clement Henry Moore, *Tunisia: The Politics of Modernization* (New York: Praeger, 1964), pp. 9–10.
10. Wael B. Hallaq, *An Introduction to Islamic Law* (New York: Cambridge University Press, 2009), p. 101.
11. Jasper Yeates Brinton, *The Mixed Courts of Egypt* (New Haven, CT: Yale University Press, 1968), pp. 6–12.
12. Nadav Safran, *Egypt in Search of Political Community* (Cambridge, MA: Harvard University Press, 1961), p. 56.
13. Hallaq, *Introduction to Islamic Law,* p. 114.
14. Safran, *Egypt in Search of Political Community,* p. 121.
15. Shafeeq Ghabra, "Islam within Islam," *Common Ground News Service,* September 15, 2009.
16. Leon Carl Brown, "The Role of Islam in Modern North Africa," in Leon Carl Brown, ed., *State and Society in Independent North Africa* (Washington, DC: Middle East Institute, 1966), p. 112.

17. Mark Tessler, William O'Barr, and David Spain, *Tradition and Identity in Changing Africa* (New York: Harper and Row, 1973), p. 279.

18. Ross Baker, *Egypt's Uncertain Revolution under Nasser and Sadat* (Cambridge, MA: Harvard University Press, 1978), pp. 104–105.

19. Kamel S. Abu Jaber, *The Arab Ba'th Socialist Party: History, Ideology and Organization* (Syracuse, NY: Syracuse University Press, 1966), p. 129.

20. Elbaki Hermassi, "Toward a Comparative Theory of Revolution," *Comparative Studies in Society and History* 18 (April 1976): 211–235.

21. John Waterbury, *The Commander of the Faithful* (New York: Columbia University Press, 1970), pp. 34–35.

22. Michael Brett, "Islam in the Maghreb: The Problem of Modernization," *The Maghreb Review* 3 (January–April 1978): 6–9.

23. Sandra Mackey, *The Iranians: Persia, Islam and the Soul of the Nation* (New York: Penguin, 1996), pp. 221–222.

24. John Voll, *Islam: Continuity and Change in the Modern World* (Boulder, CO: Westview Press, 1982), p. 171.

25. See, for example, the chapters in Ali Dessouki, ed., *Islamic Resurgence in the Arab World* (New York: Praeger, 1982).

26. Fouad Ajami, *The Arab Predicament: Arab Political Thought and Practice since 1967* (Cambridge: Cambridge University Press, 1981), p. 52.

27. Ibid., pp. 55, 69.

28. Ziya Onis, "The Political Economy of Islamic Resurgence in Turkey: The Rise of the Welfare Party," *Third World Quarterly* 18 (1997): 756.

29. Guilain Denoeux, "The Forgotten Swamp: Negotiating Political Islam," *Middle East Policy* 9 (June 2002): 60–61.

30. Gwenn Okruhlik, "Understanding Political Dissent in Saudi Arabia," *Middle East Report Online,* October 24, 2001, http://www.merip.org/mero/mero/102401.

31. Guilain Denoeux, *Urban Unrest in the Middle East: A Comparative Study of Informal Networks in Egypt, Iran and Lebanon* (Syracuse, NY: Syracuse University Press, 1993), p. 150.

32. Elbaki Hermassi, "La société tunisienne au miroir islamiste," *MaghrebMachrek* 103 (1984): 39–56.

33. Afsaneh Najmabadi, "Depolitization of a Rentier State: The Case of Pahlavi Iran," in Hazem Beblawi and Giacomo Luciani, eds., *The Rentier State* (London: Croom Helm, 1978).

34. Denoeux, *Urban Unrest in the Middle East,* pp. 159–160.

35. Dale Eickelman, "Communication and Control in the Middle East: Publication and Its Discontents," in Dale Eickelman and Jon Anderson, eds., *New Media in the Muslim World: The Emerging Public Sphere,* 2nd ed. (Bloomington: Indiana University Press, 2003), pp. 38, 40–41.

36. "L'Islam contestataire en Tunisie," *Jeune Afrique,* March 14, 21, and 28, 1979.

37. Annabelle Bottcher, "Islamic Teaching among Sunni Women in Syria," in Donna Lee Bowen and Evelyn Early, eds., *Everyday Life in the Muslim Middle East,* 2nd ed. (Bloomington: Indiana University Press, 2002), p. 291.

38. Emmanuel Sivan, *Radical Islam: Medieval Theology and Modern Politics* (New Haven, CT: Yale University Press, 1985), p. 126.

39. Ibid., p. 125.

40. Ibid., p. 126.

41. James Bill, *The Eagle and the Lion: The Tragedy of American-Iranian Relations* (New Haven, CT: Yale University Press, 1988), p. 185.

42. James Gelvin, *The Modern Middle East: A History* (New York: Oxford University Press, 2005), p. 285.

43. Bill, *The Eagle and the Lion*, p. 217.

44. Ibid., p. 186.

45. Ali Mirsepassi-Ashtiani, "The Crisis of Secular Politics and the Rise of Political Islam in Iran," *Social Text* 38 (Spring 1994): 67.

46. Bill, *The Eagle and the Lion*, p. 218.

47. Mirsepassi-Ashtiani, "The Crisis of Secular Politics," 77.

48. Christopher Alexander, "Opportunities, Organizations and Ideas: Islamists and Workers in Tunisia and Algeria," *International Journal of Middle East Studies* 32 (November 2000): 465–490.

49. Sami Zubaida, "Trajectories of Political Islam: Egypt, Iran and Turkey," *The Political Quarterly* (August 2000): 60.

50. Robin Wright, "Lebanon," in Shireen T. Hunter, ed., *The Politics of Islamic Revivalism: Diversity and Unity* (Bloomington: Indiana University Press, 1988), p. 57.

51. Dirk Vandewalle, "Autopsy of a Revolt: The October Riots in Algeria" (Hanover, NH: Institute of Current World Affairs, 1988).

52. Willis Witter, "Moroccans See Good, Evil in Possible Economic Boom," *Washington Times*, September 22, 1993.

53. Mark Tessler, "Anger and Governance in the Arab World: Lessons from the Maghrib and Implications for the West," *Jerusalem Journal of International Relations* 13 (Fall 1991): 7–33.

54. Mark Tessler, "The Origins of Popular Support for Islamist Movements: A Political Economy Analysis," in John Entelis, ed., *Islam, Democracy, and the State in North Africa* (Bloomington: Indiana University Press, 1997), pp. 97–98.

55. Tessler, "Origins of Popular Support for Islamist Movements," p. 114.

56. Azzedine Layachi and Abdel-kader Haireche, "National Development and Political Protest: Islamists in the Maghreb Countries," *Arab Studies Quarterly* 14 (Spring/Summer 1992): 76.

57. Ibrahim Karawan, "'ReIslamization Movements' According to Kepel: On Striking Back and Striking Out," *Contention* 2 (Fall 1992): 172.

58. Carrie Wickham, *Mobilizing Islam: Religion, Activism and Political Change in Egypt* (New York: Columbia University Press, 2002), pp. 12–14.

59. Amr Hamzawy, "Party for Justice and Development in Morocco: Participation and Its Discontents," *Carnegie Papers*, no. 93 (July 2008): 1.

60. Alexander, "Opportunities, Organizations and Ideas," 466.

61. Azzam S. Tamimi, *Rachid Ghannouchi: A Democrat within Islamism* (Oxford: Oxford University Press, 2001), pp. 68–71.

62. François Burgat and William Dowell, *The Islamic Movement in North Africa* (Austin: University of Texas Press, 1993), p. 281; Martin Stone, *The Agony of Algeria* (New York: Columbia University Press, 1997), p. 167.

63. Youssef Ibrahim, "Jordan Feels Change Within as Muslims Pursue Agenda," *New York Times*, December 26, 1992.

64. Abla Amawi, "Democracy Dilemmas in Jordan," *Middle East Report* 174 (January–February 1992): 27.

65. Nathan J. Brown, "Jordan and Its Islamic Movement: The limits of Inclusion?," *Carnegie Papers*, no. 74 (November 2006).

66. Lara Deeb, "Hizballah: A Primer," *Middle East Report Online*, July 31, 2006, http://www.merip.org/mero/mero073106; see also Augustus Richard Norton, *Hezbollah: A Short History* (Princeton, NJ: Princeton University Press, 2007).

67. Jenny White, Islamist Mobilization in Turkey: A Study in Vernacular Politics (Seattle: University of Washington Press, 2002), p. 79.

68. Amr Hamzawy, "Between Government and Opposition: The Case of the Yemeni Congregation for Reform," *Carnegie Papers*, no. 18 (November 2009); Jillian Schwedler, *Faith in Moderation: Islamists Parties in Jordan and Yemen* (Cambridge: Cambridge University Press, 2006).

69. F. Gregory Gause, *Oil Monarchies: Domestic and Security Challenges in the Arab Gulf States* (New York: Council on Foreign Relations, 1994), pp. 91–92, 158–159.

70. Emile Sahliyeh, *In Search of Leadership: West Bank Politics since 1967* (Washington, DC: The Brookings Institution, 1988), pp. 144–147.

71. Glenn Robinson, *Building a Palestinian State: The Incomplete Revolution* (Bloomington: Indiana University Press, 1997), pp. 21–27.

72. Mark Tessler, *A History of the Israeli-Palestinian Conflict* (Bloomington: Indiana University Press, 2009), pp. 694–695.

73. Rami Khouri, "The Arab Dream Won't Be Denied," *New York Times*, December 15, 1990.

74. Gundrun Kramer, "Liberalization and Democracy in the Arab World," *Middle East Report* (January/February 1992): 23.

75. Serene Halasa, "Arab Scholars Call for New Order Based on Democracy, Urge End to Iraq Sanctions," *Jordan Times*, May 30–31, 1991.

76. Amaney Jamal and Mark Tessler, "Dimensions of Democratic Support in the Arab World," *Journal of Democracy* 19 (January 2008): 97–110; also Mark Tessler and Eleanor Gao, "Gauging Arab Support for Democracy," *Journal of Democracy* 16 (July 2005): 83–97.

77. Tessler, Jamal, and Robbins, "Arab Attitudes toward Democracy and Governance," 91.

78. Fares Braizat, "Muslims and Democracy: An Empirical Critique of Fukuyama's Culturalist Approach," in Ronald Inglehart, ed., *Islam, Gender, Culture and Democracy* (Willowdale, ON: de Sitter Publications, 2003), pp. 46–76.

79. *Arab Human Development Report* (New York: United Nations Development Programme, 2005), p. 29.

80. *In Support of Arab Democracy: How and Why?* (New York: Council on Foreign Relations, 2005), p. 10.

81. See Glenn Robinson, "Can Islamists Be Democrats? The Case of Jordan," *Middle East Journal* 51 (Summer 1997): 373–388; also Tarek Masoud, "Are They Democrats? Does It Matter?," *Journal of Democracy* 19 (July 2008): 19–24; Bassam Tibi, "Why They Can't Be Democratic," *Journal of Democracy* 19 (July 2008): 43–48.

82. Lisa Anderson, "Politics in the Middle East: Opportunities and Limits in the Quest for Theory," in Mark Tessler, with Jodi Nachtwey and Anne Banda, eds., *Area Studies and Social Science: Strategies for Understanding Middle East Politics* (Bloomington: Indiana University Press, 1999), p. 6.

83. Marsha Pripstein Posusney and Michele Penner Angrist, eds., *Authoritarianism in the Middle East: Regimes and Resistance* (Boulder, CO: Lynne Rienner, 2005), p. 14.

84. Eva Bellin, "Coercive Institutions and Coercive Leaders," in Posusney and Angrist, *Authoritarianism in the Middle East*, pp. 27–28.

85. Larry Diamond, "Why Are There No Arab Democracies?," *Journal of Democracy* 21 (January 2010): 93.

86. Shadi Hamid, "The Islamist Response to Repression: Are Mainstream Islamists Groups Radicalizing?," *Brookings Doha Center Policy Briefing*, August 2010, p. 7.

87. Ibid., pp. 1, 7.

1. A Two-Level Study of Attitudes toward Political Islam

1. The first part of this discussion draws upon Mark Tessler, *Public Opinion in the Middle East: Survey Research and the Political Orientations of Ordinary Citizens* (Bloomington: Indiana University Press, 2011), introduction.

2. The following volumes provide useful overviews of the status of survey research devoted to Arab political and social orientations in the early and mid-1980s: Monte Palmer, *Survey Research in the Arab World: An Analytical Index* (London: Menas, 1982); Tawfic Farah, ed., *Political Behavior in the Arab States* (Boulder, CO: Westview Press, 1983); Mark Tessler, Monte Palmer, Tawfic Farah, and Barbara Ibrahim, eds., *The Evaluation and Application of Survey Research in the Arab World* (Boulder, CO: Westview Press, 1987). See also Tessler, *Public Opinion in the Middle East.* This volume reprints thirteen public-opinion journal articles based on findings from political attitude research in the Middle East and North Africa carried out since the late 1960s.

3. I. William Zartman, "Political Science," in Leonard Binder, ed., *The Study of the Middle East: Research and Scholarship in the Humanities and Social Sciences* (New York: Wiley, 1976), p. 267. See also Gabriel Ben Dor, "Political Culture Approach to Middle East Politics," *International Journal of Middle East Studies* 8 (January 1977): 43–63.

4. Malcolm Kerr, "Foreword," in Farah, *Political Behavior in the Arab States,* p. xi.

5. Michael Hudson, "The Political Culture Approach to Arab Democratization: The Case for Bringing It Back In, Carefully," in Rex Brynen, Bahgat Korany, and Paul Noble, eds., *Political Liberalization and Democratization in the Arab World* (Boulder, CO: Lynne Rienner, 1995), p. 69.

6. William Quandt, "Hume and Quandt on Contemporary Algeria," *Middle East Policy* 6 (February 1999): 145.

7. Lisa Anderson, "Politics in the Middle East: Opportunities and Limits in the Quest for Theory," in Mark Tessler, ed., with Jodi Nachtwey and Anne Banda, *Area Studies and Social Science: Strategies for Understanding Middle East Politics* (Bloomington: Indiana University Press, 1999), p. 7.

8. Iliya Harik, "Some Political and Cultural Considerations Bearing on Survey Research in the Arab World," in Tessler, Palmer, Farah, and Ibrahim, *Evaluation and Application of Survey Research in the Arab World,* pp. 66–67.

9. Quoted in ibid., p. 68.

10. Mustapha Hamarneh, *Revisiting the Arab Street: Research from Within* (Amman: Center for Strategic Studies, University of Jordan, 2005).

11. Amaney Jamal, *Barriers to Democracy: The Other Side of Social Capital in Palestine and the Arab World* (Princeton, NJ: Princeton University Press, 2007); Amaney Jamal, *Of Empires and Citizens: Pro-American Democracy or No Democracy at All?* (Princeton, NJ: Princeton University Press, 2012); Shibley Telhami, *The World through Arab Eyes: Arab Public Opinion and the Reshaping of the Middle East* (New York: Basic Books, 2013).

12. Daniel Corstange's thesis, "Institutions and Ethnic Politics in Lebanon and Yemen," defended in 2008, won the American Political Science Association's "Best Fieldwork" dissertation award in 2008; Eleanor Gao's thesis, "Diverse But Not Divisive: Tribal Diversity and Public Goods Provision in Jordan," defended in 2013, won the American Political Science Association's award for the best dissertation in the field of urban politics in 2013; Michael D. Robbins's thesis, "Bound by Brand: Opposition Party Support under Electoral Authoritarians," defended in 2013, won the American Political Science Association's award for the best dissertation in the field of religion and politics in 2013.

13. See http://www.arabbarometer.org/. I am a member of the Arab Barometer Steering Committee.

14. See http://www.globalbarometer.net/.

15. See http://worldvaluessurvey.org/.

16. Steven Kull, *Feeling Betrayed: The Roots of Muslim Anger at America* (Washington, DC: Brookings Institution Press, 2011).

17. The reports are distributed by the Brookings Institution. A summary of the 2010 report is available at http://www.brookings.edu/reports/2010/0805_arab_opinion_poll_telhami.aspx. Sample sizes range from 500 to 800, and data were collected in two or three major cities in each country. Summaries of key findings and some of the data going back to 2003 are available at http://sadat.umd.edu/new%20surveys/surveys.htm.

18. See Tessler, *Public Opinion in the Middle East*.

19. The construction of this unique dataset has been made possible by a generous Islamic Scholar award from the Carnegie Corporation of New York. The dataset is being deposited with the Inter-University Consortium for Political and Social Research at the University of Michigan and the Association of Religion Data Archives at Pennsylvania State University for use by others.

20. See Karen Long Jusko and W. Phillips Shively, "Applying a Two-Step Strategy to the Analysis of Cross-National Public Opinion Data," *Political Analysis* 13, no. 4 (2005): 327–344; and Karen Long Jusko, Orit Kedar, and W. Phillips Shively, "Strategies for Analysis of Multi-Country Individual-Level Data," *Comparative Politics Newsletter* 16, no. 2 (2005): 5–7. These authors also discuss other strategies for assessing the impact of macro-level factors on within-system micro-level relationships.

2. Islam in the Lives of Ordinary Muslims

1. Bernard Lewis, *The Shaping of the Modern Middle East* (New York: Oxford University Press, 1994), p. 22.

2. Nicholas S. Hopkins and Saad Eddin Ibrahim, *Arab Society: Class, Gender, Power and Development* (Cairo: American University in Cairo Press, 1997), p. 499.

3. Donna Lee Bowen and Evelyn A. Early, *Everyday Life in the Muslim Middle East* (Bloomington: Indiana University Press, 2002), pp. 3–4.

4. Lebanon is a strong outlier on the question of identity. Eighty-one percent of the Muslim respondents in the 2007 Lebanese survey selected nationality as the most important component of their identity; only 6 percent stated "above all I am a Muslim." For this reason, responses to the item on identity in the 2007 Lebanese survey have not been included when preparing the other tables in this chapter. The question about identity was not asked in the 2010 Lebanese survey.

5. In Saudi Arabia, 10 to 15 percent of the population is Shi'i, and Saudi Arabia was included among the countries with a significant Shi'i population in a separate comparative analysis. The distributions of personal religiosity in this analysis were very similar to those shown in table 2.2.

6. The two dimensions of development are empirically as well as conceptually distinct. Although the correlation between per capita GDP and the UN Human Development Index is statistically significant, the coefficient is only .180; one-third of the surveys were conducted in countries with a higher rating on one measure and a lower rating on the other measure, rather than a higher rating on both or a lower rating on both. As a result, despite considerable overlap, the two comparisons presented in table 2.3 do not involve identical subsets of countries. There is stronger overlap between the UN Human Development Index and the percentage of

the population living in cities, which was considered in table 2.2. In this case, only five of the countries surveyed are higher on one measure and lower on the other. Despite this overlap, the two attributes are conceptually distinct, and the respective response distributions pertaining to personal religiosity are not identical.

7. For a detailed discussion of the debate leading up to the reforms in Morocco, see Léon Buskens, "Recent Debates on Family Law Reform in Morocco: Islamic Law as Politics in an Emerging Public Sphere," *Islamic Law and Society* 10, no. 1 (2003): 70–131. For a more general account of the debates surrounding legal reform in Muslim countries, see Abdullahi Ahmed An-Na'im, *Islam and the Secular State: Negotiating the Future of Shari'a* (Cambridge, MA: Harvard University Press, 2008).

8. Buskens, "Recent Debates," 103–104. Women demonstrating in opposition to the reforms carried banners with slogans like "Yes to integration of women in development. No to Westernization and submission." The head of the women's association affiliated with Morocco's Islamist party told interviewers that "we are not against reform, but this should be carried out on the basis of the Qur'an and the Sunna."

9. For a study that uses survey data to examine this question in an Arab country, see Mark Tessler, Carrie Konold, and Megan Reif, "Political Generations in Developing Countries: Evidence and Insights from Algeria," *Public Opinion Quarterly* 68 (Summer 2004): 184–216.

10. Erwin I. J. Rosenthal, *Islam and the Modern National State* (Cambridge: Cambridge University Press, 1965), p. 24.

11. Wael B. Hallaq, *Shari'a: Theory, Practice, Transformations* (New York: Cambridge University Press, 2009), pp. 368–369.

12. John Esposito and Natana J. DeLong-Bas, *Women in Family Law* (Syracuse, NY: Syracuse University Press, 2001), pp. 153–154.

13. For a fuller discussion, see Hallaq, *Shari'a*, pp. 110–111.

14. Ali Unal and Alphonso Williams, *Advocate of Dialogue: Fethullah Gülen* (Fairfax, VA: The Fountain, 2000), p. 52; quoted in John Voll, "Fethullah Gülen: Transcending Modernity in the New Islamic Discourse," in M. Hakan Yavuz and John L. Esposito, eds., *Turkish Islam and the Secular State: The Gülen Movement* (Syracuse, NY: Syracuse University Press, 2003), p. 238.

15. Responses of "Strongly agree" and "Agree" have been combined, as have responses of "Disagree" and "Strongly disagree." Six surveys also offered the response option of "Neither agree nor disagree," and this response was chosen by some of the respondents. In no case was this response option chosen by more than 5 percent of all respondents in the dataset, however, with 2 percent or 3 percent being much more common. In order to make attitudinal tendencies stand out more clearly, these respondents are not included in the tables dealing with Islamic interpretation.

16. See Philip Converse, "The Nature of Belief Systems in Mass Publics," in David Apter, ed., *Ideology and Discontent* (New York: The Free Press, 1964), p. 208.

17. See note 5 above regarding a separate analysis that includes Saudi Arabia.

18. See note 6 above for information about the relationship between the two dimensions of development and also about the relationship between the UN Development Index and the percentage of the population living in cities.

3. Why Individuals Hold Different Views about Islam's Political Role

1. The 3,645 non-Muslim respondents in the dataset are not included in table 3.1. Also excluded are the two surveys in the dataset that do not include questions pertaining to political Islam.

2. Leila Ahmed, *Women and Gender in Islam* (New Haven, CT: Yale University Press, 1992), p. 23. For a useful account of Arab women's labor force participation during this period, see Seteney Shami, Lucine Taminian, Soheir Morsy, Zeinab El Bakri, and El-Wathig Kameir, *Women in Arab Society: Work Patterns and Gender Relations in Egypt, Jordan and Sudan* (Paris: UNESCO, 1990).

3. See Steve Crabtree, "Two-Thirds of Young Arab Women Remain Out of Workforce," *Gallup World*, April 2, 2012, http://www.gallup.com/poll/153659/two-thirds-young-arab-women-remain-workforce.aspx.

4. Ann Mayer, *Islam and Human Rights: Tradition and Politics* (Boulder, CO: Westview Press, 2006); Abdullahi Ahmed An-Na'im, *Islamic Family Law in a Changing World: A Global Resource Book* (New York: Zed Books, 2002).

5. Yvonne Haddad, Byron Haines, and Ellison Findly, *The Islamic Impact* (Syracuse, NY: Syracuse University Press, 1984), p. 97. See also Mohammed Arkoun, *Rethinking Islam: Common Questions, Uncommon Answers* (Boulder, CO: Westview Press, 1994), pp. 60–61.

6. For a data-based study arguing that the subordination of women is a major reason for the absence of democracy in many Muslim countries, see Steve Fish, "Islam and Authoritarianism," *World Politics* 55 (October 2002): 4–37. See also Ronald Inglehart and Pippa Norris, "The True Clash of Civilizations," *Foreign Policy* 135 (March–April 2003): 62–70.

7. Denis Sullivan and Sana Abed-Kotob, *Islam in Contemporary Egypt: Civil Society vs. the State* (Boulder, CO: Lynne Rienner, 1999), p. 111; for historical perspective on women's activism in pursuit of legal reform, see Judith Tucker, *Women, Family and Gender in Islamic Law* (Cambridge: Cambridge University Press, 2008), p. 32.

8. Bruce Rutherford, *Egypt after Mubarak: Liberalism, Islam, and Democracy in the Arab World* (Princeton, NJ: Princeton University Press, 2008), p. 58.

9. Léon Buskens, "Recent Debates on Family Law Reform in Morocco: Islamic Law As Politics in an Emerging Public Sphere," *Islamic Law and Society* 10, no. 1 (2003): 70–131.

10. See Stephanie Wilman Bordat and Saida Kouzzi, "The Challenge of Implementing Morocco's New Personal Status Law," *Carnegie Endowment for International Peace Arab Reform Bulletin* 2, no. 8 (2004).

11. Charles Kurzman and Ijlal Naqui, "Do Muslims Vote Islamic?," *Journal of Democracy* 21 (April 2010): 57–58. For a fuller discussion, see Robin Wright, ed., *The Islamists Are Coming: Who They Really Are* (Washington, DC: Woodrow Wilson Center Press, 2012). Wright reports that most Islamist parties today do not embrace theocratic rule, even if they are not willing to adopt a completely Western model of democracy. For an account of the 2004 "reform initiative" of the Egyptian Muslim Brotherhood, see Shadi Hamid, "The Islamist Response to Repression: Are Mainstream Islamist Groups Radicalizing?," *Brookings Doha Center Policy Briefing* (August 2010).

12. Mark Tessler, "The Origins of Popular Support for Islamist Movements: A Political Economy Analysis," in John Entelis, ed., *Islam, Democracy, and the State in North Africa* (Bloomington: Indiana University Press, 1997), pp. 93–126.

13. Ibrahim Karawan, "'ReIslamization Movements' According to Kepel: On Striking Back and Striking Out," *Contention* 2 (Fall 1992): 162.

14. Rami Khouri, "A Lesson in Middle East History and Humanity," *Jordan Times*, May 28, 1991.

15. Rami Khouri, "The Arab Dream Won't Be Denied," *New York Times*, December 15, 1990.

16. Dirk Vandewalle, "From the New State to the New Era: Toward a Second Republic in Tunisia," *Middle East Journal* 42 (1988): 617.

17. David Seddon, "The Politics of 'Adjustment' in Morocco," in Bonnie K. Campbell and John Loxley, eds., *Structural Adjustment in Africa* (New York: St. Martin's Press, 1989), p. 263.

18. Jamal Al-Suwaidi, "Arab and Western Conceptions of Democracy: Evidence from a UAE Opinion Survey," in David Garnham and Mark Tessler, eds., *Democracy, War and Peace in the Middle East* (Bloomington: Indiana University Press, 1995), p. 13.

19. Abdulwahhab El-Affendi, "Islamic Movements: Establishments, Significance and Contextual Realities," in *Islamic Movements: Impact on Political Stability in the Arab World* (Abu Dhabi: Emirates Center for Strategic Studies and Research, 2003), pp. 23, 46.

20. Youssef Ibrahim, "Militant Muslims Grow Stronger as Algeria's Economy Grows Weaker," *New York Times*, June 25, 1990.

21. Amaney Jamal, "Actors, Public Opinion and Participation," in Ellen Lust, ed., *The Middle East* (Washington, DC: CQ Press, 2011), pp. 204–205.

22. See, for example, Emile Nakhleh, *A Necessary Engagement: Reinventing America's Relations with the Muslim World* (Princeton, NJ: Princeton University Press, 2009), p. 32. See also Ellen Lust-Okar, "Elections under Authoritarianism: Preliminary Lessons from Jordan," *Democratization* 13 (2006): 456–471.

23. See, for example, Carrie Wickham, *Mobilizing Islam: Religion, Activism and Political Change in Egypt* (New York: Columbia University Press, 2002); Jenny White, *Islamist Mobilization in Turkey: A Study in Vernacular Politics* (Seattle: University of Washington Press, 2002); Melanie Cammett and Sukriti Issar, "Bricks and Mortar Clientelism: The Political Geography of Welfare in Lebanon," *World Politics* 62 (July 2010): 381–421; and Ellen Lust, "Institutions and Governance," in Ellen Lust, ed., *The Middle East* (Washington, DC: CQ Press, 2011), pp. 183–184.

24. See, for example, Amaney Jamal, *Of Empires and Citizens: Pro-American Democracy or No Democracy at All?* (Princeton, NJ: Princeton University Press, 2012), p. 85.

25. See also, for example, Mona El-Ghobashy, "The Metamorphosis of the Egyptian Muslim Brothers," *International Journal of Middle East Studies* 37 (2005): 373–395.

26. Ronald Inglehart, Miguel Basanez. Jaime Diez-Medrano, Loek Halman, and Ruud Luijkz, *Human Beliefs and Values: A Cross-Cultural Sourcebook Based on the 1999–2002 Values Surveys* (Mexico City: Siglo XXI Editores, 2004), p. E079.

27. Ibid., p. F104.

28. Mark Tessler, "Religion, Religiosity and the Place of Islam in Political Life: Insights from the Arab Barometer Surveys," *Middle East Law and Governance* 2 (2010): 221–252.

29. Although this is by no means a new phenomenon, journalistic reports emphasize the importance of these well-educated but unemployed individuals in recent protests in Tunisia and Morocco. See, for example, "Maroc: Les 'diplômés chômeurs' manifestent à la veille des élections," *Le Monde Afrique*, November 24, 2011; and "L'employabilité des diplômés de l'enseignement supérieur," *The North African Journal*, August 26, 2013.

30. Robert Lee, *Religion and Politics in the Middle East* (Boulder, CO: Westview Press, 2014), pp. 35–36.

31. See, for example, Lisa Blaydes and Drew Linzer, "The Political Economy of Women's Support for Fundamentalist Islam," *World Politics* 60 (July 2008): 576–609; Mark Tessler, "Islam and Democracy in the Middle East: The Impact of Religious Orientations on Attitudes Toward Democracy in Four Arab Countries," *Comparative Politics* 34 (April 2002): 337–354; Mark Tessler and Jodi Nachtwey, "Explaining Women's Support for Political Islam: Contributions from Feminist Theory," in Mark Tessler, with Jodi Nachtwey and Anne Banda, eds., *Area Studies and Social Science: Strategies for Understanding Middle East Politics* (Bloomington: Indiana University Press, 1999), pp. 48–61.

32. The following surveys were conducted in countries governed by a regime with a strong Islamic connection: Iran 2005; Iraq 2004, 2006, and 2011; Lebanon 2007; Palestine 2006; Saudi Arabia 2003 and 2011; Sudan 2011; Turkey 2001 and 2007.

33. Ibrahim, "Militant Muslims Grow Stronger."

34. Blaydes and Linzer, "Political Economy of Women's Support."

Bibliography

Abu Jaber, Kamel S. *The Arab Ba'th Socialist Party: History, Ideology and Organization.* Syracuse, NY: Syracuse University Press, 1966.

Ahmed, Leila. *Women and Gender in Islam.* New Haven, CT: Yale University Press, 1992.

Ajami, Fouad. *The Arab Predicament: Arab Political Thought and Practice since 1967.* Cambridge: Cambridge University Press, 1981.

Alexander, Christopher. "Opportunities, Organizations and Ideas: Islamists and Workers in Tunisia and Algeria." *International Journal of Middle East Studies* 32 (November 2000): 465–490.

Al-Suwaidi, Jamal. "Arab and Western Conceptions of Democracy: Evidence from a UAE Opinion Survey." In David Garnham and Mark Tessler, eds., *Democracy, War and Peace in the Middle East.* Bloomington: Indiana University Press, 1995, pp. 82–115.

Amawi, Abla. "Democracy Dilemmas in Jordan." *Middle East Report* 174 (January–February 1992): 26–29.

Anderson, Lisa. "Politics in the Middle East: Opportunities and Limits in the Quest for Theory." In Mark Tessler, with Jodi Nachtwey and Anne Banda, eds., *Area Studies and Social Science: Strategies for Understanding Middle East Politics.* Bloomington: Indiana University Press, 1999, pp. 1–10.

An-Na'im, Abdullahi Ahmed. *Islam and the Secular State: Negotiating the Future of Shari'a.* Cambridge, MA: Harvard University Press, 2008.

———. *Islamic Family Law in a Changing World: A Global Resource Book.* New York: Zed Books, 2002.

Arab Human Development Report. New York: United Nations Development Programme, 2005.

Arango, Tim. "In Iraq: Bottoms Up for Democracy." *New York Times,* April 16, 2011.

Arkoun, Mohammed. *Rethinking Islam: Common Questions, Uncommon Answers.* Boulder, CO: Westview Press, 1994.

Baker, Ross. *Egypt's Uncertain Revolution under Nasser and Sadat.* Cambridge, MA: Harvard University Press, 1978.

Bellin, Eva. "Coercive Institutions and Coercive Leaders." In Marsha Pripstein Posusney and Michele Penner Angrist, eds., *Authoritarianism in the Middle East: Regimes and Resistance.* Boulder, CO: Lynne Rienner, 2005, pp. 21–41.

Ben Dor, Gabriel. "Political Culture Approach to Middle East Politics." *International Journal of Middle East Studies* 8 (January 1977): 43–63.

Bill, James. *The Eagle and the Lion: The Tragedy of American-Iranian Relations.* New Haven, CT: Yale University Press, 1988.

Blaydes, Lisa, and Drew Linzer. "The Political Economy of Women's Support for Fundamentalist Islam." *World Politics* 60 (July 2008): 576–609.

Bordat, Stephanie Wilman, and Saida Kouzzi. "The Challenge of Implementing Morocco's New Personal Status Law." *Carnegie Endowment for International Peace Arab Reform Bulletin* 2, no. 8 (2004).

Bottcher, Annabelle. "Islamic Teaching among Sunni Women in Syria." In Donna Lee Bowen and Evelyn Early, eds., *Everyday Life in the Muslim Middle East*, 2nd ed. Bloomington: Indiana University Press, 2002, pp. 290–299.

Bowen, Donna Lee, and Evelyn A. Early, eds. *Everyday Life in the Muslim Middle East*. Bloomington: Indiana University Press, 2002.

Braizat, Fares. "Muslims and Democracy: An Empirical Critique of Fukuyama's Culturalist Approach." In Ronald Inglehart, ed., *Islam, Gender, Culture and Democracy*. Willowdale, ON: de Sitter Publications, 2003, pp. 46–76.

Brett, Michael. "Islam in the Maghreb: The Problem of Modernization." *The Maghreb Review* 3 (January–April 1978): 6–9.

Brinton, Jasper Yeates. *The Mixed Courts of Egypt*. New Haven, CT: Yale University Press, 1968.

Brown, Leon Carl. "The Role of Islam in Modern North Africa." In Leon Carl Brown, ed., *State and Society in Independent North Africa*. Washington, DC: Middle East Institute, 1966, pp. 97–122.

———. "Stages in the Process of Change." In Charles A. Micaud, with Leon Carl Brown and Clement Henry Moore, *Tunisia: The Politics of Modernization*. New York: Praeger, 1964, pp. 3–66.

Brown, Nathan J. "Jordan and Its Islamic Movement: The Limits of Inclusion?" *Carnegie Papers*, no. 74 (November 2006): 1–23.

Burgat, François, and William Dowell. *The Islamic Movement in North Africa*. Austin: University of Texas Press, 1993.

Buskens, Léon. "Recent Debates on Family Law Reform in Morocco: Islamic Law as Politics in an Emerging Public Sphere." *Islamic Law and Society* 10, no. 1 (2003): 70–131.

Cammett, Melanie, and Sukriti Issar. "Bricks and Mortar Clientelism: The Political Geography of Welfare in Lebanon," *World Politics* 62 (July 2010): 381–421.

Converse, Philip. "The Nature of Belief Systems in Mass Publics." In David Apter, ed., *Ideology and Discontent*. New York: The Free Press, 1964, pp. 206–261.

Crabtree, Steve. "Two-Thirds of Young Arab Women Remain Out of Workforce." *Gallup World*, April 2, 2012. http://www.gallup.com/poll/153659/two-thirds-young-arab-women-remain-workforce.aspx.

Deeb, Lara. "Hizballah: A Primer." *Middle East Report Online*, July 31, 2006. http://www.merip.org/mero/mero073106.

Denoeux, Guilain. "The Forgotten Swamp: Negotiating Political Islam." *Middle East Policy* 9 (June 2002): 60–61.

———. *Urban Unrest in the Middle East: A Comparative Study of Informal Networks in Egypt, Iran and Lebanon*. Syracuse, NY: Syracuse University Press, 1993.

Dessouki, Ali. ed. *Islamic Resurgence in the Arab World*. New York: Praeger, 1982.

Diamond, Larry. "Why Are There No Arab Democracies?" *Journal of Democracy* 21 (January 2010): 93–104.

Eickelman, Dale. "Communication and Control in the Middle East: Publication and Its Discontents." In Dale Eickelman and Jon Anderson, eds., *New Media in the Muslim World: The Emerging Public Sphere*, 2nd ed. Bloomington: Indiana University Press, 2003, pp. 33–44.

El-Affendi, Abdulwahhab. "Islamic Movements: Establishments, Significance and Contextual Realities." In *Islamic Movements: Impact on Political Stability in the*

Arab World. Abu Dhabi: Emirates Center for Strategic Studies and Research, 2003, pp. 7–52.

El-Ghobashy, Mona. "The Metamorphosis of the Egyptian Muslim Brothers." *International Journal of Middle East Studies* 37 (2005): 373–395.

Esposito, John. *Islam: The Straight Path*. New York: Oxford University Press, 1988.

Esposito, John, and Natana J. DeLong-Bas. *Women in Family Law*. Syracuse, NY: Syracuse University Press, 2001.

Farah, Tawfic, ed. *Political Behavior in the Arab States*. Boulder, CO: Westview Press, 1983.

Fish, Steve. "Islam and Authoritarianism." *World Politics* 55 (October 2002): 4–37.

Gause, F. Gregory. *Oil Monarchies: Domestic and Security Challenges in the Arab Gulf States*. New York: Council on Foreign Relations, 1994.

Gelvin, James. *The Modern Middle East: A History*. New York: Oxford University Press, 2005.

Ghabra, Shafeeq. "Islam within Islam." *Common Ground News Service*, September 15, 2009.

Gomaa, Ali. "In Egypt's Democracy, Room for Islam." *New York Times*, April 2, 2011.

Haddad, Yvonne, Byron Haines, and Ellison Findly. *The Islamic Impact*. Syracuse, NY: Syracuse University Press, 1984.

Halasa, Serene. "Arab Scholars Call for New Order Based on Democracy, Urge End to Iraq Sanctions." *Jordan Times*, May 30–31, 1991.

Hallaq, Wael B. *An Introduction to Islamic Law*. New York: Cambridge University Press, 2009.

———. *Shari'a: Theory, Practice, Transformations*. New York: Cambridge University Press, 2009.

Hamarneh, Mustapha. *Revisiting the Arab Street: Research from Within*. Amman: Center for Strategic Studies, University of Jordan, 2005.

Hamid, Shadi. "The Islamist Response to Repression: Are Mainstream Islamists Groups Radicalizing?" *Brookings Doha Center Policy Briefing*, August 2010.

Hamzawy, Amr. "Between Government and Opposition: The Case of the Yemeni Congregation for Reform." *Carnegie Papers*, no. 18 (November 2009): 1–25.

———. "Party for Justice and Development in Morocco: Participation and Its Discontents." *Carnegie Papers*, no. 93 (July 2008): 1–23.

Harik, Iliya. "Some Political and Cultural Considerations Bearing on Survey Research in the Arab World." In Mark Tessler, Monte Palmer, Tawfic Farah, and Barbara Ibrahim, eds., *The Evaluation and Application of Survey Research in the Arab World*. Boulder, CO: Westview Press, 1987, pp. 66–74.

Hermassi, Elbaki. "La société tunisienne au miroir islamiste." *Maghreb-Machrek* 103 (1984): 39–56.

———. "Toward a Comparative Theory of Revolution." *Comparative Studies in Society and History* 18 (April 1976): 211–235.

Hopkins, Nicholas S., and Saad Eddin Ibrahim. *Arab Society: Class, Gender, Power and Development*. Cairo: American University in Cairo Press, 1997.

Hudson, Michael. "The Political Culture Approach to Arab Democratization: The Case for Bringing It Back In, Carefully." In Rex Brynen, Bahgat Korany, and Paul Noble, eds., *Political Liberalization and Democratization in the Arab World*. Boulder, CO: Lynne Rienner, 1995, pp. 61–76.

Ibrahim, Youssef. "Jordan Feels Change Within As Muslims Pursue Agenda." *New York Times*, December 26, 1992.
———. "Militant Muslims Grow Stronger as Algeria's Economy Grows Weaker." *New York Times*, June 25, 1990.
Inglehart, Ronald, Miguel Basanez, Jaime Diez-Medrano, Loek Halman, and Ruud Luijkz. *Human Beliefs and Values: A Cross-Cultural Sourcebook Based on the 1999–2002 Values Surveys*. Mexico City: Siglo XXI Editores, 2004.
Inglehart, Ronald, and Pippa Norris. "The True Clash of Civilizations." *Foreign Policy* 135 (March–April 2003): 62–70.
In Support of Arab Democracy: How and Why? New York: Council on Foreign Relations, 2005.
Jamal, Amaney. "Actors, Public Opinion and Participation." In Ellen Lust, ed., *The Middle East*. Washington, DC: CQ Press, 2011, pp. 193–237.
———. *Barriers to Democracy: The Other Side of Social Capital in Palestine and the Arab World*. Princeton, NJ: Princeton University Press, 2007.
———. *Of Empires and Citizens: Pro-American Democracy or No Democracy at All?* Princeton, NJ: Princeton University Press, 2012.
Jamal, Amaney, and Mark Tessler. "Dimensions of Democratic Support in the Arab World." *Journal of Democracy* 19 (January 2008): 97–110.
Jusko, Karen Long, Orit Kedar, and W. Phillips Shively. "Strategies for Analysis of Multi-Country Individual-Level Data." *Comparative Politics Newsletter* 16, no. 2 (2005): 5–7.
Jusko, Karen Long, and W. Phillips Shively. "Applying a Two-Step Strategy to the Analysis of Cross-National Public Opinion Data." *Political Analysis* 13, no. 4 (2005): 327–344.
Karawan, Ibrahim. " 'ReIslamization Movements' According to Kepel: On Striking Back and Striking Out." *Contention* 2 (Fall 1992): 161–179.
Kerr, Malcolm. "Foreword." In Tawfic Farah, ed., *Political Behavior in the Arab States*. Boulder, CO: Westview Press, 1983.
Khairallah, Chedley. *Le Mouvement Jeune Tunisien*. Tunis: Bonici, n.d.
Khouri, Rami. "The Arab Dream Won't Be Denied." *New York Times,* December 15, 1990.
———. "A Lesson in Middle East History and Humanity." *Jordan Times,* May 28, 1991.
Kramer, Gundrun. "Liberalization and Democracy in the Arab World." *Middle East Report* (January/February 1992): 22–25, 35.
Kull, Steven. *Feeling Betrayed: The Roots of Muslim Anger at America*. Washington, DC: Brookings Institution Press, 2011.
Kurzman, Charles, and Ijlal Naqui. "Do Muslims Vote Islamic?" *Journal of Democracy* 21 (April 2010): 50–63.
Layachi, Azzedine, and Abdel-kader Haireche. "National Development and Political Protest: Islamists in the Maghreb Countries." *Arab Studies Quarterly* 14 (Spring/Summer 1992) : 69–92.
Lee, Robert. *Religion and Politics in the Middle East*. Boulder, CO: Westview Press, 2014.
"L'employabilité des diplômés de l'enseignement supérieur." *The North African Journal*, August 26, 2013.
Lewis, Bernard. *The Shaping of the Modern Middle East*. New York: Oxford University Press, 1994.

"L'Islam contestataire en Tunisie." *Jeune Afrique*, March 14, 21, and 28, 1979.

Lust, Ellen. "Institutions and Governance." In Ellen Lust, ed., *The Middle East*. Washington, DC: CQ Press, 2011, pp. 143–192.

Lust-Okar, Ellen. "Elections Under Authoritarianism: Preliminary Lessons from Jordan." *Democratization* 13 (2006): 456–471.

Mackey, Sandra. *The Iranians: Persia, Islam and the Soul of the Nation*. New York: Penguin, 1996.

"Maroc: Les 'diplômés chômeurs' manifestent à la veille des élections," *Le Monde Afrique*, November 24, 2011.

Masoud, Tarek. "Are They Democrats? Does It Matter?" *Journal of Democracy* 19 (July 2008): 19–24.

Mayer, Ann. *Islam and Human Rights: Tradition and Politics*. Boulder, CO: Westview Press, 2006.

Mirsepassi-Ashtiani, Ali. "The Crisis of Secular Politics and the Rise of Political Islam in Iran." *Social Text* 38 (Spring 1994): 51–84.

Najmabadi, Afsaneh. "Depolitization of a Rentier State: The Case of Pahlavi Iran." In Hazem Beblawi and Giacomo Luciani, eds., *The Rentier State*. London: Croom Helm, 1978, pp. 211–227.

Nakhleh, Emile. *A Necessary Engagement: Reinventing America's Relations with the Muslim World*. Princeton, NJ: Princeton University Press, 2009.

Norton, Augustus Richard. *Hezbollah: A Short History*. Princeton, NJ: Princeton University Press, 2007.

Okruhlik, Gwenn. "Understanding Political Dissent in Saudi Arabia." *Middle East Report Online*, October 24, 2001. http://www.merip.org/mero/mero/102401.

Onis, Ziya. "The Political Economy of Islamic Resurgence in Turkey: The Rise of the Welfare Party." *Third World Quarterly* 18 (1997): 743–766.

Palmer, Monte. *Survey Research in the Arab World: An Analytical Index*. London: Menas, 1982.

Posusney, Marsha Pripstein, and Michele Penner Angrist, eds. *Authoritarianism in the Middle East: Regimes and Resistance*. Boulder, CO: Lynne Rienner, 2005.

Quandt, William. "Hume and Quandt on Contemporary Algeria." *Middle East Policy* 6 (February 1999): 141–149.

Robinson, Glenn. *Building a Palestinian State: The Incomplete Revolution*. Bloomington: Indiana University Press, 1997.

———. "Can Islamists Be Democrats? The Case of Jordan." *Middle East Journal* 51 (Summer 1997): 373–388.

Rosenthal, Erwin I. J. *Islam and the Modern National State*. Cambridge: Cambridge University Press, 1965.

Rutherford, Bruce. *Egypt after Mubarak: Liberalism, Islam, and Democracy in the Arab World*. Princeton, NJ: Princeton University Press, 2008.

Safran, Nadav. *Egypt in Search of Political Community*. Cambridge, MA: Harvard University Press, 1961.

Sahliyeh, Emile. *In Search of Leadership: West Bank Politics Since 1967*. Washington, DC: The Brookings Institution, 1988.

Schwedler, Jillian. *Faith in Moderation: Islamists Parties in Jordan and Yemen*. Cambridge: Cambridge University Press, 2006.

Seddon, David. "The Politics of 'Adjustment' in Morocco." In Bonnie K. Campbell and John Loxley, eds., *Structural Adjustment in Africa*. New York: St. Martin's Press, 1989, 234–265.

Shami, Seteney, Lucine Taminian, Soheir Morsy, Zeinab El Bakri, and El-Wathig Kameir. *Women in Arab Society: Work Patterns and Gender Relations in Egypt, Jordan and Sudan*. Paris: UNESCO, 1990.

Sivan, Emmanuel. *Radical Islam: Medieval Theology and Modern Politics*. New Haven, CT: Yale University Press, 1985.

Stone, Martin. *The Agony of Algeria*. New York: Columbia University Press, 1997.

Sullivan, Denis, and Sana Abed-Kotob. *Islam in Contemporary Egypt: Civil Society vs. the State*. Boulder, CO: Lynne Rienner, 1999.

Tamimi, Azzam S. *Rachid Ghannouchi: A Democrat within Islamism*. Oxford: Oxford University Press, 2001.

Telhami, Shibley. *The World Through Arab Eyes: Arab Public Opinion and the Reshaping of the Middle East*. New York: Basic Books, 2013.

Tessler, Mark. "Anger and Governance in the Arab World: Lessons from the Maghrib and Implications for the West." *Jerusalem Journal of International Relations* 13 (Fall 1991): 7–33.

———. *A History of the Israeli-Palestinian Conflict*. Bloomington: Indiana University Press, 2009.

———. "Islam and Democracy in the Middle East: The Impact of Religious Orientations on Attitudes toward Democracy in Four Arab Countries." *Comparative Politics* 34 (April 2002): 337–354.

———. "The Origins of Popular Support for Islamist Movements: A Political Economy Analysis." In John Entelis, ed., *Islam, Democracy, and the State in North Africa*. Bloomington: Indiana University Press, 1997, pp. 93–126.

———. *Public Opinion in the Middle East: Survey Research and the Political Orientations of Ordinary Citizens*. Bloomington: Indiana University Press, 2011.

———. "Religion, Religiosity and the Place of Islam in Political Life: Insights from the Arab Barometer Surveys." *Middle East Law and Governance* 2 (2010): 221–252.

Tessler, Mark, and Eleanor Gao. "Gauging Arab Support for Democracy." *Journal of Democracy* 16 (July 2005): 83–97.

Tessler, Mark, Amaney Jamal, and Michael Robbins. "Arab Attitudes toward Democracy and Governance: Findings from the 2010–2011 Arab Barometer." *Journal of Democracy* 23 (October 2012): 83–103.

Tessler, Mark, Carrie Konold, and Megan Reif. "Political Generations in Developing Countries: Evidence and Insights from Algeria." *Public Opinion Quarterly* 68 (Summer 2004): 184–216.

Tessler, Mark, and Jodi Nachtwey. "Explaining Women's Support for Political Islam: Contributions from Feminist Theory." In Mark Tessler, with Jodi Nachtwey and Anne Banda, eds., *Area Studies and Social Science: Strategies for Understanding Middle East Politics*. Bloomington: Indiana University Press, 1999, pp. 48–69.

Tessler, Mark, William O'Barr, and David Spain. *Tradition and Identity in Changing Africa*. New York: Harper and Row, 1973.

Tessler, Mark, Monte Palmer, Tawfic Farah, and Barbara Ibrahim, eds. *The Evaluation and Application of Survey Research in the Arab World*. Boulder, CO: Westview Press, 1987.

Tibi, Bassam. "Why They Can't Be Democratic." *Journal of Democracy* 19 (July 2008): 43–48.

Tucker, Judith. *Women, Family and Gender in Islamic Law.* Cambridge: Cambridge University Press, 2008.

Unal, Ali, and Alphonso Williams. *Advocate of Dialogue: Fethullah Gülen.* Fairfax, VA: The Fountain, 2000.

Vandewalle, Dirk. "Autopsy of a Revolt: The October Riots in Algeria." Hanover, NH: Institute of Current World Affairs, 1988.

———. "From the New State to the New Era: Toward a Second Republic in Tunisia." *Middle East Journal* 42 (1988): 602–620.

Voll, John. "Fethullah Gülen: Transcending Modernity in the New Islamic Discourse." In M. Hakan Yavuz and John L. Esposito, eds., *Turkish Islam and the Secular State: The Gülen Movement.* Syracuse, NY: Syracuse University Press, 2003, pp. 238–251.

———. *Islam: Continuity and Change in the Modern World.* Boulder, CO: Westview Press, 1982.

Waterbury, John. *The Commander of the Faithful.* New York: Columbia University Press, 1970.

White, Jenny. *Islamist Mobilization in Turkey: A Study in Vernacular Politics.* Seattle: University of Washington Press, 2002.

Wickham, Carrie. *Mobilizing Islam: Religion, Activism and Political Change in Egypt.* New York: Columbia University Press, 2002.

Witter, Willis. "Moroccans See Good, Evil in Possible Economic Boom." *Washington Times*, September 22, 1993.

Wright, Robin, ed. *The Islamists Are Coming: Who They Really Are.* Washington, DC: Woodrow Wilson Center Press, 2012.

———. "Lebanon." In Shireen T. Hunter, ed., *The Politics of Islamic Revivalism: Diversity and Unity.* Bloomington: Indiana University Press, 1988, pp. 57–70.

Zartman, I. William. "Political Science." In Leonard Binder, ed., *The Study of the Middle East: Research and Scholarship in the Humanities and Social Sciences.* New York: Wiley, 1976, pp. 265–325.

Zubaida, Sami. "Trajectories of Political Islam: Egypt, Iran and Turkey." *The Political Quarterly* (August 2000): 60–78.

Index

MARK TESSLER is Samuel J. Eldersveld Collegiate Professor of Political Science at the University of Michigan. His books include *Public Opinion in the Middle East: Survey Research and the Political Orientations of Ordinary Citizens* (IUP, 2011); *A History of the Israeli-Palestinian Conflict* (IUP, 2009); and (edited, with Jodi Nachtwey and Anne Banda), *Area Studies and Social Science: Strategies for Understanding Middle East Politics* (IUP, 1999).